The Last Witness From a Dirt Road

A FICTIONALIZED MEMOIR

BOOKS

Copyright © 2005 Bill Hunt
All Rights Reserved
ISBN 978-0-9790454-0-0 (previously ISBN 1-4196-1883-0)

Library of Congress Control Number: 2006901331

PRINTED IN THE UNITED STATES OF AMERICA

®
LIGHTNING SOURCE
La Vergne, TN

The Last Witness From a Dirt Road

A FICTIONALIZED MEMOIR
BY
Bill Hunt

2005

PRAISE for

THE LAST WITNESS FROM A DIRT ROAD

"Author Hunt presents a moving account of one boy's young life and how his perceptions of a world once considered ideal become suddenly turbulent and then increasingly painful, a realization that unfolds as memorable and graphically as the story's carefully honed narrative itself." NYT Best Selling Author, Ellen Tanner Marsh.

"Its message is timeless and universal." K. Middleton, Reviewer (AL)

"I think it has helped me better understand people I come in contact with now, and have known all through my life." Village Voice (LA)

"...the charming and informative lecture/reading/book signing. What a wonderful treat for me and for my students!" Dr. B. Shaw, Athens State University (AL)

"Mr. Hunt paints a beautiful and poignant story that brings the reader into a specific time and place of an entertaining, gentle and marvelous era." G. McClure (RI)

"I could have lived in that book." L. Pope (LA)

"Finally, I also admire a young boy who could see the chasm between Black and White, yet still easily move across it to share his life with his friends on the dirt road." Dr. J. Bassham (AL)

"This is a great human interest story that appeals to anyone. I think it should be in every library in this country." C. Kayser (MN)

"I was greatly moved by this story's poignancy and reality. It is told in the same vein as 'To Kill A Mocking Bird' in that it reveals an adult world seen first through the naïve but honest eyes of a young boy, the author himself." J. Davis, Reviewer (AL)

"Through good humor and lively dialogue, the reader develops an affectionate attachment to the characters and the way their lives were woven together. You'll close the book, wishing for a sequel." C. A. Roberts Dumond, MS, CMS, M.Ed. (LMS) (MA)

"Billy's slow realization of the silent pain and suffering of this underclass mirrored my own experience." J. Haydel (TX)

ACKNOWLEDGEMENTS AND THANK YOUS

Because so many helped me...reading, expressing opinions and more than anything, inspiring me to go on. With all of my gratitude, I want to acknowledge those who stand at the forefront, and say "thank you," over and over. It is unlikely that anyone will fully understand how much each has contributed to this book, and there is no order in which his or her name appears, except the first one:

Grace, my wife...who had heard all of the stories many times, but endured them over and again for forty years. Dr. Penny Laubenthal, who unknowingly, challenged me. Carol Dumond, a fabulous teacher and librarian in Boston, who first read the stories as a truth that should not die with time. Judge Henry Blizzard and his wife Lilia, both recognized a value, and an interest in the content of the stories. Dr. Bob and Barbara Searcy, great teachers who had so much patience and encouragement, and dealt with me with a kind gentleness. Dr. Elizabeth Brett, a marvelous teacher who understood the makings in the life of a young child, and was thus inspired to write her own story. Dr. Betty Logan, another teacher from whom I learned very much, when she worked so hard to help me. Tom Kayser, who has the ability to "sit" in your mind, and stir. Todd Foret, who finally convinced me that a computer wasn't my enemy. Van Trent...almost a son, who enthusiastically made every step with Billy, and cheered for him. My four children, Carl, David, Carole and Claire, all of whom inspire me daily with their families, and never cease to love me, regardless of how bossy I am. Carolyn Crow, a teacher who has a little bookshop on the square, and came late into the picture, but dealt a hand of continuous encouragement and enthusiasm. And Bonnie Roberts, an extraordinarily accomplished Poet of international fame, and a teacher, who keenly brought out the best in each story, but more so, was willing to help me along with patience and kindness.

There are others, not named here, who have contributed one way or another, and to them, too, I say thank you, thank you.

The Last Witness From
a Dirt Road

A FICTIONALIZED MEMOIR

NOTE

A PORTION OF THE AUTHOR PROCEEDS

FROM THE SALE OF THIS

BOOK ARE DISIGNATED TO BE GIVEN TO

BOYS & GIRLS CLUBS OF AMERICA

SPECIFICALLY

TO ESTABLISH A BOYS AND GIRLS CLUB

IN

BUNKIE, LOUISIANA

THE VENUE OF THE STORIES IN THIS BOOK.

BOOKS

NOTE

EXCEPT FOR FAMILY MEMBERS AND RELATIVES, THE NAMES OF THE PEOPLE IN THE STORIES OF THIS BOOK HAVE BEEN CHANGED AND ARE THE RESULT OF THE AUTHOR'S IMAGINATION. ANY RESEMBLANCE TO ACTUAL PERSONS, LIVING OR DEAD, OR TO THE EVENTS TOLD IN THIS BOOK, ARE TAKEN FROM HEARSAY AND CONVERSATIONS HELD OVER AN EXTENDED PERIOD OF TIME, RECONSTRUCTED FROM THE AUTHOR'S MEMORY, THEN COUPLED TO THE AUTHOR'S IMAGINATION. THE SUBSTANCE AND TONE OF THE STORIES, THE DIALOGUE AND DIALECT ARE AS PRECISE AS MEMORY PERMITS, AND ARE THE BEST RECOLLECTION OF THE AUTHOR, ALSO COUPLED WITH THE AUTHOR'S IMAGINATION.

Bill Hunt
Author

"The Last Witness From A Dirt Road"

A FICTIONALIZED MEMOIR

✳✳✳

✿✿✿

Based on a unique childhood,
lived in an era that will never be again,
and is lost in time.
Bill Hunt
Author
THE LAST WITNESS FROM A DIRT ROAD

The Memories In My Heart And Mind I Dedicate To My Parents And To My Sisters And Brother - My Blood Family. The Stories In This Book Are Dedicated To The Many Families Whose Lives Intertwined With Ours When Our Families Lived Together On The Dirt Road. This Book, In Whole - Everything From Front To Back Cover, Is Dedicated To Every Soul Whose Chances, Choices And Hopes, Were Taken Away From Their Life By A Dirt Road Of Some Kind, Somehow, Somewhere.

CHAPTER 1

Juneteenth had finally come, our biggest and best holiday on the plantation every year. The morning was wet and rainy, and everybody was home getting food and all the good stuff ready for the celebration. I could hear the far off sound of an airplane coming, and finally the plane flew very low, its motor making an awful racket while crossing just a little above the tops of the tall pecan trees in our yard at the Big House. For two days, a quiet, slow drizzle had cooled us off, giving the field hands a rest from the fields and the summer heat, and also, plenty of time to get ready to celebrate *emancipation day*. But I was disappointed a whole lot, figuring the ball game would have to be put off because it was too wet and the grass was too tall in the pasture where we played ball, next to the Big House.

Playing under the pecan trees near the fishponds, and wearing only short britches, I quickly edged my way through the barbed wire fence on the backside of the hedges so I could get a better look at the plane. Running through the knee-high grass in the side pasture, I recognized the silver fighter plane as the one owned by Danny McBride. He had been a pilot during the war, and just two weeks before he had visited with my dad at our house, wearing his khaki uniform with the ribbons and awards. He even said hi to me, and shook my hand. Because of the stories I'd heard about Danny McBride, I wanted to be a fighter pilot, too, like him. He was a friend of my family's, a favorite person to me, and he was one of my heroes.

Flying low, the plane headed south from our house on Shirley Plantation, where my family lived. All of a sudden, it made a big loop above the top of the sugarcane in front of me, and I stopped in my tracks, waiting to see it again when it would rise above the cane tops; but a second later I heard a loud bang, and I knew it had plowed into the ground. In the drizzling rain, I ran down the muddy turn-row through the sugarcane field, and arrived at the crash.

About the same time, a big blue Lincoln slid to a halt in the gravel road beside the pasture where the plane had crashed. I could see the fear and pain on the face of Danny McBride's dad while he jumped out of his car. He crossed the shallow ditch to where I was holding apart the strands of barbed wire so he could crawl through. Together we ran through the grass toward the wreckage. Muddy and wet, we tried with all our might to lift Danny's torn-up body from the cockpit, but we couldn't do it.

While we both stood waiting for someone to come help, the smell of oil and fuel, water, and blood—so much blood splattered about the cockpit and across the instruments—made me sick to my stomach. I tried really hard not to look, but my eyes kept going back to the broken face and body of my friend, and to the blood.

The hot engine lay about twenty yards away, and, with every tiny raindrop that fell on it, a little cloud of steam rose in the cool, damp air. After what seemed like a long time to me, several men came, lifted Danny's body from the cockpit, and laid it on one of the wings. My dad was one of the men. After a couple of minutes, he walked to his truck, then returned with a shovel and dug a hole in the grassy dirt near where I stood at the cockpit. I watched while he carefully buried Danny's brains deep in the ground. Feeling my stomach turn over again and again, I placed my hand over my nose, hoping to shut out the odors, but then the blood was smeared across my face, nose and cheeks, making the odor worse. I reached into the cockpit and wiped the *red* from the glass of one of the instruments, a little clock. A bit past ten, it looked like to me: time had stopped at a little bit past ten on June 19, 1946, for my hero, Danny McBride.

He died on Freedom Day, and I cried.

Looking at the group of men, I could see them moving about in slow motion, their lips saying something, but I heard nothing, only a muffled, low rumbling. Danny's father started crying, and with both his hands cupped over his face, he knelt over Danny's body. I couldn't move, and I felt the sting of my fingernails biting my palms, while colorful circles began moving about in my eyes; my knees and legs felt tired and weak. I wished that I had not been there, right in the middle of a terrible thing, and I knew right away that it was rooting itself deep into my mind; odors and pictures I would never forget. I stumbled a couple of times as I walked through the wet grass to reach my dad's truck, about fifty yards away, parked on the gravel road beside the pasture. My fists remained tightly clinched while I rolled onto the tailgate, crawled to the front, and sat against the truck cab. I looked down at Danny's blood on my arms and chest while the tiny raindrops began turning the red to a soft pink, slowly washing the blood away. When I unclenched my fists, the bright red blood was thick in my palms and quickly I wiped them on my britches, turning the cloth red. Leaving my hands open to the rain, I wished with all my might that what I was seeing and smelling were only a bad dream and it would soon be over. But it wasn't a dream, and the little puddle of water that I was sitting in was pink. Everywhere I looked, and everything I smelled, was a shade of *red*.

***

Well over fifty years after Danny McBride crashed his plane, my mind still recalls quite often the red memories of that day. Smells of fresh raindrops on hot concrete, exhaust from a car passing by, a drop of blood from a minor cut, and visions of early morning dampness on the green grass of a quiet pasture are a few of the triggers that still thrust me back to that day, June 19, 1946, Freedom Day.

Freedom Day was also the day when I was badly *shackled* by the memories planted deep in my mind, and for the first time the innocence of my childhood was suddenly broken, and I was thrust into the start of my youth.

A couple of days after the crash, Dad sent a crew of men to pick up the pieces of the silver plane. They placed the wreckage under two big oaks about a hundred yards from our house on Shirley Plantation. Alone, I played in the shade under the trees, sitting in the plane's cockpit where its pilot had died, softly crying for him, and for me. Over and over, I lived that bloody day, hoping my mind would tire of remembering and free me from the horror that had rooted itself so deep inside.

I became anxious for school to start. It was a feeling I seldom had under normal circumstances, but I wanted to get away from the plantation and, especially, away from the silver plane. Every day something drew me to the wreckage—to see it, examine it carefully, cry quietly, and make wishes I knew would never come true; and the next day I would wander again to the oaks where the wreckage lay. The silver plane was ugly now, tormenting, and after several days it seemed to have developed into *something* other than a pile of twisted rubble, something with powers of its own, pulling me, stirring in my mind, and sometimes whispering sounds the big trees and I could hear, but I couldn't understand. Every evening at bedtime I counted the days left in the summer before school would start, figuring with my friends at school I might forget about Juneteenth, about the day when Danny McBride crashed his silver plane and I was there. And maybe one day when school was over and I came home, the silver plane might be gone from under the oaks.

But, like my heart or my hand, I knew the silver plane and the blood had become a part of me.

The summer of 1946 finally came to an end.

And I started the fifth grade.

CHAPTER 2

Being an overseer and manager of a big sugar plantation in central Louisiana, my dad was always able to find jobs for me in his attempt to keep me busy, supposedly productive, and, hopefully, out of trouble. When school started in September of 1946, I was anxious and ready to return to my friends in Bunkie; I also hoped that moving into a different building, with students in the two grades above me, the fifth grade might be a new adventure for me.

The lives of everyone who lived in the little town of Bunkie, and along the country roads all around it, were simple, but the social and economic levels found their roots mostly in the land-who owned it, who controlled the vast acreages of sugarcane and cotton, and, especially, who controlled the laborers who worked in the fields. This agrarian society was like a heavy fabric, hot and burdensome, woven in many patterns of social layers and classes, sometimes strange and difficult, with some layers being denied any attachment to other more prominent layers. But the main and dominant colors still neatly woven through this fabric in 1946 were black and white, always separate except in a workplace setting, and even then, it seemed barely out of a long era of servitude. Like the dust from their sandy, pinkish dirt, the great sugar plantations in the middle of Louisiana, hovered like a smothering, dusty cloud over the lives of those whose roots were deep into the little-changed economic system that had existed for hundreds of years. In the fall of 1946, the aging fabric of the old structure and order began showing countless broken threads and an occasional opening from which a few heavily laden souls sought to climb out and away from the torment of the dirt roads where they had barely survived for generations.

Like the tall, green, sugarcane, always in motion from the gentle breezes that moved across the flat fields of central Louisiana, our rural and agrarian lives, too, swayed in the breezes that swept through our little town of Bunkie. In my family, the stormy winds of World War II blew very great, fearful and anxious, taking eight of my cousins to war, and bringing the deaths of my older brother early in 1944 and both my grandfathers in the fall of 1945. And then, in 1946, an airplane crash, which weighed heavily on my mind, had broken the heart of the entire community.

***

My Grandfather—we called him Paw Paw—lived in the Big House on Shirley Plantation with my family. He used to tell me over and over that the

Germans and the Japs were really mean. He didn't like the *Reds* either; in fact, he hated the Reds and he always said, "Now, Billy, I want to tell you, we ought to get rid of the Reds while we're at it." I believed him, and I wanted to get rid of the Reds, too, but I didn't know who the Reds were. Every Monday morning at about ten, Paw Paw would walk down the dirt road to the mailbox at the gravel road to fetch his *Sunday Times Picayune* from New Orleans; then, every evening for two or three hours, he sat in his big red chair, with arms so big that I could straddle one of them, while we listened to his Zenith radio, or until he got tired of me hanging around. The Zenith stood tall and real handy-like, and with his fingers, Paw Paw beat out some kind of little rhythm on the left arm of his big chair, just a few inches from the knobs on the Zenith. And he could answer any question anyone would ask about the war. After he died, I missed my grandfather, my own Paw Paw, but I was glad the war was over, and we didn't have to worry about it anymore.

It was awfully hot when school let out that September day. The old yellow school bus rattled down the dry gravel road, every hole making us bounce against each other; some of us laughed about it, but some of the girls whined about the heat and the dust. The hot air swarmed through the open windows, but offered very little to cool us off. We were heading out of Bunkie to deliver the noise and energy inside the bus to the rightful owners. Our driver, poor ole Mister Armand, a tiny little man with a big French accent, fussed an awful lot, mostly in French, but no one ever paid any attention to him. As the old bus squealed to a stop at the dirt road where Shirley Plantation began, a cloud of dust surrounded it, filling the inside with a rich tan color and making the kids yell and scream more, even with a few dirty words. I never used any dirty words, but I knew all of them. Mama would have killed me if I did, but it didn't matter much to Dad.

Everybody on the plantation was my friend. They were all hard workers, and had worked for years in the cotton and sugarcane fields. Most had been born somewhere close by, and their lives had been spent like all of their people ahead of them, working from daylight to dark. They were good people, and I knew all of them.

My little brother, Mickey, and I stepped off the school bus into a slow-moving cloud of dust, and crossed the graveled highway onto the dirt road leading through the Quarters all the way to the other end, to the Big House where we lived. The little devil kept falling behind and whining that the dust on the dirt road was hot on his bare feet. We had taken our shoes off, and I walked in the grass on the side of the road while calling him a sissy, knowing that would make him mad and give him something to fuss about. When we turned the corner at the end of the hedgerow, Pal ran to meet us. I loved my ole yellow dog. I loved him the very first day Mister Brown brought him to me as a little puppy. He could really wag his big yellow tail, he was always glad to see me, and when he laid his ears back, it looked like he was smiling. Mickey trotted on ahead of Pal and me. I figured he was hurrying to tattle to Mama about my teasing him. His whine soon turned into a loud whimper as he clutched a couple of books under his arm and his shoes in one hand. Mama's car was in the garage, so I knew she was home. That was a good feeling. Every Friday was fish day at school, because there were so many Catholic kids, and it hadn't been enough to eat, at least for me. I didn't like soup made with fish—it didn't smell very good and didn't taste good either, but I would get Mama to make me something. I had almost forgotten how black Pal's nose was, and wet. He licked my hand to say *hello*, and I skipped down the side of the Big House and rounded the corner of the screened porch. Mrs. Prosser's brand new Chevy was parked at the other end of the porch, and I stopped.

Nineteen forty-six was a good year for Chevy. At least that's what my Dad said. It was the first year new cars had been made since the war ended, but not very many people could get a new car just yet. I ran over and touched the bright chrome door handles one by one. Its black paint was clean and shiny, and I wanted to open the door to look inside, but figured that maybe Mrs. Prosser wouldn't like that. Mrs. Prosser might have seen me, and she didn't have any kids, and would have complained to Mama. She had already fussed about my riding my horse across her yard last winter, claiming the hoof prints left holes in the grass. I hopped up the back steps onto the porch and quietly walked into the kitchen where Mag was still cleaning up after serving Mama and Mrs. Prosser some coffee. Mag was my favorite person who worked in the Big House. She was my friend, and I loved her, even though she got onto me a lot. After dropping my books onto the kitchen table, I slid my shoes under the edge, getting ready to beg her to fix me something to eat. Before I said a word, she started in on me.

"Boy, you takes dose upstairs. Ya Mama's gon be in heah, and I knows she don wants no stinkin shoes in dis heres kitchen, an me neitha," and she pointed her long finger toward the dining room door. "Ya heah me, Billy?"

She faced the sink and continued washing the cups and saucers, humming one of her songs. I picked up a shoe and ran over and hit her on her big round rear end. She turned around and tried to grab me, but I had already dropped the shoe and ran onto the porch. Mag couldn't run very good, but she could really fuss, and she liked to fuss, especially at me.

She stopped at the kitchen door and with one hand on her hip she shook her finger at me again and yelled, "I's gon tell ya Daddy hows ya treats me, ya rascal! Ya gon be sorry bout dat. I sho wish I could catch ya jist one time, ya lit'le devil. Jist one time's all I need. Lawdy, Lawdy, I sho pity yo po wife."

While shaking her head, she turned and went back to the sink, mumbling something as she went. Mag loved me and I loved her. She and Gilbert Frank didn't have any kids. Besides, I didn't have to worry about my "po wife." I wasn't even twelve yet.

I went back to get another look at Mrs. Prosser's new Chevy. Opening the door made the light in the top come on. That was new for me. Our old Ford didn't do that. I closed the door as quietly as I could, crept up the back steps, and tiptoed to the kitchen door. Mag heard me and quickly turned around, figuring, I guess, that I might try to hit her on her big butt again.

I leaned on the door-facing, looked down at the floor, and whimpered, "I'm sorry, Mag. Would you *please* fix me a sandwich?" and I stuck my bottom lip out as far as I could.

She turned partway around, looked at the fresh loaf of store-bought bread, fussing again, "I oughts not to, yous so mean, but don'cha set foot in dis heah kitchen. Ya heah me, boy?"

I waited at the door, and she brought me two slices of bread with fresh cream between them, sprinkled with sugar. Mag liked sugar. Me too. Her light brown skin was shiny with sweat, and it was past time for her to go home. She looked at me and smiled, her white teeth showing bright against her brown skin and painted red lips, then she pushed my hair to the side of my forehead, commanding, "Now ya git outta heah and leaves me lone, I gots to goes home, boy. Sides, I's tired 'a foolin wis ya!" She shook her head, making her long earrings dance about her neck. She reached to pinch my cheek, but I jerked away just as her hand went by.

Taking my sugar and cream sandwich, I went out to the fishponds under the pecan trees where the air was a little cooler. Pal had to have a bite, and he just gulped it down without really tasting the cream and sugar. He wanted another bite, but I kicked at him while he ran his tongue across his black lips. That's the way he ate all the time, and I guess I did, too, except on Sundays. It seemed like we had the preacher and his family for dinner almost *every* Sunday. Mama made me be careful how I ate at the dinner table on Sunday. I had to use a few good manners, but Pal; he didn't have any manners at all.

I hoped that Papa would come to play. Papa was a little older than I was, but he was my best friend and favorite playmate, and he was Hoss's boy. He had a tall head, and Hoss had to tell him everything to do. Papa never went to school, so I had to read comic books to him. He really liked comic books, especially *Superman.*

Mag had put a lot of sugar on my sandwich. I liked it.

Sure enough, just when I reached down in the cool water in one of the ponds to try to catch a goldfish, Mrs. Prosser drove down the side of the house in her new black Chevy. While I waved to her, I wished that Dad would buy us a new Chevy just like it. Before the dust could settle, Mag came walking down the side of the Big House, headed home for the day. She and Gilbert Frank lived at the far end of the Quarters, where the dirt road met the gravel road going into town.

She shook her fist at me and called out, "Me and yous is gon have it out one a dese days, Billy. I's gonna git cha, jist ya wait an see. Ya sho gon be sorry, too."

I ran after her as though I was going to hit her on her butt again, but she never turned around. She just twisted her big behind more, and sashayed on down the long driveway. "See ya, Mag," I called out, and she waved her hand in a flutter, and made her big flowery skirt swing from side to side. Glancing at my hand, I saw blood oozing from my knuckle, bringing back bad memories of the airplane crash. I figured I must have hit a rock in the pond, causing the cuts, but Pal was right there with me, wagging his tail, so I sat on the old grindstone at the ponds and let him lick the cut till it stopped bleeding. Paw Paw said that if you let a dog lick a cut like mine it would go away quicker. We always did that, and Pal liked to do it, too.

Jumping on Pal, I rolled with him in the grass. He tried to lick my lips for the sugar and cream; he really smelled bad. He must have been digging after the armadillo that lived under the steps at our front porch. I didn't want to take a bath, so I pushed him off of me and ran to the back porch, into the kitchen.

Mama frowned at me and said, "Oh my, you smell worse than Pal. Go wash-up, Son. Supper will be ready in a little while." Mama had a terrific smeller.

Before I could leave the kitchen, she ordered me to pick up my books from the table and take them and my shoes upstairs. I thought Mag would have done it, but she didn't. I would have to get even with her for that. She liked for me to pick at her, so she could pick back, but if she got close enough she would grab a handful of my hair and would pull it, until I said *uncle*. Then she would laugh out loud and pinch my cheek. The cheek pinching hurt worse than the hair pulling.

I asked Mama if I could take the Keller bus to Aunt Sook's store in the morning.

Aunt Sook had the best country store around. Everybody who lived south of town in Eola bought groceries from Aunt Sook. Mama said it was okay, but only if I had my own quarter to pay my way on the bus. I had a lot of quarters in my trunk upstairs, but I also knew where my sister hid her change in a little white box from the jewelry store. Some stupid boy had given her a present in that box. I figured I could borrow a quarter from the little box, and my sister would never know. Aunt Sook would give me a dollar or two if I stacked groceries for her, giving me enough money to last a week or so. I loved Aunt Sook. She was always glad to see me and was always neat and pretty. Other than my Mama and Mag, Aunt Sook was my favorite grown person. I had to watch out for Uncle Gathard, though. I think he must have had a stomach ache all the time, or something was wrong with him in the head. He frowned most of the time and looked like he was mad about everything. He even sounded mad every time he talked to me, so I figured he didn't like me, or something.

The Keller bus was almost as bad as our school bus, noisy and dirty. It was dusty and hot all the way to Aunt Sook's store, about a half mile past The Four-Way Café at the four-way stop in Eola. A cloud of dust rolled around the bus as the brakes squealed, bringing it to a halt in front of the store, just when the driver called out "Harper's Grocery." That was unnecessary, since I knew it was Harper's Grocery and I was the only person on the bus. I flat-footed off the high step and landed on a rock in the grass, hurting my foot really bad. I waited for the bus to pull away before I got up out of the tall grass and limped across the gravel road, hoping the rock hadn't broken the skin. I couldn't see any blood, but I thought to myself, "That's a hell of a note. Now I'll have to limp around all day on a sore foot! Uncle Gathard will laugh about it if he finds out and he'll call me a sissy."

The screen door, with the big *Holsum Bread* handle, opened easily and I stepped inside, smelling all the good stuff in the store. Fresh potatoes, onions and strings of garlic dangling from a wire all mixed with the smells of fresh bread and the coffee in the kitchen. I kept pulling in the smells, but very quickly I realized that something was wrong. Something must have happened before I got there. All the way from the back of the store I could hear Aunt Ida jabbering to Uncle Gathard, and I could see her shaking her finger at him every now and then, like she was getting ready to smack him. I wished she would smack him. Now was no time for me to ask questions, so I just stood by the drink box at the door, trying to figure out what had made Aunt Ida so excited. The Coca Colas standing in the cold water in the drink box looked really good, and my mouth started watering a little bit, but I hadn't done any work yet so I figured I needed to wait a while. Besides, Uncle Gathard would have gotten onto Aunt Sook if I had taken a Coke without having done some work. Aunt Sook would have just laughed about it and would have told the ole goat, "Ah, Gathard, he's just a child. Would you leave us alone, please?" Then she would smile and wink at me. I liked it when she winked at me, but I wanted her to tell him, "Just shut-up, and quit fussing...smile a little bit."

Aunt Ida was going full steam at Uncle Gathard and shaking her finger every time she glanced at him. Everybody said Aunt Ida was a good cook, and I believe she was. She lived with Aunt Sook and Uncle Gathard and took care of the kitchen and the house. But she could really lay on some words when she wanted to, and today she was letting them fly, not smiling and not stopping even to catch her breath.

Uncle Gathard was cutting meat for the Saturday customers, while Aunt Sook was writing up groceries and talking to a colored lady with solid white hair. Aunt Sook looked up and smiled at me, but never stopped talking. By her smile

I could tell she was glad I came, so I went to the back of the store and spoke to Aunt Ida and Uncle Gathard, but neither one stopped talking long enough even to see me. I got a box of canned black-eyed peas and started stacking the shelves. I didn't care much for black-eyed peas. After the colored lady left, Aunt Sook came over, hugged me, and said she was glad that I had come to help her. Also, she reminded me that *Pete week* on Augusta and Oak Hall Plantations had ended Friday, so everybody would have money to buy groceries. Pete week was the second week after the last payday, when all of the money and food was gone. By then, ole *Pete* had gotten everything! Nobody liked Pete week.

I glanced into Aunt Sook's face and I could tell she loved me. She and Uncle Gathard didn't have any kids either, like Mag and Gilbert Frank. I asked her what was wrong with Aunt Ida, so excited and talking so much.

"Oh, Mister Levy stopped by the store and left his truck partly on the road; Bobby Joe came by and scraped the rear fender on Mister Levy's truck, and he wants Bobby Joe to pay for it," Aunt Sook said and patted me on my head.

Aunt Sook was really pretty, and smelled good all of the time. Her hair was really black. She glanced at the cans of black-eyed peas, and then continued; "Aunt Ida and Uncle Gathard think that Mister Levy shouldn't have left his truck on the roadway." Bobby Joe was my cousin. Not knowing whose fault it was, I just kept stacking the cans on the shelves, but I didn't want Bobby Joe to have to pay for it. He didn't have any money that I knew of.

Aunt Sook gently touched my arm and said, "Billy, honey, you need to mark them first." She said *honey* and *darling* a lot, and sometimes she called me *Bill Beau*. I knew the cans had to be marked first with the price, but my mind was already set on a cold Coke and my foot was still hurting. A long time later, when poor old Mister Levy died, Aunt Ida would smile and say, "Levy certainly made a beautiful corpse." No one ever told me if Bobby Joe had to pay Mister Levy or not. I don't reckon he did because if he did Aunt Ida would probably still be fussing.

About three thirty or four o'clock, Mama came to Aunt Sook's store to pick up a few groceries for Sunday dinner and to get me. While pushing my hair off my forehead with her hand she asked me if I was ready to go. It seemed like to me that all of the grown-up women liked to push my hair off my forehead. Mama told me that the preacher and his family were coming again. As usual at about that time of day, Mama was dressed real pretty, and I could smell the Coty powder. She liked red lipstick and smiled a lot, and she always smelled good, too. She loved Aunt Sook. They had been childhood friends since grammar school and were the same age. Mama's hair was coal black. Aunt Sook's was coal black, but she had to dye hers to keep it black, and everybody in the world knew it. Aunt Murel and Aunt Madiline always said that Aunt Sook's hair would be "solid white" if she didn't dye it, then they always said, "Poor Sook." In fact, everything they ever said about Aunt Sook they always ended it with "Poor Sook." Their hair was some odd color, and I could tell that they dyed theirs, too, but Aunt Sook was a whole lot prettier than they were. I think that's why they always said, "Poor Sook."

When we arrived back at Shirley Plantation, Mama dropped me off at the Gaspard's house, next to the barn lot. Alfonse Gaspard was the plantation *horseler* and took care of the mules and the barns. I told Mama that I would be home before dark, hoping that Cathrine would want to play gin rummy for a while. Maybe Caroline would be there, too. Cathrine's mama, Mrs. Mazie, made bread every day and she would give me a roll sometimes. If she didn't, then I would usually ask for one, but sometimes she said she didn't have any. She always had bread around, and I knew it, but you had to watch Mrs. Mazie pretty close. In fact, really close! She usually stayed a step ahead of everybody, and she liked to get onto me, too. She fussed in French most of the time.

Mrs. Mazie came out onto the porch and looked at me just as I stepped toward the swing where Cathrine was sitting. I spoke softly, "Miz Mazie, Cathrine, how y'all doin'?" But they didn't say anything. Poor Mrs. Mazie didn't have any teeth, at least that I could see, and I was afraid of her sometimes. She talked real fast with a lot of French words mixed in and fussed a lot at Cathrine and Mister Alfonse, too. When she talked all in French I figured she was talking about me, but she didn't know I knew a few French words, too. Mostly curse words, like *sacre'nom*.

Mrs. Mazie looked down at my bare leg and said, "Billy, I'm gonna get rid of that 'so' on ya leg," then she turned and went into the house. That scared the daylights out of me; I had had the sore a long time, and I hated it, but I sure didn't want Mrs. Mazie fooling with it.

I was sitting in the swing talking to Cathrine when Mrs. Mazie returned with a wash pan of water and a big piece of dark gray soap. She made her soap, too, and it was always dark gray.

She did a crooked little grin and ordered, "Stan-up and put yo' foot in dis heah pan, Billy." Then she looked at me really mean. I figured I needed to do what she said, and besides, I was wishing she had some kind of secret so she could get rid of my sore.

Squinting with fear, I put my foot into the pan of water and she washed my leg with an old rag and the gray soap. It burned a lot, but I tried to look like I was grateful. When Mrs. Mazie wasn't looking, I acted like I was crying: rubbing my eyes with my fist. Cathrine started smiling bigger and bigger and finally rolled up in a ball on the swing, laughing out loud.

Mrs. Mazie turned around and scolded, "Hush-up Cathrine, ya' might be nex." Cathrine sat up straight in the swing. She was as afraid of Mrs. Mazie like I was, I figured. Mrs. Mazie ordered me to come back every evening for three or four days in a row so she could wash my leg. And sure enough, after about the third day the sore quit draining the yellow stuff and started to dry up, making me think that maybe Mrs. Mazie *could* do a little magic. But Cathrine said it was the *lye* soap that made it go away, and I was sorry Mrs. Mazie couldn't do a little magic, but every day she gave me a roll and I didn't have to beg her for it. One time it even had butter on it. Mrs. Mazie always went barefooted in the summer, like all the kids, and sometimes in the winter, too, if it wasn't really cold. She sure had big feet for a little ole woman. I guessed it wasn't magic after all, but I was sure glad Mrs. Mazie made my sore go away. And it never came back, either.

***

The darkness was coming and the locusts and crickets were beginning their songs, while the row of small, unpainted houses on both sides of the dirt road through the Quarters seemed to slowly hide away in the dwindling light and the pinkish haze. The smells in the evening along the dirt road were familiar to me as anything in the whole world. With the smoke from the stoves and the constant hint of dust in the calm air, the glow of the setting sun turned every evening into a soft, dusty pink. Through the night, the dust would settle, but would quickly stir again when the dirt road burst alive at the first glimmer of the rising sun. The dust was always there in the summer, turning to a sandy mud when the rain came. Both the dust and the mud were part of our lives on Shirley Plantation, where we lived, where we played a lot, where we often fought, worked hard, and where we laughed with each other. But always, we knew, on every dusty or rainy day, when evening came and the stoves were warm with supper, and while peace and quiet surrounded us, we were home.

As I turned the corner at the hedgerow, I could barely see Pal coming to meet me. Under the darkness of the giant oaks in our front yard I could see the tall, lighted windows of the Big House. This faded gray house was where my family lived, where every summer we drank iced tea on its long, wide porches, where we played in the shade of the big trees all around it, and where we rode our horses through the broad, flat fields of sugarcane and cotton. In the winter, we gathered around its big brick fireplaces to keep warm, talk, laugh, be children, and patiently wait through our youth to grow up. I wondered why anyone would ever want to leave this magical kingdom. This big, old house was tall and graceful, and I imagined that it held thousands of secrets in its shadowy corners and long hallways. When the winds blew and rain pounded its tin roof, I could sometimes hear the house groan, and its windows would rattle in anguish. At other times, when a soft, gentle breeze blew against it, it seemed to laugh, or cry softly, while it remembered the happiness or the heartaches of the families who had lived there for over a hundred years. I imagined it was like a proud *King* sitting happily on his throne, surrounded by ever-moving shades of green, and believing that he would rule forever. That was the Big House, solemn, dignified and majestic. That was my family's home.

The sun had fallen below the woods in the west. Hoss and Wesley had finished their chores in the barns and around the Big House and had gone to their homes in the Quarters. The lamps were on in the front rooms, and the dimly lit windows seemed to be calling to me to come home. As I walked with Pal close to my side, I felt every little rock pressing into the soles of my bare feet. The locusts and crickets were singing to me from all directions, and I hummed along with all the evening sounds that were part of the enchantment around me. As the Western sky turned to lavender and purple, it cast a glow over the proud King and his big kingdom. He liked every minute of it, and he wished that every day would end just this way.

The screened door squeaked when I swung it open wide, then let it slam loudly behind me to announce my arrival. I crossed the porch and squinted, stepping into the brightly lit kitchen.

Mama, in her housedress and apron, was pouring milk into the glasses. At that very moment, almost in a trance, I felt the love, happiness, and beauty that surrounded my life. She looked at me, and with her glistening blue eyes, she smiled, "Well, young fellow. Just in time. Supper's all ready!"

I smiled, too, and knew where I belonged.

CHAPTER 3

It was Sunday and we always went to Sunday school and to church—twice on Sunday—at The Eola Baptist Church, about five miles below Bunkie. Limping from step to step down the long stairway in the main hall of the Big House, my foot was hurting because of the jump from the bus at Aunt Sook's store. It looked a little bit bigger than the other one, but I always thought it was little bit bigger anyway, so I looked at it real close and didn't see anything like a cut.

My stomach growled a little just when I got to the kitchen, where a hot biscuit and ham were waiting for me on the table. After I ate, I pleaded with Mama in my best whiney voice, telling her that I just couldn't go to Sunday school and church with a sore foot like mine, but she shook her finger at me and threatened, "Boy, if you're not ready in forty-five minutes, I'm gonna skin you alive," and she didn't smile at all. That was one of her threats when the answer was "No," and I knew that when she used a really mean one, then I shouldn't push her any farther. Sometimes, if I did, her blue eyes would turn almost solid black. I limped really badly when I left the kitchen, every step begging for a little bit of sympathy, hoping to maybe make her feel bad about saying no so quickly, but Mama never even looked my way. She just kept on cooking dinner for the preacher.

Since the preacher and his family were coming after church, Mama had already cooked most of what we would have for Sunday dinner. The food smelled really good, and after she went to get dressed I had planned to sneak a fried drumstick and go to the fishponds to eat it. Pal could have the bone, and no one would ever know. I really didn't mind the preacher and his wife, Mrs. Olivia, and little Fredrick coming, but Eunice Ellen could stay at home, as far as I was concerned. Eunice Ellen was as mean as the Devil. She was at least two years older than me and was a big ole girl with curly red hair and a lot of red freckles. Everybody called her Red, which I think she didn't like. Still, I called her Red all the time and just stayed away from her as much as I could. She didn't like me anyway; in fact, I don't think she liked anybody.

There was a bunch of kids at church, and I believe Eunice Ellen got mad at all of us in Sunday school because she was the slowest person during the *sword drill*, when, as the preacher's daughter, she should have been the fastest at finding Bible verses. At least, that's what I figured. She let it be known real quick that she would "Get um," and I knew she would get me first when they would come to our house after church.

Church lasted a long time, ten or fifteen minutes past twelve o'clock. The preacher was awfully loud and waved his arms a lot. He said someone had gotten drunk during the week, and he had to get him out of jail, and talk to the man's wife. The preacher didn't say if the man drank wine or whiskey, but by the way he was carrying on I figured it must have been whiskey because wine didn't make a fellow really drunk as bad as whiskey, from what I had heard. Besides, the word *whiskey* just seemed to me to be a lot tougher than the pretty little word *wine*.

But anyway, Mister Buck led us through all twelve verses of "Just As I Am," before my stomach began a little growl, and I could almost feel it moving inside me. Two ole maid sisters sitting at the end of the pew started whimpering and sniffing around the tenth verse, so I just lowered my head and closed my eyes like I was praying. Mama sang out pretty loudly from the choir. She really liked "Just As I Am." It was hot, all of the windows were open, and people were fanning themselves, and I started sweating, so I took my tie and sport coat off, which would probably make Dad a little mad at me because he figured everybody needed to suffer at least a little bit to be a good church-goer. The two ole maids left their seats, went up to the front and shook the preacher's hand, then put their arms around him. They went back to their seats, still sniffing and each wiping their eyes with little white handkerchiefs, and one of them blew her nose real soft-like. Just then she looked over at me, like I ought to go up and shake his hand, too, and maybe tell him something. But, I figured they just needed someone to say a few words to, and needed a hug from a man. The preacher didn't often repeat what anyone ever told him, so I figured that whatever anyone said to him must have been some kind of secret. I never had anything to tell him, and I didn't think I had any secrets either, except the airplane crash and the blood, but I wasn't going to tell anybody about that anyway. And besides, the preacher was big, and that day was too hot to hug anybody. I never even hugged my Dad anymore, so I knew I didn't care to hug the preacher, but Mrs. Olivia hugged me almost every time she saw me. She always smelled good, just about as good as the perfume counter at Parrino's Drug Store, and was really pretty. In fact, to me, Mrs. Olivia was downright beautiful. Everybody thought that, and I even figured she could be in a picture show one day if she ever went out to Hollywood. I had gotten to be a little taller than Mrs. Olivia and, in fact, I was getting close to being as tall as my dad.

But anyway, the preacher prayed the last prayer, and a few of the men spoke out, "Amen!" That was the signal I waited for, and as usual, several people stood around and talked out in front of the church. My friends and I always talked about cars, and today was special because the McCoys had just gotten a new Hudson, dark red, and it was the only new 1946 parked out front. Several of the boys went over to look at the fenders, which went all the way from the front to the rear without stopping. It was sure nicer than our old Ford. I hated our old car, and I wished Dad would get us a new one. A Hudson would be better than a Chevy like Mrs. Prosser's, but I would take a Chevy anytime.

Poor Miss Hattie, tall and skinny, Poor Miss Hattie, in her black dress and a little white lace collar around her long neck, was standing by herself right off the sidewalk with her old black, shiny purse dangling from her elbow, waiting, I guess, for someone to stop and talk to her. Her lipstick and her hat were both crooked, and sometimes her eyebrows were lopsided on her forehead. Everybody called her *"Poor Miss Hatti,"* and we figured she had a few bricks short of a full load, but nobody ever said so, especially my mama or my dad. They felt sorry for Poor Miss Hattie, and I guess I did, too. All of a sudden, Poor Miss Hattie grabbed both sides of her head with her hands, mumbled something that sounded like "Dammit" to me, and she looked down. My buddies and I looked down, too, and Poor Miss Hattie's old white drawers had fallen all the way down to the grass, piled up around her ankles. She looked at us about ten feet away and stuck her tongue out, then she stepped right out of her drawers, turned around and almost ran to her car, leaving her drawers on the edge of the sidewalk. We looked at each other and started laughing harder.

I told Sam, "Pick up your aunt's drawers, Sam, and give 'um to her tonight." He turned to me and frogged me on the arm. It really hurt, but he owed me one.

Mrs. Olivia came over and picked up Poor Miss Hattie's drawers, rolled them up, and put them in her purse. She looked at us like we weren't supposed to laugh, so everybody stopped really quick and waited. Knowing how nice and sweet Mrs. Olivia was, I figured she would save them for Poor Miss Hattie. All of us boys looked back and forth at each other, and smiled as we watched beautiful Mrs. Olivia strut on back toward the church house door. She was as pretty as anyone I had ever seen, and could really walk nice, even in high-heeled shoes. But I wouldn't have touched Poor Miss Hattie's old drawers with a ten-foot pole.

Dad blew the horn for me to come on, so I jumped into the rear of our old Ford and we headed home. When we got to Four Corners, I wished we could stop at The Four Way Café and eat a good hamburger, but it was closed on Sunday anyway. Maw Stafford owned The Four Way Café and could really make good hamburgers, but Dad never wanted to eat anywhere but at home because he said it cost too much. But that day, I really didn't want to have to fool with red-faced Eunice Ellen when we got back to our house.

I ran upstairs and changed my clothes as fast as I could. My foot still hurt a little, but I figured that if I walked around on it for a while, it might stop hurting. I walked into the kitchen from the dining room at just about the time the preacher and his family were walking through the back door from the porch. Eunice Ellen stopped at the door and looked at me like she was ready for a fight, but she turned around and went to sit on the porch with her little brother and

Mickey. Mrs. Olivia crossed the kitchen and set her purse at the end of the cabinet by the icebox, and I wondered if Poor Miss Hattie's old drawers were still in it, sitting on our cabinet right next to where we kept all of our food cold.

"What can I do to help, Florence?" asked Mrs. Olivia, smiling and winking at me, reminding me how really pretty she was and how nice, too. I liked looking at her, so I smiled back, waiting and hoping she would come over and hug me like she usually did—hug me really tight.

Mama replied, "Why don't you get some trays out and put ice in the glasses. We're gonna have tea." Mrs. Olivia opened the icebox, and I could see my small can of *imported nuts* sitting on the front of the top shelf, just waiting for the right person to open the icebox.

"Miz Olivia, try one of those imported nuts. They're really good," I told her nicely, while glancing toward Mama. Mama turned, stopped in her tracks, and frowned at me with her red lips partly opened, but she didn't say anything. She just stood there with a stack of plates in her hands, waiting.

Mrs. Olivia got the can out and turned the lid. When that big spring-loaded snake jumped out of the can, the lid flew out of her hand and hit the airplane clock on top of the icebox. The big green snake hit Mrs. Olivia under the chin, and her little hat fell to the side of her head, while her beautiful auburn hair came loose and one side fell below her shoulders. All at the same time, she dropped the can, screamed, and fell to the floor right in front of the icebox, with the door wide open, letting all the cold air out. It looked to me like she was hardly breathing; her eyes had rolled back in her head, her red lips had disappeared, and her rosy cheeks had turned grey. The little can rolled slowly across the kitchen floor, stopping at Mama's feet. Mama's mouth opened wider, and her blue eyes started getting darker.

The preacher came running into the kitchen from the family room, yelling louder than he did in church, "What happened? What's the matter?" He started picking up Mrs. Olivia, while I was already headed out to the porch to face Eunice Ellen.

A few days later, I asked Mama what had happened to my can of imported nuts. She looked at me with a frown, chuckled, then she shook her finger at me and said, "Boy, you're gonna pay for those kind of tricks some day, and I hope you do." I never saw my pretty little can again.

Eunice Ellen was waiting at the sitting end of the screened porch, her lips narrow and stiff like she was trying to keep her face from exploding. She asked me what had happened, and I told her that her mama had had a little sinking spell but everything was okay.

She opened her mouth to say something else, but before she could, I suggested, "Come on, let's go out in the yard at the fishponds." I knew if we went outside and she tried to hit me with her fist or get close enough to kick me in the shin, I wouldn't be cornered, and I could surely run faster than she could. Besides, she had on her Sunday dress and good shoes. She could never catch me. We went to the fishponds under the pecan trees, and she bent over to see the goldfish. She had a big booty for just fourteen, almost as big as Mag's. I sure wanted to give her a little shove, but Pal started barking and jumping at my hand, wanting to play. Besides, Dad would have gotten really mad at me if Eunice Ellen had somehow fallen into one of the ponds, and I sure didn't want to get him stirred up with the preacher being there. Dad would be stirred up enough about Mrs. Olivia fainting. I figured she shouldn't have fainted. It was just a joke.

I told Eunice Ellen that a day or so ago I had hit my knuckle on a rock in the pond, and I let Pal lick it so the sore would go away quicker. I shoved my fist real fast at her face and nose, so she could see the scab up close. She jerked her head back; I could see her ball-up her fist, and her face started turning red. I figured she wanted to sock me in the nose and was just about to let me have it, but she gritted her teeth and yelled, "That's stupid, you idiot. You're about the most stupid boy I know."

Pal was right there, wagging his big yellow tail, with his ears back and kind of smiling up at me, and I figured he was begging me to "sic" him on Eunice Ellen. He could tear up her pretty dress in about five seconds, but if I did that Dad would kill me and maybe kill poor ole Pal, too, and I sure didn't want him to hurt Pal. So, instead, I scratched the scab off my knuckle while Eunice Ellen watched with her mouth and eyes wide open, and I squeezed the little cut to make it start bleeding, telling her, "Look at that red blood. It's red, huh, Red? Pretty, huh?" and I saw her grit her teeth while her head started to shake and I figured she couldn't stop it.

She looked at me, turned her lips down, and yelled, "You're so stupid and dirty, I hope you die!" Pal was waiting for me to let him lick the cut again like it was his duty to do that, but I wasn't afraid of dying; I was way too young to die. The only dead people I had ever seen were my two grandfathers, and they were both really old. I wasn't even twelve yet. Oh, I had seen my older brother after he died, and Danny McBride when he crashed his plane, but I knew my brother died because they couldn't get the medicines they needed during the war, and Danny died because the plane crashed. That plane killed him, tore him apart. I had seen it, but I wished I hadn't thought about that, and about Danny.

Eunice Ellen stuck her tongue out at me, then she spit toward me and missed; then she turned around and ran back toward the porch with her big butt bouncing under the flowers on her dress. Some of Uncle Nick's laying hens, mostly Rhode Island Reds that I could see, were pecking around the back walk. They squawked and ran as fast as they could when they saw Eunice Ellen coming, making me figure they wouldn't be able to lay any eggs for at least a week. But I wished that red-faced witch would step in some chicken mess in those Sunday shoes, and walk into the kitchen with it. Her mama would get on her for that. Eunice Ellen was as mean as a polecat fighting my yellow dog. Ugly, too, just like her daddy.

I waited with Pal at the fishponds, hugged him a couple times and let him lick my cheeks. I told him I would let him tear up Euncie Ellen's dress the next time she came to our house, if she was still so mean. A few minutes later, Mickey yelled from the side porch to come eat dinner, and I was really hungry, figuring it must have been at least half past one by then.

I swung open the screen door and crossed the porch into the kitchen where Mrs. Olivia was leaning over the table cutting some chicken for Fredrick. Eunice Ellen, Fredrick, and my little brother were already seated at the kitchen table, so I made Mickey change sides so I could sit opposite from the red-faced witch. Her green eyes were locked on every move I made.

Just when I sat in my chair, I hung my head a little, and said, "Miz Olivia, I'm sorry bout the nut can. I sure hope you're okay." Her fluffy dress sleeve brushed against my cheek as she continued cutting Fredrick's chicken, and she really smelled good. I tried not to look, but I could see her bosoms as she leaned over the table.

She smiled, hugged me, and pushed my hair to the side; then she kissed me on the forehead, smiled again and said, "Oh, that's okay, Billy. I'll get over it." She had rearranged her pretty hair, pinning some of it high on her head, and with a roll going almost all the way around. With a deep breath, I took in the aroma and sweetness coming from Mrs. Olivia. When she kissed me on the forehead, I looked at Eunice Ellen and thought all of her freckles had gotten together in one big red splotch, and her face was about to explode again. She stuck her long tongue out at me, and acted like she was going to vomit. Touching my forehead, I held my hand on the spot where Mrs. Olivia had kissed me, then let out the breath holding Mrs. Olivia's sweet aroma.

In my nicest and kindest voice, I asked politely, "Eunice Ellen, would you say the blessing, please?" and I sat very tall in my chair, closed my eyes, and bowed my head.

Mrs. Olivia hugged me again and said, "Oh, how sweet you are, Billy!" I closed my eyes and sniffed again, bringing in the aroma surrounding the preacher's wife. She patted me on the shoulder and I inhaled deeply again and held it in. Just as quickly, she turned and headed toward the dining room door, her high-heeled shoes tapping sweetly on the linoleum floor.

Eunice Ellen had the meanest look on her red face that I had ever seen, and was kicking at me under the table. I took a bite of my chicken leg, crossed my eyes at her, smiled, and finally exhaled Mrs. Olivia's sweet smell. Eunice Ellen gritted her teeth and kicked harder, but couldn't reach far enough to get me.

The red-faced witch never did ask God to bless our food that Sunday.

THE LAST WITNESS FROM A DIRT ROAD

The preacher and his family left our house around four o'clock since he had to prepare for the Sunday night service. My good friends would be there, and we would hang around in front of the church and talk about cars and whatever we wanted to—sometimes girls. The girls mostly stayed inside. When the singing started, the boys in my group most often sat together in the back of the church, while the older boys and girls teamed up to sit with each other. Sometimes they would hold hands under the songbooks layed open in their laps, especially if there were no grownups sitting too close to them. I guessed it wouldn't be very long before I would do that, too. But that night, I couldn't find anyone I wanted to hold hands with, surely not Eunice Ellen. She was sitting closer to the front with some other girls who were about as mean as she was, and I knew I didn't want to hold hands with any of them. But Mrs. Olivia, well, Mrs. Olivia was the prettiest lady in the church, and if I were older, I knew already, that I would like to hold her hand.

That Sunday was the last time the preacher, Mrs. Olivia and their kids came to the Big House on Shirley Plantation. No one had bothered to tell me that they were leaving, but just a week or two later they moved to another church a long way off and I missed Mrs. Olivia. Very soon, another preacher and his family came and took over at The Eola Baptist Church.

Mama made sure they, too, would come to dinner after church.

Mama was good about that.

CHAPTER 4

The sheets on my bed were damp from the air drawn through the window by the big fan at the end of the downstairs hall. Sleep was good in my cool little room overlooking the big oaks in our front yard. That morning I needed to pee very badly, so I went to the other bedroom, raised the window in the back dormer and peed through the screen, knowing that I could never pee enough for it to run all the way down the gutters to the old cistern at the back-end of the Big House. Anyway, the old cistern was left over from when we didn't have well water, and the only time we ever used the water in it was when the well pump or the electricity went out. About that time, Mama called up the stairs, "Get up! Get up! Time to get ready." I called back an "Okay," but my heart sure wasn't in it. I never liked school, even from the first grade.

I put on my short britches, a white knit shirt, and socks, trying also to put on my tennis shoes. My sore foot was still a little swollen, so I took the socks off and managed to get my shoe on. I limped down the steps and headed to the kitchen, guessing that Mag would be there, and I needed to get even with her for not taking my shoes and books upstairs a few days back. Stopping in the dining room, I could hear her humming one of her songs, and every now and then she would sing out a few words and shake her big bosums like she was going to break out dancing. Very quietly, I crossed the dining room, then I jumped into the kitchen with a loud yell, throwing my books across the kitchen floor. Mag dropped the skillet on the floor and screamed, while the French toast scattered across the linoleum. She stood with one hand on her hip and the other with a dishrag pressed against her chest. I knew then that I shouldn't have done that to poor Mag because now she would have a lot to get even for, and her brown skin looked to me like it was turning lighter. She didn't say anything, but shook her head as she bent over to pick up the skillet. I quickly opened the bottom cabinet, grabbed a can of Donald Duck orange juice, stuck a hole in the top with the ice pick, and ran out to the far end of the porch.

I could hear her yelling after me, "I's sho gon tell yo mama bout dis. Yous betta run, yous rascal! Yous almost made dat skillet burn me, boy. An look at cha, ya ain't even washed yo' face and combed yo' hair, and ya don already started wit yo foolishness."

I drank the can of orange juice and went back to the kitchen door. Mag was waiting by the sink, turned toward me, and said "Ya can jist forgits bout breakfas 'cause I ain't cookin ya nothin," and she threw a slice of French toast at me. I didn't want breakfast anyway. She stopped and planted both hands on her hips, asking, "Wat makes yous so mean, Billy? Ya oughts to be shame of yoself! Ya gon see me in hell one day, boy!" and she threw a second French toast in my direction. She shook her long finger at me and said, "I sho ain't gon invite chu to my pawdy Saddey night. Don' chu count on dat, ya lit'le rascal."

That was the first that I had heard about her party. Since it was Monday, I knew I had a few days to make it up to Mag, but she wouldn't invite me anyway, I knew that. She also knew that Dad would get mad if I was invited to a Saturday night party in the Quarters.

"Ah, Mag, I'm sorry," and I lowered my head a little, turning my lips down.

She shook her head from side to side, making her big earrings dangle around her neck, then she looked at me and said, "Lawd have mercy, I sho don' knows wat I's gon do wis you! Ya's awful, Billy. I's still shakin like a leaf, boy. I sho wunda where ya Mama and Daddy gots you from! Out da hog pen, I betcha!" She came closer to me and shook her finger right at my nose and ordered, "Ya go in dare and wash yo face and comb yo hair, 'fo ya leaves heah. Ya looks awful, goin to school dat a way." She shook her head and went back to the stove, turned and exclaimed, "Evybody gon think you ain't never lef dis ole plantation, lookin' lack a sho 'nuf contry hick," then she asked, "Is ya hongry, boy? Da skillet's still hot."

I picked up my books, but before I could answer I heard Mama backing the old Ford out of the garage and blowing the horn for me to come on. I straightened my hair with my hand, ran down the steps and called back to her, "See ya, later, Mag! *I loves ya, honey! I sho do, I loves ya, honey!*"

Standing in the kitchen door onto the porch, I could hear her yelling, "I hopes ya gits a 'F' today, and dat teacher gives ya a good whippin fo ya comes back heah."

She would get over the whole ordeal in two minutes, but would be ready to yell at me some more by the time I got home from school. Mag loved fussing as much as she loved laughing.

School was slow as molasses in the wintertime. Fifth grade was tough, and Mrs. Gilroy was tougher, but I didn't like the fifth grade any more than any of the other grades I had been through. Mrs. Gilroy was always good to me, and I liked her. The other kids, some of them anyway, like Janet, always complained about Mrs. Gilroy getting on to her, but I could tell that Janet talked too much and made everybody giggle a lot, especially the girls who sat next to her. I figured most of the kids always said they didn't like their teacher much anyway. Mrs. Gilroy was tall and thin and wore pretty clothes every day. On Wednesday, about three o'clock, we would go to the playground to play softball. One Wednesday, when I was the pitcher, Mrs. Gilroy stood in back of me calling the strikes and balls. Jack came up to bat and hit the ball over second base out into centerfield.

Harold threw the ball to Eddie on second, and Jack was almost to third. Eddie threw the ball toward home plate, and I turned toward home to see if Jack could be stopped at third. I heard a *thump* and a soft whistling sound right behind me, like somebody blowing in my ear. I turned around and found Mrs. Gilroy lying in a heap on the grass. Everybody started running toward the pitcher's mound, including the girls who were standing on the sidelines. Mrs. Gilroy was a big pile of person just lying there. I bent over her and saw the dusty print of the softball on her pretty pink blouse, right in the middle of her back. I pulled the ball from under her arm and put it in my glove, thinking poor Mrs. Gilroy might be dead, and Eddie had killed her, but I couldn't recall his ever saying he didn't like her. Some of the girls started crying and everybody was asking, "Is she breathing? Is she dead?" Harold had come in from center field, knelt by her, and shook Mrs. Gilroy really hard by her shoulder, commanding, "Wake up, you old battle ax, wake up," and about then she moved a little and the girls all started jumping up and down, yelling, "Miz Gilroy, Miz Gilroy!" I figured one of the teacher's pets would tell her what Harold had called her, but she had probably been called worse things than that, and besides, I figured she didn't care anyway.

She opened her eyes and looked around for just a second, took a deep breath, then raised herself on her elbows, and then her hands. She stood up straight like a beanpole, clapped the dust from her rear end, then her hands, and ordered, "Everybody! Back to your places! Let's play ball!"

Dammit! Just his luck, Jack had made a home run!

A drizzly little rain on Thursday afternoon cooled down everything. That night at supper Mama told me that my sister Margie was coming Friday to visit for a little while. We called her "Margie" instead of her first name, Ethel. I thought she liked that better. It didn't matter to me. I didn't like "Billy" very much, but that was my name. We all called Ethel "Margie," except Aunt Sook and my dad's other four sisters. They were just that way—they weren't about to change.

It was still drizzling on Friday when the school bus dropped us off. Mickey and I took our shoes off and walked through the mud down the dirt road to our house. As usual he whined, but that day it was about the mud. I tried really hard not to pick at him, but he could whine better than anyone I knew. I picked up a little piece of mud with a tiny rock in it and lightly threw it at his head. It stuck in his pretty little blond curls; and when he tried to get it out, it just smushed more. I knew then, Mama would make him bathe that night and wash his hair. He knew it, too, and he whined louder. Then he picked up a handful of mud and threw it at me. His aim was really bad, and I dodged it easily, which made him madder. He started crying and running after me, as he wiped his hand on his shirt, but in just a couple of steps he slipped down and his books and shoes scattered in the muddy road. He yelled some ugly words at me and said that he was going to tell Mama. I didn't know he knew so many bad words.

I told him, "Tell her, smell her, put her on the gatepost and sell her."

That made him madder, so he spit at me. I told him I was going to tell Mama about the dirty names he called me and that it was a sin to spit on somebody because people spit on Jesus a long time ago. He cried harder and his face got redder. I figured that I would get it from Mama when we arrived at the Big House.

By the time we rounded the corner at the hedgerow, he had mud all over him. Trying to help a little, I told him, "You better go wash off at the faucet before you go in the house, else Mama's gonna give you whipping, and I hope she does because of all that dirty talk."

Mama must have heard him yelling, because she was waiting at the end of the porch and made him go straight to the faucet out back and take his clothes off. He really started crying. Mama asked him what happened, and I like to think she used to laugh inside a lot about things like that. I hurried into the kitchen, got a spoon full of white beans out of the pot on the stove, spread them on a slice of bread, and headed out to the Quarters as fast as I could. My little brother was shaking from the cold water, still crying and trying to tell Mama the story while I quickly rounded the corner of the porch. He really looked funny, buck-naked, standing outside with Mama trying to wash him down. When I looked over at him, I smiled and waved, and he saw me getting away. He started crying louder and screaming some ugly words right in front of Mama. He was stomping his feet up and down and pointing in my direction. He was awful! I thought she ought to skin the little rascal for acting like that and talking ugly in front of her, but I thought I could see her laughing pretty hard. Pal and I just hightailed it down the driveway. I gave a bite of my bean sandwich to my ole yellow dog, and he took almost the whole thing, leaving just a little bite for me. I told him he was just downright greedy.

When I got to the barn lot, I could see Margie's car coming, slipping and sliding in the ruts through the muddy road. She stopped and I got in, and she leaned over and kissed me, patting me on my leg. I had always known that both my sisters were pretty, in fact as pretty as the preacher's wife, Mrs. Olivia. Just when the car started to move again, ole Kaiser knocked on the driver's side window. Kaiser lived across from the Gaspards', and every now and then she worked in our house if Rosa or Mag couldn't come. Kaiser loved Margie a lot, so she said, but I didn't trust her one bit. Margie lowered her window, smiled at her, and before Margie could say anything at all, Kaiser started singing a song about a Blueberry Hill, or something like that. She never stopped, just sang the whole thing, and Margie told her how good it was. I couldn't believe it! It made me want to vomit. I thought it stunk, in fact, just about like Kaiser stunk. When the ole devil worked in our house, she was ugly and mean, and I didn't like her. Mag was fun and happy, Rosa was quiet and nice, and Mama liked Rosa the best, but ole Kaiser was awful.

We finally pulled away and I told Margie to let me off at the hedgerow, that I was going back to the Quarters, figuring that my little brother was probably still mad at me. Margie and I said goodbye, and I wondered if maybe Margie was going to have a little baby. Her tummy was getting big, but nobody talked about that to kids like me, so I had to listen, wait, and listen some more.

I headed back down the muddy road and went to Papa's house, where he was waiting for me on his front porch swing. I whispered to him that Mag was going to have a party Saturday night, and we *had* to go to it. He shook his head "No," and said that I better not go either because his daddy would tell my daddy. Figuring that if Papa went with me, he wouldn't tell his daddy, Hoss, about it, and I told him that Mag had invited him as her special person. He liked that. Papa and I walked back to my house and went to the milkroom to play, to hide out from Mama, too, until everything cooled down and she would start cooking supper. Margie had left by the time Papa and I arrived back at the yard.

Papa and I found some old paint, "Kemtone," in the corner of the milk-room, left over from painting the inside of our house a couple of years back. I knew it was a new kind of paint, but I didn't know much about paint. I had painted my bicycle a couple of times, but that was all. We opened a can, and we decided to paint Papa's legs from his short britches down to his toes. It was re-ally white, but Papa was as proud as he could be. While we were cutting up and laughing, Hoss, Papa's daddy, came in with a couple of buckets of milk and got onto us, making us go to the faucet and wash Papa's legs. I wanted to take Papa and show him to Mag, knowing she would have shaken that long finger at me and fussed a little, too, but she would have laughed, and maybe she would have invited us to her party, for real. I could tell that Hoss was a little mad at us when he made Papa go home.

It had stopped raining by the next day, Saturday, and the plantation truck took everyone to town for payday and to buy groceries. Hoping that he had not left to go to town, I hurried down the dirt road to Papa's house. We sat in the swing and talked a little while, and I showed him my new comic books. His mama came to the open door and ordered Papa to rake the front yard, which was the same as telling me to go home. I guessed she was mad, too, about our painting Papa's legs. I told Papa I would be by about five o'clock, and we would walk down to Mag's party. He said he still didn't know if he should do that, but I told him Mag was looking for us, and she had some pop for us. I could see that he couldn't get all the white paint off his legs, as they were a dark gray. I thought maybe Hoss had given Papa a whipping because of the paint.

The dirt road had dried up really well, but hadn't turned into dust yet. In two or three days the dust would come back if the traffic were heavy enough. Every time I saw my little brother, I waited for him to get onto me about the muddy walk home the day before, but he didn't. On the other hand, though, he did talk about Mag's party, my guessing that Little Joe or Lionel had told him about it. They were his best pals, but they were all too young to go. I had to be very careful or Mama or Daddy would get the idea I was planning to go to Mag's "Saturday Night Ball." That's what she always called it. I was afraid Dad would warn me about going; then I would be in real trouble when I went. All day Saturday I played away from the Big House and tried to stay away from Mama or Dad.

CHAPTER 5

Around four o'clock I went into the kitchen where Mama was busy fixing supper.

"Mama, I'm gonna go see if Miz Mazie wants to wash my leg. I'll be back in a little while," and I opened the screened door.

Before I could jump down the steps, she called to me, "Okay, but you come on home when that party starts at Mag's."

I was already down the steps by the time she finished her command, but I pretended like I didn't hear her, and besides, that wasn't a real warning for me not to go to the party. I skipped down the driveway headed to Papa's house.

Papa was all dressed up in long pants, shoes, and a white shirt, looking like he was going to a Sunday school party. I still had on my short britches and a knit shirt, and was barefooted. We sat on his front porch till his mama went inside to check on supper before we slipped off and headed to the end of the dirt road where Mag and Gilbert Frank lived.

Their front yard was surrounded by tall bushes and had a little gate where the walkway started at the edge of the road. The house was mostly hidden behind the bushes and a big oak tree on the side of the front yard. Papa and I slowly crept to the gate and saw that several people were already there. We could hear Mag laughing while she stood on the steps at the front porch, talking across the yard to somebody. She was all dressed up in a big flowery skirt and a white top that fit really tight, with ruffles at the top of it. Her bright red shoes were as pretty as any my sisters had ever worn. All the way from where I hid at the gate I could see the long crease between her big bosoms. I told Papa to look at her big brown bosoms, but he just covered his eyes with his hands and grinned, like he was ashamed or something. We had talked about bosoms several times before, and we both wondered what they were really like. Mags were really big, and they stuck out farther than the ruffles on her top.

Mag had on some of her long earrings and brightly colored necklaces, with two or three big bracelets dangling around her wrists. She was slim and pretty. Her eyes moved quickly toward the gate, and I jumped behind the bushes leaving Papa clearly visible from the porch. I leaned over to peek around the bushes, and Mag was already at the gate right in front of me. She put her elbows on top with her hands hanging over the little gate and shook her head at Papa and me.

"Wat' in da world is I gon do wis yous two?" she asked, and moved her head saying "No, no, no." "Oh, com' on in, but chu can't stay long. Yo daddy's gon kill me, fo sho." She turned and motioned for us to follow her.

That was the first okay I had heard all week, and just when I was feeling good about it, she suddenly turned again and caught me by my hair and fussed, "I oughts to give ya a whippin right cher and take ya to ya Daddy, ya mean lil' rascal, and tel'im hows you done bust in on my pawty."

She had pulled my head down to the side where she was holding me, and I quickly said, "Uncle, uncle! I'm sorry Mag!"

She let go of my hair, and with her long fingers she brushed it to the side of my forehead. "Okay, dawlin, but don' chu tell yo Daddy bout comin heah!" Her pretty red lips spread into a beautiful smile, and I let her pinch my cheek without any objection.

I could hear the soft voice of Nat King Cole coming from the radio on the front porch. My sister listened to his radio show, too. The next party we would have, I figured I could bring my sister's little record player and some of her records. It was brand new and I liked it. Mag would like that.

Alex, Veesy, and Bernice, their daughter, were already there; Rosa's younger sister Emma was sitting on the porch swing, while Gilbert Frank was taking some of the food out to the table in the front yard, and Mag left us to go help him.

Alex looked puzzled at Papa and me, raised his eyebrows and asked, "Billy, wat'chu boys doin? I bet yo Daddy don know bout y'all commin' down heah."

Alex took me fishing a lot and was a "straw boss" for Dad. He taught me how to drive my dad's truck some time back, and he always let me drive when we went fishing to Chicot Lake or Miller's Lake, either one.

Veesy, sitting close to Alex, looked straight ahead. She never said much, as I recall, and I believe she dipped snuff. Her bottom lip always looked like it had something hiding in it. I told Alex that Mag told Papa and me to come on in. That seemed to satisfy him, but I figured that come Monday he would probably tell Dad that I was at Mag's party, especially if Dad would ask him if anything bad might have happened. Alex had a half-empty gallon jug of Port wine sitting on the ground beside his chair. Before he could ask any more questions, I walked off with Papa hanging onto the back of my shirt with one hand.

Being a "straw boss" placed Alex a little higher in the rank of the plantation field hands, a distinction that oftentimes caused a separation from old friends and neighbors in the Quarters, where they lived. However, Alex as a straw boss, and Mag with her job in the Big House, had managed to hold on to their friends in the Quarters, and were most often the ones who gathered everybody together on Saturday nights to party.

Across the yard, Ellis and Elijah were sitting in straight chairs, leaning over playing cards on the ground in front of them. Ellis was Alex's brother, and he had a glass of wine sitting by the leg of his chair. Dad said Elijah went to the little white church up the road toward town, and that he didn't drink. There were some nickels and pennies lying on the ground, so I guessed they were playing for money. Wine, gambling, and, pretty soon, dancing—it made me think that if our preacher from The Eola Baptist Church had seen this party, he could preach his whole sermon on it. Two or three women dressed up like the people in Mama's Sears and Roebuck catalogue were going in and out of the house with food and other stuff, each one drinking a bottle of Regal beer. I wanted to try one of those Regals myself, but Mag and Alex would make me go home if I went inside and got one. Maybe after it got dark I could wander inside and see if there was any Regals left. Several women would laugh and talk to Alex and Ellis. They would lean against them and whisper something in their ears, then laugh out loud. Veesy just kept looking straight ahead with her bottom lip stuck out, never saying a word. Other women who came through the gate would stop and take a sip of wine from Alex's glass, like they were trying it out, or trying to decide if they wanted some wine. Emma sat quietly on the porch swing, sipping every now and then from a small glass. Mag was laughing and singing along with the music coming from the porch, and suddenly she was dancing all by herself on the walkway, with her arms in the air and that big skirt swinging from side to side. Everybody in the little yard stopped talking and started clapping and calling out "Go, go, go!" A couple of times she picked up her skirt to where you could see above her knees, or she would turn around really fast and the skirt would fly up and out into a big circle. Papa suddenly grabbed the back of my knit shirt with both hands, almost pulling me down to the ground. Mag could really dance, but I figured she was a lot older than her big, fun heart, and a good bit older than Gilbert Frank, too.

More people were coming through the gate with bottles of wine and sometimes pots of food, while others brought in odd-shaped things wrapped in a piece of cloth or in some kind of paper. Gilbert Frank came out with two coal-oil lamps and set them on the ground in the middle of the yard, since it was getting a little dark with all the tall bushes around. Pretty soon the bugs started flying about the lamps, but I figured it wouldn't be long before no one cared about the bugs anyway. Suddenly, somebody broke the smooth sounds of Nat King Cole with a couple of dirty words and loud talk coming from under the oak tree. Ole Kaiser was cursing at J.B.: "Ya touch me agin, and I's gon cut ya, ya son ova bitch." I hadn't seen ole Kaiser come in, and I knew Mag didn't invite her—nobody liked Kaiser. Alex jumped up from his chair, crossed the yard, and told Kaiser and J.B. something. Kaiser spit some tobacco juice on the ground at Alex's feet, and it looked like some of it landed on his shiny brown shoes. Alex looked down at them and shook his head, while Kaiser put her hand in her pocket, as though she was searching for something, my figuring she probably carried a knife or maybe a straight razor. I waited while Papa pulled closer to me, my hoping that ole Kaiser would pull a knife on Alex, so he would beat the hell out of her, but she stopped and didn't make another move. Standing right where he had been when his shoes got splattered with Kaiser's tobacco juice, Alex balled up his fist and the muscles came alive in his cheeks, while he told her something right in her ugly face. Kaiser spit again, then she took off, almost running toward the little gate, and never looked back. She was mean and ugly, and I was glad she had left, but I really wanted Alex to bloody her nose with his big fist and flatten her out on the ground. Alex looked at J.B., gritted his teeth and told him something, then he walked back toward his chair by the gate.

Mag slowly danced over and stood on the steps near where Alex's daughter, Bernice, was sitting. She clapped her hands a couple of times and called out, "Evybody, come serve ya plate! Suppa's ready! Don be bashful, now. Com'on fo it gits cold," and she motioned toward the table, loaded with food.

With a big grin on his face and his white teeth shining, J.B. strutted over and sat on the steps by Bernice. I hoped he would touch her like he did Kaiser, figuring that Alex would beat the hell out of him really quick. In fact, I had heard about the fights at the Saturday night parties, and I wanted to see one, especially one where Alex would beat the hell out of either ole Kaiser or even J.B. But nobody moved after Mag's announcement, except Mag herself, and she headed toward the table where the food was laid out. When she came to me, she caught my arm and whirled me around to the music, laughing and swaying from side to side. I got caught up in her big skirt, and she wrapped it around me all the way to my chin, singing and dancing to the music. Papa had almost ripped my shirt before he finally let go. Gilbert Frank walked over to Emma, sitting on the swing, took her hand and led her off the porch to the food table. Mag had let go of me, and Papa and I moved a little toward the gate. He was holding on to my shirt again and stayed in back of me. When we got to the food table, I asked him if he wanted anything. His eyes were wide open looking at the dancers, and his jaw had dropped, while he just shook his head *no*. I looked across the table and Mag handed me a plate covered with more food than I had eaten in three days. Then she asked, "Papa, wat chu want boy?" and she bit down on a small pickle.

I took my plate from her, answering, "Thanks. Papa won't eat anything, Mag." I knew I didn't like everything she had piled on my plate, but I ate the bread and the fried baloney. I didn't want the greens and especially the black-eyed peas, but they sure smelled good.

The little yard started getting crowded, and the talking became louder. Nat King Cole wasn't singing anymore, and I didn't know who was, but someone called out real loud, asking, "Who dat singin? Dat's good!"

Mag broke in and called back, "Dat's Ella, honey. Miss Ella Fitzgerald! She bout good as Lena Horne huh'sef!" I didn't know Ella or Lena, but everybody at the party who wasn't eating was dancing up tight with each other. I knew that, and like Papa, I watched.

Most of the food was gone after about fifteen minutes. I looked over to the porch where Gilbert Frank and Emma were sitting in the swing, talking and nibbling at their food. They each had a glass of wine and would sip from the glass every now and then, while they smiled at each other. Alex went over and hugged Mag and whispered in her ear. The music changed to a slow rhythm, just as Mag leaned her head back, laughed a little and brushed her fingers through her soft brown hair. She turned her head and glanced toward Papa and me, while Alex walked toward his brother Ellis.

Very quickly Mag came over to where we were, put her arms on our shoulders, and said to both of us, "Now, ya boys don seen a 'nuff. Yous betta head on home."

I frowned and whined to her, "Ah, Mag, I'm not ready to go," then pointed to Alex's almost empty jug, still sitting on the ground by his chair. "Can I have a glass of that wine, Mag?"

She looked at me really hard, frowned, shook her head, and mean-like, asked, "Are you crazy, Billy?"

"No, I just want a taste, Mag, just a little bit, please, come on."

"Billy," and she hesitated for a second, " jist look at me!" She came closer to my face and angrily said in a loud whisper, "Ya oughts not be heah a' tall. Jist look at dese folks. Da's colored people, boy, and ya ain't fittin in heah! Dis ain't yo pawdy, anyway! Git goin right now!" All the while she was pointing toward the dirt road.

Papa pulled at my shirt and pushed us toward the gate, while still looking back at the dancing crowd. He was hitting my shoulder lightly with his other hand, mumbling, "Dis ain't yo pawdy, dis ain't yo pawdy."

"Just shut-up, Papa! I don't wanna hear that crap," I said, and quickly his lips began to quiver. He looked at me as though I had hit him in the mouth and he was about to cry.

J.B. had turned off the coal-oil lamps and set them on the porch, but in the bright moonlight I could see brown skins glisten with sweat, and shiny, damp cloth sticking to the backs of hot bodies. There was no breeze around us, only a stillness that seemed even to slow the dancing to almost no movement at all. The smell of sweet perfumes, the hot bodies, and the aroma of fresh pomade aroused my thoughts and deepened my curiosity. I wanted to dance, too. I wanted to laugh and sing, and I wanted to sweat just like my friends were doing, their holding tight to someone with their eyes closed, letting their bodies melt together while moving smoothly to the rhythm of the soft music. Something in the little yard had taken over completely, something I had never seen, but I knew that same *something* had made me anxious and excited. I wanted the feelings I could see all around me, the thoughts I imagined running through the minds of the dancers, and I wanted to catch *the moment*, holding it, until I, too, would close my eyes, melt into someone's arms and dance. Dance, to the slow sweet music that engulfed us.

A big moon seemed trained onto the little yard, happily watching the dancers and listening to the music. Mag followed Papa and me to the gate, and then she grabbed my arm and hugged me while tears moved slowly down her cheeks. At the same time, we both glanced toward the porch where Gilbert Frank was sitting in the swing with Emma, laughing and holding her hand. I didn't like what I saw, and when Mag turned and looked into my face I knew she didn't like it either.

She picked up the bottom of her big skirt to wipe the tears away, and said softly, "Bye, now, my dawlings. I'll see y'all later," and she brushed my hair to the side with her fingers. Gently, she placed her warm hand on my cheek, looked straight into my eyes again, and smiled. I turned quickly and walked through the gate onto the dirt road.

Mag's Saturday Night Ball had started, but not the way she had wanted.

✵✵✵

The sun had long ago set behind the woods in the west and the bright moon lit the way for Papa and me while we walked slowly toward home. When we came to Papa's house, he finally let go of my shirt, turned and ran up the narrow path to his front porch, not saying a word. I continued in the soft dirt, thinking how it was cool on my bare feet. In the heavy damp air, the smoke from the wood burning stoves fell onto the dirt road, as the crickets and locusts sang loudly from the long spreading limbs of the big oaks. My heart beat fast, while my mind raced through the evening and I took in the enchantment around me. Reaching the start of our graveled drive, I felt myself strutting to the slow, sweet sounds of *Ella* somebody, feeling as though I was going on twenty instead of twelve, and I was suddenly ten feet tall, knowing that Mag had opened a big window for me to see into another side of life along the dirt road. It was new to me, and it was there for me, and I wanted to be a part of it. I liked it.

Just when I turned the corner at the end of the hedgerow, Pal came running and barking in the night, protecting his family. I called his name and laughed out loud at myself, promising that the next party I would dress up in long pants, shoes and a sport shirt, and I, too, would dance. Alex would let me dance with Bernice. She was pretty, and I would like to dance with her.

Pal recognized my voice and came to meet me. We ran, as fast as my sore foot and the gravel would let me, through the moon-made shadows under the big trees, all the way down the side of the Big House to the back porch.

THE LAST WITNESS FROM A DIRT ROAD

The screened door squeaked when I jerked the handle, and I let it slam loudly behind me.

Neither Mama nor Dad asked where I had been that night, though I'm sure they knew. They also knew that I wouldn't go far and that everyone I would meet was a friend, even at Mag's party.

Squinting in the brightness of the kitchen lights, I sat at the little table and nibbled the supper that Mama had waiting for me, smiling to myself, and thinking big and exciting thoughts about the way we lived on the dirt road.

After that Saturday Night Ball in 1946, we gathered on other Saturday nights along the dirt road and listened while Nat, Ella, and Lena sang to us sad but sweet sounds about hard times and good times, about lost love and gained love. They made us believe they knew *us* and how we lived, and maybe they too, had once lived along a dirt road like ours. We ate good food with good friends, and we danced.

We danced, and we danced.

Our lives were good.

I liked it.

And I liked who I was.

CHAPTER 6

A quarter, a nickel, and three pennies were all I had left from the two dollars Aunt Sook had paid me the last time I had worked at her store. That would be enough money to last until the next Saturday when I planned to work again. Mag's party had cost me fifty cents; a quarter for me and a quarter for Papa went into her party jar, and I gave Papa two nickels and three pennies, also. Papa couldn't work and make his own money, and he liked to have a little change in his pockets. I saved a quarter in my trunk in my bedroom closet, and with some other change I had hidden away, I planned to go to The Sweet Heart Banquet on Valentine's Day at First Baptist Church in Bunkie. I was planning to ask a girl to go with me, since I would be twelve in a couple of months, and I was also going to ask Dad to let me take the old Ford. He knew I was a good driver. Driving tractors and his truck on the plantation for at least a year or more made me feel good, big, like a grown-up man.

Dad didn't say anything to me about Mag's party. There wasn't any bad stuff that happened, at least that I knew of, so I guessed he figured the party went okay. My little brother didn't go to school that Monday, probably feeling puny, so I had no one to pick on while walking through the Quarters after the school bus dropped me off.

When I reached the gate into the barn lot, J.B. was closing it behind him. He had just put up Josie, his mule, and had put out some corn and hay for her, and cleaned her stall. J.B. drove the water cart from one work crew to the other, all over the plantation, and he knew everybody and picked on everybody.

Many of the field hands accused him of sneaking food from their lunch buckets. Sometimes when I rode with him we both would sneak a bite or two from the buckets, and hoped the owner of the bucket wouldn't notice anything missing. J.B. picked on me a lot, but I liked him anyway. He lived with his Aunt Colleen and her husband Shine.

I met up with J.B. and asked him how the party finished up on Saturday night. He threw his arms around me and raised me a few inches from the ground, then dropped me with a loud yell. My foot was still sore, but I wasn't about to tell him about it, or he would have teased me some way. He looked at me with a big smile, and said, "Dat's the best pawdy we done had in a long time, and guess what? Me an Bernice's gon gits togetha."

"Alex and Veesy'll kill you, too. You know Bernice's too young for you, and too pretty for you, J.B. You need somebody as ugly as you," and I backed away a bit before he could grab me again.

BILL HUNT

"No, she ain't," he said, "and 'sides, Alex and Veesy don know nuttin bout it." Then he reached to grab me, but missed.

"You better leave Bernice alone, or Dad and Shine will get all over you if Alex doesn't." I couldn't figure out how anyone, especially Bernice, would want to marry J.B. Anyway, I didn't want Bernice to marry J.B. ever. She was my good friend.

We had passed the tool shed by then, and I walked toward our driveway while J.B. headed across the wooden bridge over Bayou Boeuf, toward the Quarters on the north side of the plantation. At supper that night, Dad said that there was going to be a wedding next Saturday evening. He told Mama about it, but I couldn't hear enough, with my little brother jabbering at me, to make out what was going to happen. It must have been for grownups only because he never directed any of his conversation toward me nor my little brother, Mickey. He said something about a broom, and the couple would do something with the broom. I had been to only one wedding and that was when my sister Margie got married a couple of years back, and there weren't any brooms there. I guessed that J.B. and Bernice would be the couple getting married. I hated that idea, and I wanted to ask my Dad about it, but he would have only brushed off my question.

Early Saturday morning, Mama drove me to town to catch the Keller bus that would take me to Sook's store. When we got to the paved highway through town, we came to some brand new cars parked in front of the old lumber company building, about four or five bright and shiny Chevys.

Excited, I said, "Look, Mama, some new cars! I wish Dad would buy us a new one like that," and I pointed to the one with the green top. She didn't say *yes* or *no* or anything, but I figured that she would like to have a new car, too. Our old Ford was seven or eight years old and had been wrecked a few years back, and was downright ugly.

She finally looked at me, smiled and said, "Well, those are black market cars, and they cost a lot more than a new one from the dealer. We'll just have to wait on one." I didn't know what black market cars meant. I just wanted a new Chevy like Mrs. Prosser's.

"What's a blackmarket car, Mama? That doesn't sound too good."

She smiled and said, "Well, when there is a bigger need for certain things, like cars for instance, people who have one will sell them for a lot more than they paid for them." She drove on for a block or two and added, "It won't be long before the factories will be putting out plenty of new cars again, now that the war's over!" I remembered a lot of other blackmarket things sold during the war, such as tires, gasoline, and even sugar. I still wouldn't mind having one of those blackmarket Chevys.

The Keller bus dropped me off at Aunt Sook's store and pulled away. I had waited for the driver to call out Harper's Grocery, but he didn't. I crossed

38

the road and opened the screened door, and, as usual, I had on short britches, a knit shirt, and was barefooted. Uncle Gathard was standing behind the counter, counting the money in the cash register.

He looked up and said, "Boy, if you don't start wearing some clothes your mama won't be able to find you in the dark," and he smiled a crooked little grin, with rows of wrinkles above his heavy eyebrows. I had turned a dark brown from the sun, but he sure didn't have to make fun of me. It wasn't any of his business anyway, but he ordered, "Go to the kitchen. Your Aunt's waitin' for you."

"What for?" And he kept his eyes locked onto my every move, afraid that I might sneak a bottle of pop from the drink box and hide behind the shelves of groceries to drink it. I could read his mind very easily.

Trying to fool me with a smile, he ordered again, "Go on! She's been waitin' for thirty minutes!" I was scared she didn't want me to work, and I needed some money really bad.

I walked to the back, jumped up the steps into the kitchen, and found Aunt Sook and Aunt Ida drinking coffee at the kitchen table. Aunt Ida smiled, lowered her head a little to look at me through the top of her glasses, while Aunt Sook stood up and put out her arm to hug me. I could smell her perfume, clean and sweet, even better than the aromas that met me while I walked through the store—all smells I loved. Aunt Ida went to the stove and poured a cup of coffee for me while I sat at the table waiting, hoping Aunt Sook wouldn't tell me she didn't need me to work.

"Well, Bill Beau, I'm so glad you came today," and my heart started beating again. She called me Bill Beau a lot when she was feeling good and was happy. I knew she took a lot of medicine for something and had a lot of headaches, but I was just glad that she had wanted me to come today. Margie, my sister, sometimes called me Bill Beau, too. I kind of liked that name.

Aunt Sook "O'ed" her lips and said, "I've got something for you!" She got up from the table and went through the living room to her bedroom, and brought back a nice-sized box from Godchaux's Department Store. "Open it right now," she said and smiled.

"This is for me?" I felt a little embarrassed, but I pulled on the strings really hard, struggling to break them, when Aunt Ida reached over with a little knife and cut them for me. I opened the box, laid back the white paper and looked at a new pair of brown pants and a shirt to match.

"These are from Aunt Ida, Uncle Gathard and me. How do you like them, Bill Beau?"

"I like 'um! They're great. I sure do thank you."

"Go try them on, and let's make sure they fit," and she pointed toward the living room.

I took them and put them on over my short britches and knit shirt and returned to the kitchen. Aunt Ida was still sitting at the table and Aunt Sook was standing with her hands on her hips. She looked at me, smiled, and said, "Perfect, just absolutely perfect!" She reached over and straightened my collar and pushed my hair off of my forehead. They really didn't feel too perfect. I seldom wore long pants in the summer, and they scratched my legs a little, but I hoped that I would get used to it quickly. I ducked back into the living room and took the pants and shirt off, folded them and put them back in the Godchaux's box. I would wear them to church tomorrow. That would make Aunt Sook happy.

Mama came about three o'clock to pick up a few groceries for Sunday dinner and to get me. I wasn't quite finished stacking the shelves but Aunt Sook said that was okay. She gave me a dollar bill and two quarters that day. I asked her to give me three quarters and five nickels for the dollar bill, since I had planned to give Papa two nickels. I thought his mama took his money some time, but Papa never said so. Mama had her groceries bagged and told me to put them in the car—that we had to go before the rain might start.

"The car's parked on the side in the driveway," Mama said, and smiled her red smile at me.

I put one sack under each arm, kicked the screen door open with my foot and rounded the corner of the building. The old Ford wasn't there, and my prayers had come true! Dad had bought one of those black market cars, a brand new Chevy, green on the top and tan on the bottom. I turned around and smiled while Mama and Aunt Sook stood under the porch cover, enjoying my second surprise that day. Aunt Sook handed Mama my box from Godchaux's and raised her hand, gesturing, "Bye, y'all, we'll see you tomorrow," knowing that we would all be at church on Sunday morning. Mama opened the car door and the light in the top came on. That was nice. I never told anyone that I had been praying for a new car. Mama wouldn't have liked that.

The new Chevy was quiet, not like our old Ford, which was noisy and even smelled bad. The seats in the new car were soft and the dashboard looked like wood. A big round clock was part of the dashboard right in front of me, and matched the speedometer in front of the driver. "Mama, this is really nice. How much did it cost?" And I wiped the glass over the clock's face.

"Oh, I don't know. Your Dad takes care of those things." I wondered how he could buy a black market car. Every time I asked for something, like a bicycle, or for anything at all, he always told me he didn't have any money. I figured God probably knew Dad needed the money if we were going to get a new Chevy, and maybe I ought to ask Dad if God sent him the money. But anyway, we had a new car, and we wouldn't have to put up with that junky old Ford anymore.

When we reached the north side of town and left the paved road, Mama said, "Come on. Let's trade places. You can drive home." She showed me how to shift. I had driven Dad's truck, and our old Ford, but they both had the shift on the floor. She told me, "Now think of an 'H,' just like the shift on Dad's truck but sideways." That said everything, and I learned right away how to shift our new Chevy. When we got to the Quarters, I put it back in second gear and eased slowly through the Quarters, very slowly, never looking from side to side. I don't know if anyone saw me or not; I was hoping that Papa was on his porch, and if he saw me, he would come to the house to look at the new Chevy, but his swing was empty. When we got to the garage, Mama said, "Stop here, Son, I'll put it up." I was glad not to have to pull the brand new car into a tight spot like the garage.

"Thanks, Mama. It's great. I'll be back after while. I'm going to the Quarters, okay?"

"No, you better come in and clean up. Your Dad said you could go to the wedding with him later." I asked her who was getting married, hoping that it wasn't J.B. and Bernice. She looked at me and smiled just a little, reached out of the window and pushed my hair off my forehead, and said, "Gilbert Frank is going to marry Emma Camp."

My stomach turned over and dropped all the way to my knees, and then I wished in my mind that it were J.B. and Bernice. What was poor Mag going to do without Gilbert Frank?

CHAPTER 7

My heart was broken for Mag, and Mama knew it. I walked slowly to the steps, sat on the top step, and leaned against the screen. Pal came up, and I let him lick my cheeks. I hugged him, and he smiled at me with his ears pulled back, but all I could think about was my other friend, Mag.

When Dad called upstairs to me, I was putting on my new pants and shirt, and my best shoes. I quickly finished dressing, ran down the long stairway, through the dining room, and found Mama and Dad talking in the kitchen. Dad had on starched and ironed khakis with a white shirt and tie. He looked at me, exclaiming, "Wow, look at those brand new britches and that matching shirt!" then asked, "Well, what do you think of the new Chevy?" I told him that I drove it all the way from town. He looked over to Mama, and she just smiled at him, but I'm sure he had wanted to give me some strict warnings of *dos* and *don'ts*. I was waiting to hear his commands, but he said nothing more about it, so I asked him what was Mag going to do without Gilbert Frank. He said, "Oh, Mag will make it. Don't worry about her." I knew that she was getting too old to start working in the fields again, and the company wouldn't let her keep her house without a man who could work as a field hand. We left to go to the wedding.

Dad let me drive his truck across the wooden bridge to Shine and Aunt Colleen's house, where the wedding was going to take place. All of the little kids, like me, called her "aunt," because that's what J.B. called her. A light rain had stopped an hour or so before, and as I looked through the windshield I saw a rainbow wandering all the way across the sky in front of us.

"Dad, is there really a pot of gold at the end of a rainbow?"

"Oh, I don't know for sure, but I really doubt it."

I quickly countered, "I bet there is, and I'm gonna find it one day."

He looked toward me and said, "Oh, forget the pot of gold, Son. Just look for the rainbows, and you'll be a lot better off." He smiled and took a puff on his pipe; the blue smoke curled out the open window.

I didn't know exactly what he meant, but I knew that everybody looked for rainbows after every little ole rain, and Mama always said that a rainbow was a promise from God that the world would never be destroyed by water again like it was during Bible days. Every time she saw a rainbow, she would tell us that, like it was something she didn't want us ever to forget. And I always thought it was good to know, but I never told Mama that the pot of gold was what I wanted.

Shine was Dad's main straw boss, and he and Aunt Colleen lived in a bigger house than the other field hands, with a picket fence around the yard. Shine and Aunt Colleen had worked for Dad for a long time, like twenty years or more. Fifteen or twenty people were already standing around in the front yard of Shine and Aunt Colleen's house, most of them from the North Quarters, with a few people sitting on the porch. I looked for Papa, wanting to remind him to bring my two new *Superman* comics back on Sunday, after he had looked at the pictures ahead of time, but he wasn't there.

Aunt Colleen was a big woman, tall and heavy, and usually wore white. She never worked in the fields any more—I figured she was too old and too fat—so she seldom left her house except to help in birthing babies or when someone was sick in the Quarters. She always had a remedy for anybody who needed it. Everybody said she could put a *spell* on someone you didn't like if you paid her a few pennies. Aunt Colleen could read and write, was a city girl from Opelousas, and had light brown skin. She was standing at the bottom of the porch steps with a small spelling pad in her hand and a little white Bible, while a new broom leaned against the top step. Dressed in a long white dress that came almost to her ankles, she had a white scarf wrapped high on her head, tied about half way up, in a big bow. When Dad and I walked through the gate, Aunt Colleen smiled and nodded to Dad, and he went on to the steps to stand next to her, my figuring they had done this wedding thing before. In a faded brown suit, Shine was sitting on the porch with several other men. Looking around the group of people I couldn't find Mag either, but at just about that time Aunt Colleen clapped her hands, raised her arms high, and everybody stopped talking. The men on the porch stood up.

Aunt Colleen smiled, and spoke really loud. "We wants to thank Mista Carl for comin heah today to witness this weddin," and Dad raised his hand to the brim, and tipped his hat. She didn't mention me, so I just stood over by J.B. When he put his hand on my back, I expected him to do something to me. Aunt Colleen called out, "Emma Camp and Gilbert Frank, please come forth, my churin." Shine held open the screened door, and Emma stepped through it onto the porch. Tall, and dressed in a dark purple dress and a little hat on the side of her head, it seemed like it made everybody take a deep breath when they saw her. Gilbert Frank was following her, holding her hand. They went down the steps slowly, side by side, and both smiling.

Emma was as beautiful as Miz Olivia, the preacher's wife. She lived with her Mama and Dad around the long bend in Bayou Boeuf; in a big house that I guessed had once been a planter's home before the Civil War. It was called Oak Grove, but now was a part of Shirley Plantation. Gilbert Frank was dressed in a gray suit, and they both looked as pretty as some of the people in Mama's Sears and Roebuck catalogue. Emma's mama and dad were standing at the side of the steps. Nearby were Rosa and her three girls; all named for my Mama, Florence, and my sisters Ethel and Jerry. Aunt Colleen stood very tall facing the people in the yard, and when Emma and Gilbert Frank reached the bottom of the steps they turned to face her. She leaned forward and whispered something to them, and they both nodded a *yes*. Everyone was quiet, except for a few throats being cleared and a cough or two. Aunt Colleen handed Emma the broom, and Emma held it out in front of her, then Gilbert Frank jumped over it, like he was playing a game of leapfrog. Some folks giggled. Aunt Colleen took the broom and handed it to Gilbert Frank. He held it out in front of himself and Emma stepped lightly across it while holding up her skirt a little, like a lady stepping across a mud puddle. Gilbert Frank moved back to his spot and handed the broom to Aunt Colleen. She bent over a little and held it out in front of her. Holding hands, both Emma and Gilbert Frank stepped across it together, turned to face each other, and smiled.

Aunt Colleen took a deep breath, then, asked, "Emma Camp, do yous take this man to be yo husband?"

Smiling, Emma answered, "Yes, Ma'am, I do." She held her eyes on Gilbert Frank.

Aunt Colleen looked at Gilber Frank, and asked, "Gilbert Frank, do you take this woman to be yo wife?"

Gilbert Frank choked a little and stammered very softly, "I, I do, Ma'am."

Aunt Colleen raised one eyebrow, leaned forward and asked, "Did I heah uh 'I do?'"

Gilbert Frank grinned and said, "Yes'sum, Yes Ma'am," and several people chuckled out loud.

Aunt Colleen opened the little Bible, raised her other hand high toward the sky, and read, "There is no fear in love; but love casteth out fear," then she turned directly toward the small group in the yard, announcing, "Yous have been witness to these young people makin theah vows to each otha as man and wife. Let nobody heah ever forget that this is done with the blessin' of the Lawd God Almighty, from our homes in the heavens we all look far evy day we live on dis Earth. We all must hol'um up and giv'um courage, dese two young fokes, to go forward for all da days of their lives. Let us pray to da Lawd." She bowed her head, raised her hand high again with the little Bible and the spelling pad, and continued, "We thank you Dear Lawd fo these young folks, and pray that ya will always giv 'um da strength to endure thru this life; giv'um da courage to face what lies ahead and da love to hold each otha's heart fo eva and eva. In tha name of da Lawd, Jesus, we pray. Amen." Several "Amens" popped out of the crowd.

She looked around the small group and handed the little spelling pad to my Dad. He wrote something on it, signed his name, and handed it back to Aunt Colleen. She tore the sheet out, opened her arms and hugged Emma and Gilbert

Frank, and gave them the small sheet of paper, the little white Bible and the new broom.

"Ya can kiss yo new wife," she said, and Gilbert Frank kissed Emma real hard, right on the mouth. Everybody started clapping and talking, then they took turns coming over to Gilbert Frank and Emma; they said a few words, smiled a lot, and patted them on their backs. Aunt Colleen had made a stack of *teacakes* to go with the Port wine.

I felt J.B. move his hand down my back, and he pinched me really hard on the butt. I jumped and kicked at his shin as hard as I could, and I got the bastard a little bit above his left ankle. He frowned at me with his big lips tightly pursed, hobbled toward the steps, and sat down.

Smiling about my great achievement, I walked slowly through the crowd to the food table and picked up two of Aunt Colleen's big teacakes.

The wedding was over, and another Saturday Night Ball was about to begin.

CHAPTER 8

On Sunday morning I woke a little early, wanting to rinse off our new Chevy before we went to Sunday school and church. It was pretty cool, reminding me that cane-cutting time must be getting close. Fieldhands liked cane-cutting time, too, because they were paid a higher wage than regular day wages, giving them a little more money from before Thanksgiving and lasting sometimes nearly to Christmas.

I put on clean short britches and a knit shirt, then quietly went down the long stairway, tiptoed past the door to my mama and dad's bedroom, crossed the hall, then increased my speed through the family room and the dining room. Hoss had started making a fire in the kitchen stove, and would be making coffee in a little while.

"Hi, Hoss, did you see our new Chevy?" I asked. He grunted at me and shook his head. I couldn't tell if it was a *yes* or a *no*. He was like that. He never had much to say except when he got on to me about something. I sat at the kitchen table and did a big morning stretch.

Finally, having never looked directly at me, he replied, "It gon be ready in a minute."

I knew he was talking about the coffee. When my sisters lived at home, in the winter, Hoss and my dad would wake us up with coffee in our bedrooms. If there were any biscuits left over from supper the night before, he would break them up and put one in our coffee with a little cream and sugar. He always entered the room saying, "Git up, git up, dis'll make ya slap yo daddy." I never understood why he said that, because I knew that if I even *looked* like "slapping my daddy" my dad would let me have it quick. With his white hair and slumped shoulders, Hoss looked really old, but none of us knew how old he really was. He always said, "I's ova eighty or mo." Dad let Wesley come every day to do the harder work so Hoss could have a payday every two weeks for him and Helen, and my friend Papa.

I told Hoss I was going to back the new Chevy out, go to the fishponds and rinse it off. He never said anything. After getting a towel from the bathroom, I ran out to the garage, backed the new car out very slowly, turned and headed out by the side of the house pulling onto the grass at the fishponds. I rinsed it off, and started drying it, then wished that I had on some shoes, long pants, and a long sleeve shirt. It was cold. Early November was usually cool, but I could feel cold air that made me shiver. I finished drying off the new Chevy, wiped the dust off the dashboard, and drove it over to the front of the house to the big steps, knowing that in an hour or two we would load up and head for church.

When I stepped into the warm kitchen, Hoss was pouring some coffee for him and me, with an empty cup sitting near by for Dad. We sat at the table and drank our coffee, not saying anything.

Then, staring at me from where he sat at the table, Hoss cleared his throat and softly scolded, "Billy, ya oughts not to' a painted Papa's legs da ways ya did da otha day. Dat's wuz ugly."

I had been waiting for several weeks for him to bring up the leg painting, my knowing that he had been mad at both Papa and me when we had painted Papa's legs.

"I'm sorry, Hoss, we were just having a little fun."

Hanging his head down, Hoss looked to the floor and spoke very slowly, "Ah knows dat." Then he looked straight into my eyes and said, "But Papa ain't no white boy, an he ain't neva gon be one. Papa gotta knows dat and 'memba dat, too. Iffin he forgits dat and acts lik'a white boy, somebody gon hurt him bad, maybe even kill 'im. Ah knows ya don want dat to happen to po Papa, do's ya, Billy?"

Before I could think of anything to say, he finished his coffee, stood up and patted me on my back, then slowly left the kitchen to go milk his cows and start his long day's work. I knew then that the leg-painting problems were probably over, and I felt better; but he left me with a sadness and fear inside me. I wondered about what Hoss had said about Papa, but I had never figured that anyone would ever want to hurt Papa. I wanted to cry, but I was getting too big.

Wesley had come to the kitchen while I was washing the car, but he had already gone to the milk shed. They would take care of all the chores and the milk. Hoss was a real gentleman, and everybody on the plantation loved and respected him. It was plain to me, however, that he liked my mother and my two sisters better than my little brother and me, since he seemed to be happy when they were around and he joked with them. On cold winter mornings he would bring a washpan of warm water upstairs to their bedrooms so they could wash their faces when they woke up. Dad said he spoiled them and did whatever they wanted, but to Dad everybody was spoiled except him.

I drove all the way to church that day, even through town, with Dad riding in the front with me. When we turned at the Four Way Café, Dad said to put my arm straight out of the window, giving the car behind me a signal that we were turning left. I did that, but I had a hard time turning the wheel with one hand. We went very slowly. I was hoping that most of my buddies were already at church and waiting out front so they could see me driving our shiny new Chevy. When I turned in to park, four of them came to meet me, and while my mama, dad, and little brother got out of the car and headed toward the church, I hung back with my buddies, leaned against the front fender with one leg crossing the other at my knee, and my arms crossed at my chest. I was the *big man* that day. All four of my friends looked in the new Chevy and all around it. Then, two of them came from the front, and two from behind, and, grabbing me, they threw me down in the grass. Two of them jumped on me and frogged me on the leg. I had on my new brown pants and matching shirt that Aunt Sook gave me the day before. We all started laughing. One of my knees was green now. We got up, hurried into the church, and went into our Sunday school class. No one said anything, but I knew our new Chevy was the talk going around that day, and my friends liked it. If Eunice Ellen, the red-face Devil had been there, she would have made fun of it and would probably have spit on it. That day at church, nobody would have noticed if Poor Miss Hattie had lost her drawers again.

After dinner, Dad and my little brother went to take a nap in Mama's bedroom. The crispness of the early morning November air had gone, so I put on my short britches and a knit shirt, and headed out to the Quarters. About fifty yards from Papa's house, I could see him waving his comics to me to come on to the porch to read them. I called to him from the road that I would be back in a few minutes. He sat down in the swing and let his lips and head droop, pouting like a spoiled kid.

I called to him, "Don't worry, I'll be right back, Papa. I gotta go see Mag for a minute." He never moved from his spoiled kid look.

Walking quietly to the little gate, I heard Mag humming. She didn't see me because she was busy getting things out of her house onto the porch.

"Hi, Mag."

She turned around really fast, and her beautiful smile crossed her face. I opened the gate, and she started toward me, but stopped at the steps while I walked toward the porch. Missing her usual flowered skirt, white blouse, and long earrings, I knew something was very different—and wrong—about what was going on. She wore blue overalls and a light blue work shirt with her soft brown hair tied up in a red bandana.

Looking past her toward the porch, and with a frown creased on my forehead, I asked her, "What are you doing? What's happening?" She had pulled four or five pieces of furniture out of the house, along with several boxes, and two big washtubs full of dishes and clothes. I stood on the porch looking back and forth from her to her belongings laid out in front of me, making me feel a little sick to my stomach.

She raised her arms, looked at me with a great big smile, announcing "I's movin tomorra mornin, t'ank da Lawd, Billy."

"Where are you going, Mag? Where to?"

She reached toward me and brushed my hair to the side, then held me by my shoulders, explaining, "Well, it ain't fer an' ya gotta come ta see me when I gits settle down. I's jist goin to Bubenzer," and she threw her head back a little, chuckling.

"Bubenzer?" I questioned.

"Sho 'nough, Billy! Yo Daddy don talk to 'um, and got me a job ta work in da Big House on Bubenzer."

"When? You can't leave like this, Mag. When are you going?"

"Da truck'll be heah early in da moanin'. Ain't dat som'um," and her smile began to fade.

Bubenzer was the plantation a mile or two north of Shirley, and was run by the landowners. I knew that working directly for the owners of Bubenzer Plantation would be several steps up for my friend, but that didn't matter to me. "Mag, you don't know anybody on Bubenzer! You gonna just leave all your friends here on Shirley?"

Her smile quickly faded; she sighed, answering, "I ain't got no place else ta go, Billy. I'sl be okay. I can work fer a long time in da Big House there, and evythangs gon be fine. Jist ya wait an see," and she smiled again. She reached up and ruffled my hair as though she was waiting for me to say something good about her going to live on Bubenzer Plantation.

I could feel my stomach turn over, almost like it did at the airplane crash. I didn't want this move from the plantation to happen, but I knew that I could do nothing to change it. We stood there looking face to face with each other, her hands latched onto my shoulders, and finally I said, "Bye, Mag. I gotta go. Papa's waiting for me to read my comics. Bye."

Before I could move, she pulled me to her, her hand pressing the side of my head against her cheek. I could barely see the other as she wiped the tears from her eyes. She pressed harder, whispering softly, "I's gon miss ya, my bad *little white child*, an' ya betta come to see me! An I mean it! Okay?" and she pushed back from me, forcing a quivering smile

***

It was a sad moment for both Mag and me. I looked at her through my own watery eyes, bewildered, realizing that this aging black woman, with so much grace, beauty, and dignity, was almost as near to my heart as my mother. She had been a part of our house, and my life, every day since I was born. Walking quickly away, I came to the gate onto the dirt road. After flinging it open as wide as it would go, angrily, I slammed it closed, stopped, and turned to look back one more time. I raised my hand, and without moving from where she stood, Mag raised hers, and her big smile, where her heart showed through, faded away. She pressed her long fingers to her lips, and with her hands together as though she was praying, she looked away from me, up into the blue fall sky.

The air was cool, gently moving the leaves on the big oaks along the dirt road, and my bare feet brought chills throughout my body while I walked slowly to Papa's house.

The Bubenzer truck came sometime during the next morning, while I was at school, to move my friend away from Shirley Plantation. Most of the time, I looked the other way when the school bus dropped me off or when we passed by the little house on our way to town. Mag's house was the last in the row of houses in the Quarters and sat at the line where the plantation ended. I had already felt that each time I crossed that line, something inside me changed, and I changed, too. From that day on, Mag's house would be another reminder of how fast everything around us was changing, especially the changes in my little world on the plantation, the place I loved.

But we had had several big parties there, in Mag's little house and yard, and I remembered Ella, Lena and Nat, singing smooth sweet sounds, while the moon watched us dance, sweat, and dance again and again, then lit our way as we walked along the dirt road late into the evening. Ten feet tall. Then, I had been ten feet tall.

But when I flung open the little gate in a confused state of anger, and slammed it closed for the last time, I waved goodbye to Mag, feeling that I was a sad and surprisingly angry little *white child*, being thrust out of his childhood into an unknown and uncertain place—a new place for me that made me wonder about the separation of my friends at school and church from my friends on the plantation, where most of my life was spent. Looking along the graveled road toward Bunkie made me anxious and nervous, as though my friends were waiting for me there, waiting for me to join them, and I knew that *a life* and *a place* were there for *me*. Slowly turning, and with tears in my eyes, I looked at the rows of small, unpainted houses on each side of the dirt road, where I knew everyone and everyone knew me, and they, too, were my good friends, and most of all, the dirt road was our home.

In my heart and mind a sickening and growing fear crept upon me, as though I was treading very near to the edge of a wide, long ditch, deep and dark: a chasm that meandered along, like Bayou Boeuf and its brown waters, slowly moving through the plantation. Feeling a weakening sadness, I felt compelled to look to the other side, my thinking that I should maybe cross the chasm, the divide, into another place, to a different place, a place that seemed always to be calling me, and reaching for me. There was a struggle inside, pulling my heart and confusing my mind about everything I knew about the way we lived on the plantation, about our lives and my friends, a struggle pulling so hard in different directions.

In my mind, I could see dense movement, a growing movement of strange shadows, some dark and others light, like the ever-moving shadows that play beneath the waters of a developing picture.Each shadow reached out and, as always, beckoned to me to come. Come!

CHAPTER 9

My intentions were good that Sunday afternoon when I said goodbye to Mag, thinking I would visit her at her new home only two miles away, at Bubenzer. Eighteen years later, long after I had married and had two children of my own, I found my way to look for my old friend. Angry with myself and filled with deep regret for not having visited her sooner, I hoped I wouldn't be able to find her that day. Driving slowly along those familiar roads, we stopped and asked a man mowing grass at the Big House on Bubenzer if he knew Mag Williams.

"I sure do," and he pointed to a little house about two hundred yards down the road. "She lives right over there, and I'm sure she's at home." We thanked him and drove on, stopping in front of the small house. I told my wife and two sons to wait in the car until I could check to see if she was there.

When I reached the front porch, most of which was hidden by tall bushes, there sat a very elegant black lady, her chin held high, arranging a red silk scarf tied in her soft, graying hair. She straightened her clothes while she sat very tall in a small rocking chair. She must have heard the car stop and was waiting to hear a voice at her front steps.

"Hello, who is it? Who's there, please?" she said distinctively, in a low voice. It was my friend Mag, but I immediately recognized from her speech that she had made adjustments in her personal presentation in order to work for the *landowners* at Bubenzer. She spoke with precision and had discarded the earthy beauty of the local dialect, which was strongly flavored by the French language of the area.

I spoke to her in a question, "Mag?"

"Yes, Sir," and she looked toward me.

Stepping onto the porch, I could tell that her eyesight had faded.

"Mag, I'm your old friend. This is Billy!" Her eyes, in a watery gaze, stayed fixed on me, but in a second her red-tinged lips parted into a broad smile that lit up her face. The light in her eyes had dimmed, but the fire in her heart that made the person I had known and loved many years before began to flame again.

With both arms outstretched, her eyes swelled with tears and she reached toward me. "Oh, Mista Billy, you've finally come to see me. I've been waiting for an awfully long time." I had never heard her call me Mister. She patted my hand, her long fingers tipped with red, and in the next sentence she returned to her real self, the person I had known, and the one I had come to see.

"Well, ya sho do looks good, and look at dat black hair, and you done learned to comb it." Both of us laughed, and she said softly, "I sho hopes you doin good," and she continued holding my hand, then she added, "Oh, Lawdy, I jist can't believes yous heah with me, Mista Billy."

Having waved to my wife to come, she and the boys had reached the porch.

"Mag, I have my wife and boys with me. This is Grace, this is Carl, and the little one is David," and I smiled, waiting for her reply. She smiled as she reached toward the boys, but they looked down and wrapped their arms around their mother's legs.

Mag took a deep breath, smiled again and said to them, "Don't be scared, I's jist ole Mag," and she pointed toward Carl, saying, "That one's named after yo daddy, huh?"

"Yes, and the other one for my mother's family, Armand."

Her smile broadened. She looked up at me, pointed her finger, and said, "That there lil'one got some meanness in 'im too. Like his daddy, but I ain't gonna tell 'um bout how bad ya was and how terrible awful ya use to treats me." She leaned her head back and laughed out loud while still grasping my hand. Her long earrings came out of the fold in the light shawl that covered her back and neck. "Mista Billy," she asked, "where y'all been living all dese yeahs? And yo wife, ain't she beautiful!" All the time, she was expressing herself with her other hand, bringing it to her chest and extending her arm as though she was reciting a great monologue in a big theater. Before I could answer her question, she announced, "Mista Billy, ole Shirley ain't da same. Sho ain't. Evybody done up and moved to California: Alex and Veesy, J.B., Little Joe and Lionel, and even Gilbert Frank and Emma and dey's two kids. Dey's was the first to go. Evybody don been gone a long time, now." She was still doing her monologue in full drama.

I said, "Yeah, I see that all the houses in the Quarters are gone, and what happened to the Big House?"

She put her hand to her forehead, sat upright in her rocker, and exclaimed, "Dey burned it to da ground! We's all taught da cane fields was caught on fire. We could see da smoke all da way from Bubenzer, but deys was burning the Big House. What a shame, dat is! Dey sayes some folks come all da way from New Awlins and took all da mantle pieces and da doors, and dat great big glass cabinet out da dinin room. Ya remember that big glass cabinet, Mista Billy?"

"I sure do," and I smiled.

"Yes, sir, yo Mama use to keep her fruit cakes and whiskey in da top of dat ole cabinet. Way up high, sos ya couldn't reach it. I knows ya used to git up dere. I just never told yo Mama. Ya was a bad lit'le ole boy." She leaned toward me and in a low voice, asked, "Ya don't drinks too much, do ya?" and she laughed out loud, reached over and tapped me on the arm. "Yes, sir, yous was bad! A lotta times, iff'in I's couda caught ya, I'da giv ya a good one. Yo good ole daddy use to tells me, 'Give it to him, Mag!' But I's wont gon hurt 'chu none," and she laughed out loud again, still holding my hand.

We talked and visited for a while longer until a young girl came through the door onto the porch and whispered in Mag's ear.

With disappointment showing clearly on her face, she announced, "Mista Billy, dis here's Ella Mae. I lives wit'her Mama and Daddy. Yes sir, tings has been good fer me here at Bubenzer." She hesitated, and asked, "Can y'all come back ta-morra? I gots to go lay down a while," and she finally let go of my hand.

She was beginning to pale a little and her breathing became shortened.

I knelt by her rocker, took her hand, saying softly, "Mag, I'm sorry it took so long to come see you, but I'm glad that you have a good place here," and I slipped a small roll of money into her hand. She wrinkled it in her palm, reached up with her other hand, and wiped away the tears in her eyes. Her face changed, and she began to cry softly, never taking her eyes from mine, then she reached up and ran her fingers through my hair, feeling it. Slowly, she moved her warm hand down to my cheek, then gently across my forehead, over my nose, until her fingers crossed my lips.

Never taking her eyes from my face, she spoke softly, "Yous changed, Billy, yous a man now, I can tell. But, to me, you'll always be a lit'le boy," and her lips quivered into a slight smile.

Grace and the boys had already walked down the steps and on toward the car. Mag again grasped my hand in hers, squeezed it, and brought it up, kissed it and held it to her lips.

I stood. She looked up at me with a faint, quivering smile, and said slowly, and again, very distinctly, "Billy, you were the only child I ever wanted to be mine, and my heart was broke when I left you. You shudda come to see me *long* before now, but I thank you anyway!"

Realizing that Mag had had no choice but to let her heart bleed for almost twenty years because of lost love and suppressed silence, I cried inside. Gently, I pulled my hand from hers while her grip tightened. I turned and walked down the steps, neither of us saying another word. Halfway to the car, I stopped, turned to look at her again, and raised my hand. Mag had raised hers, too. That big beautiful smile had vanished, and I could see the red tips of her fingers as they moved to cover her lips. The strong smell of fresh cut grass in the distance encircled me while I shaded my eyes from the sun. Softly, I heard myself say, "Goodbye, Mag, and thank you! Thank you."

We both knew that our goodbyes on that warm summer day would probably be our last. For years, deep inside of me I had felt that I had deserted so many friends with whom I had lived on the dirt road, and Mag was foremost. Because of her, for all of my life I would relate clearly to the realities of a black woman, alone in a harsh world, struggling against the cruelties of dependence, suppression, and racism.

That day we closed an old and unfinished chapter in our lives—a chapter that ended with a young white man finally understanding his relationship with a strong and courageous black woman. For both of us, she had been my *black mother*, and I had been her *white child*.

My old friend had done it—she had endured—and I understood the dignity, the pride and the power of the heart that filled Miss Magdeline Williams. Her strength, courage, and goodness enabled her to transcend the oppressive reality of a dark era in history.

Everything had changed, yet everything was the same.

✸✸✸

CHAPTER 10

That Sunday afternoon when Mag was packing her belongings to move to Bubenzer, and in anger I had slammed the little gate shut, I walked slowly down the dirt road to Papa's house. He was still waiting on the swing for me. I had wiped away the tears, but when I got to the steps he teased, "Wat'chu be cryin bout, Billy? Is ya a cry-baby?"

"Yeah, I guess I am, Papa. Come on, let's read Superman!" and I flipped through the first pages of one of the comics.

Suddenly a gray bird swooped down into the porch and clipped the top of my head. Papa jumped up, waving it away, apologizing, "Don pays it no mind, Billy. Da's jist's a mockin' burd. She live heah, anyway."

I stood, rubbing the spot on my head, and watched the bird as it lit in a tall bush about twenty yards away, keeping an eye on Papa and me. I looked at Papa sitting calmly in the swing, waiting for me to start reading. Still rubbing the top of my head, I told him, "Next time I come, I'm gonna bring my BB gun and kill it."

Papa quickly stood up, fussing, "No ya ain't! Dat's God's burd! Ya ain't s'pose ta kill no mockin' burd, Billy! Don chu be talkin' bout no BB gun round one of God's burd."

"Who the devil told you that? That's crazy!"

His eyes seemed to glaze a little and he spoke slowly, all the while point-ing a forbidding finger at me, "Ma daddy don' said that when God made all da burds, he give evy one'a song, and when he got finish, he had a bunch'a songs lef ova, and..."

"Yeah, and I bet he decided to make one more bird, and he put all the left over songs in that bird, and he called it His Mocking Bird. Right?"

"Dat's right, Billy, an ya ain't s'pose to kill no mockin' burd. Ya hear me?" He shook his finger at me and warned, "Neva, so don'chu bring no BB gun heah, an shoot dat mockin' burd, else God'll sho be mad wis ya. Maybe wis me, too."

I sat down in the swing, shook my head, smiled and announced, "Yeah, I've heard that old story, too, Papa," and I handed him the comic book. He quickly started concentrating on the picture of Superman gliding around the spiral of a tall building, and I thought, "I'll bet that rascal believes that Superman is real and he can fly."

He turned to one of the stories that he had earlier picked out. I had already read it to him at least three times, and I asked him, "Papa, do you really want to read this one?" He nodded yes, and looked at me with his usual begging grin.

He liked for me to point to every line while I read it, and many times I had to explain the pictures to him. He would often call out the letters forming the words, and every now and then he knew a word or two. Sometimes he got so excited that he would shake his legs and ball up his fists and laugh, and wave his arms wildly. Papa wanted to learn to read, and I hoped that he could. I had taught him the alphabet and how to write the letters, which took almost a year. I'd tried to teach him how to sign his name, but he got awfully tired of trying and me saying the same thing over and over. I got tired, too. His name was Isaac Vead, but he believed his name was Papa.

As I read the last page of the *Superman* story, he handed me the other comic book and we turned to another story he had picked out. I started reading it when he interrupted. "Wat wuz ya cryin bout while ago Billy?" he asked. "Ya sho is a cry-baby, I sho can tell."

"Mag's moving in the morning to Bubenzer," I mumbled, and thumbed through the pages of the next comic book.

He quickly said, "Well, dat aint's fer. We's can walk dat lit'le piece. Billy ya jist a big ole cry baby, ain't chu?"

Looking at Superman fly through a cloudless sky, I replied, "Yeah, I guess I am, but we won't be able to go to anymore of her parties."

He quickly focused his eyes to the other end of the porch, and said, "Dat's awright wit me. I don like 'er pawdys. Dey's bad, and yous ought to quit goin' to dem, too, cause ma daddy says ya gon git hurt. Somebody gon git mad at chu, and hurt chu." All the while he was shaking his head with his big round eyes opened wide. I guessed that his dad and mama had told him that; and if he went to the party they would give him a whipping. But he continued, "I's heard my daddy tell my Mama he's gon tell yo daddy 'bout yous goin to da pawtys all da time. Ya daddy sho gon be mad, and whip yo butt good," and he laughed. "He gon make ya really cry, ya ole cry-baby."

I asked him, "Did your daddy whip your butt after the last party you went to?" He latched his eyes onto Superman and said nothing. I punched him in the ribs with my elbow and asked again, "Did he?" He lowered his head and shook it *yes*; then, a couple of big tears welled in his eyes.

I watched his head droop almost to his chest and waited for a second. "Okay, Papa, let's read Superman!"

I read both comics to him and he wanted to start over. "No, I gotta go, Papa. I have to get ready to go to church." It was getting really cold on the porch, and I had to walk home barefooted with just my short britches and a knit shirt to shield me from the cool air. I took my comics and told him I would see him later.

Reaching in my pocket, I found the two nickels I had saved for him, and I gave them to him. He smiled and said, "I's gon git me some Bazooka when da

'Rollin Sto' come." Papa liked bubble gum, and the Rolling Store, which roamed from one plantation to another every week, always had plenty of candy and Bazooka. He stood up while I walked through the yard to the dirt road. I started a little trot in the soft dirt on the road, and glancing back I saw Papa waving to me with a smile as broad as a new moon. The air felt cold.

When I came to the Gaspard house, Cathrine was standing in the road talking to some other girls and playing hopscotch. I said *hi* to them and handed Cathrine my two new comics. She would take care of them and give them back in a day or two. "See if Caroline wants to read them," I said, then, I started trotting again toward home.

After church was over, everyone left quickly because of the cold. The temperature had dropped since early evening. Mickey and I sat in the back of the Chevy, and Dad and Mama were talking in the front. I watched the trees while they quickly passed the window of the moving car, with nothing more than a recount of the day going through my mind. Turning toward the front, and looking at the back of the hat sitting high on Dad's head, I said to him, "I think Hoss whips Papa a lot, Dad."

He was saying to Mama, "Yeah, it looks like it's going to frost in the morning, and we can probably start cutting by Thursday or Friday." Realizing this wasn't the time to talk to him about Papa, I said nothing more.

I knew that cane-cutting time was nearing, and everybody on the plantation would be busy getting ready for the next couple of days. Everyone would be excited because of the extra money and knowing that the sugarcane was the last crop to be harvested.

***

The *flags*, the long, slender, sharp-edged leaves on each stalk of sugarcane, would be killed by the frost, which would dry them and turn them brown in a day or so. The fields would be set on fire to burn the flags just hours before the cutters came in. Not having to *strip* the cane of its flags made cutting easier, and harvesting would go a lot faster than cutting it while it was green. It was a good season that year because the first frost had come at the right time, and the rain was still a few weeks away. We had a lot to do. Some of the older kids on the plantation would stay out of school for two or three days in a row for three or four weeks to help get the cane out and to the sugar mills before the winter rains set in.

The women and the men worked side by side in crews of about fifteen or twenty. The lead crewman set the pace and was always the fastest cutter. Others had to stay up with him as best they could. Members of the crew who fell behind would be quietly rotated into a slower crew. After about the first three or four days, the faster cutters ended up working together in one area. The slower cutters were together in another area, but away from the faster cutters. The women who might be slower but wanted to work side by side with their husbands often depended on their husbands to keep them moving in line with the other cutters while the crew worked across a newly burned field. It was backbreaking and dirty work. The physical closeness of the job would oftentimes lead to arguments and an occasional fight between crewmembers. The straw boss, like Shine, had to keep the peace between workers and be alert to other problems that field hands often brought out to the fields. The job of straw boss as peacekeeper continued long past quitting time, and most often didn't end until cutting season was over, when the crewmembers slowly dissipated into their homes in the Quarters. Some arguments that started in the cane-cutting season lasted from one season to the next and, often, would last a lifetime. Working so hard and under so much pressure was a detriment to husbands and wives, not only because of the physical closeness of crewmembers, but most often because of loose tongues and gossip. Relationships developed, changed, or were destroyed completely during cane-cutting time; however, neither meanness nor anger could be tolerated with a cane knife in the hand of a field worker.

✿✿✿

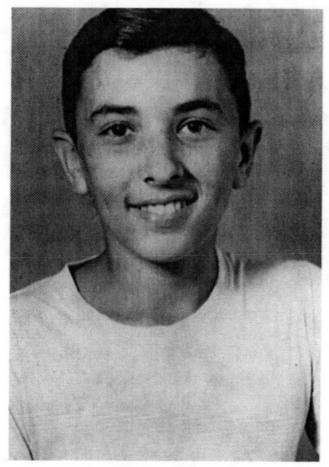

Billy   1946

PAPA   1944

CHAPTER 11

School was slow on Monday as I looked forward to getting home to ride my horse to the cane fields. I turned at the hedgerow, finding Papa sitting on the old grindstone at the fishponds. The ponds were big, round-bottomed, iron syrup kettles sitting about a foot deep into the ground. With the grindstone, they were remnants of the big sugar mill, which many years before had been a very big part of Shirley Plantation.

Pal was sitting next to Papa, letting Papa rub his ears. Papa had on a short-sleeved shirt with long pants, and was barefooted. He came to meet me. "We's gon read t'day, Billy?" I told him that I was going out to the cane fields as soon as I could saddle my horse and before the cutters knocked off for the day. It was pretty cold, and I could see that Papa was feeling it.

"Papa, don't you know it's cold, boy. Where's your coat and shoes?"

He shrugged his shoulders and slowly spoke, answering, "I don' know. I guess I don got any."

"Well, come on. Let's go to the kitchen," I told him, knowing he had shoes but probably saved them for dress up on Sundays. We turned the corner at the screened porch, went up the steps, and I pulled on the screened door. Crossing the porch together, I opened the door into the warm kitchen.

Rosa was putting wood into the stove. "Hi, Rosa," I greeted her, and she turned around and looked at Papa. Before she could say anything, I commanded, "Papa, go warm up by the stove," and I waited to see if Rosa might object. Rosa, like Mag, had worked in the Big House for many years, placing her and her family at a different level in the rank of the workers on the plantation. She had little to do with the other workers whose jobs as *field hands* placed them away and apart from workers like Mag, Rosa, Hoss, and Wesley, all of whom worked in the yard and in the Big House.

Rosa didn't like Papa anyway, and certainly didn't want him in the kitchen that she had finished cleaning an hour or so before. Rosa looked at me but still said nothing. She was never jolly or a cutup, like Mag was, and I knew I had to treat her differently. Mama liked Rosa better than anyone else who worked in the Big House. Rosa was a tall, big woman with light skin, and had worked for Mama since she was about twelve years old and knew our family very well. She was married to Jo, and they had three little girls, all named for my mama and my two sisters. She expected that anytime I wanted something from the kitchen, and she was there, then she would be asked to get it. When Rosa wasn't there, our use of the kitchen and everything in it was centered on the idea that we must remember that Rosa would return to the kitchen the next day, and we must keep it as neat and orderly as possible.

"Rosa, would you fix Papa and me a bite to eat, please?" She said nothing, but she opened the icebox and got out a short stick of baloney, cut two thick slices and put them between two slices of white bread. She put my sandwich on a plate but just handed Papa's to him. "Thanks, Rosa." Then I told Papa, "Papa, tell Rosa thank you." He already had a mouth full; he stopped chewing, then looked at Rosa and nodded a couple of times, with his eyes open wide. He was afraid of Rosa, and he didn't like being in the kitchen when she was there.

The new Chevy was in the garage, so I knew Mama was at home some-where. I asked Rosa about Mama, and never looking toward me she replied "Miz Florence's in her bedroom sewin, Mista Billy." She called me *mister* all the time.

Turning to Papa, I asked, "Are you sure you don't have a coat and some shoes, Papa?" He had his hands about three inches from the side of the stove, and was chewing a bite from his sandwich.

He looked at me, shook his head *yes*, and with a mouth full, he quickly said, "I's sho, Billy. I ain't got none, I promise. I sho don't."

I looked at Rosa and asked her, "Is he lying, Rosa, or do you think that's right?"

She turned around toward me with her back to Papa and said softly, "I guess dat would be bouts right, Mista Billy, po lil' ole thang." I left the kitchen to go see if Mama had any ideas as to solving Papa's coat and shoe problem. Rosa called to me, "Tells Miz Florence I's goin. I'll see huh ta'morra."

I told Mama what Rosa had said and about Papa's problem with no coat and no shoes. She leaned on the back of her chair in front of her sewing machine as if she was trying to catch her breath. Finally, she said, "Well, maybe some of your dad's shoes will fit him. He needs some socks, too, poor fella. We'll see," and she leaned toward her machine again.

I knew what "We'll see" meant—"Don't bother me right now." But I whined to her, "Mama, I need them now! Papa's in the kitchen waiting and trying to warm up! I need to hurry!"

She looked surprised, but got up from her sewing machine and went over to Dad's closet. She pulled out two long-sleeved flannel shirts and found three pairs of white socks in the bureau drawer. Handing them to me, she instructed, "Take these, and go look in the porch closet. There's an old pair of your dad's rubber boots that he won't wear anymore. I guess they leak. See if they'll fit Papa. He might have to put on two pairs of socks." She turned to her sewing machine again and ordered, "You get Papa to help you haul in some wood for the fireplaces so Hoss can go on home. It's getting cold."

I took the shirts and socks to the kitchen, held them up so Papa could see them, set them on the table, and went out to the porch closet to get the boots. When I returned to the kitchen, Papa was still standing at the end of the stove, grinning from ear to ear. He rubbed his hands together and said, "Boy, dis ole stove sho feel good." He had finished his sandwich and had taken a big bite out of mine, but had put the rest back on the plate.

He was really hungry, I guessed, but I scolded, "You ate my sandwich, you dirty dog!" With his jaws packed full, he started smiling. "Take the rest of it, you rascal." He looked at the remainder of the sandwich, and then at me, and with his grin slowly disappearing he picked up the plate. I told him again, "You can have it, Papa. It's okay." He turned and started warming himself again at the stove.

Impatient, and wanting him to hurry, I said disgustedly, "Papa! Put on one of those shirts and some socks. See if these boots fit you! Shake them out!" Spiders were always looking for a place to hide. Sometimes, I felt like Papa didn't try very hard. He just waited to be told everything. "Hurry up, Papa," I said, "You gotta learn to take care of yourself, boy. Your mama and daddy can't do it forever. And I can't either!"

He put on one of the shirts, dropped his arms to his sides and stood in front of me as if to say, "Well, here I am! You do the rest!" I sighed heavily, gritted my teeth, and shook my head, knowing that I wasn't going to the cane fields that day. Papa's grin had gone, and he looked at me as though he was about to cry.

After making only one roll in the sleeves, I went on and buttoned the shirt for him, then straightened his collar. He sat down in a chair and started putting on the boots when I stopped him. "No, no! Put the socks on first. Papa, think a little bit, would you? You're not helpless; and, if you don't start trying a little, I'm not gonna help you one bit."

He dropped the boot, started putting on the socks, and mumbled, "Fuss, Fuss, Fuss! Yous gittin jist like my Daddy! Fuss all da time. I's sho ya wanna *whip* me, too." His comment snapped the meanness I was feeling at that moment, and I was sorry to have fussed at him.

The boots were almost a perfect fit. He stood up, then looked down at his boots and the flannel shirt, and started to grin again.

"Well, maybe we can find a coat for you tomorrow. I guess you want a glass of milk now, huh?" He grinned bigger, and shook his head. I took a glass from the cabinet, went to the icebox, and poured him a big glass of milk. He drank the whole thing without stopping, banged the glass onto the table, and looked at me with a big smile while his tongue swept across his lips. He suddenly belched really loud, and then he bent over laughing and patting his butt with both hands. He stood up straight, raised his arm and fist, and with his other hand placed at his waist he did a fancy little jig with his feet and legs, and sang out loudly, "Rosa done gone, gone, gone, tank da Lawd 'a mighty. Les's read *S u p e r m a n*...BILLY!"

How could anyone want to hurt Papa, I wondered.

CHAPTER 12

One more day and it would be Thanksgiving. During the night, a bad storm came in from the west with plenty of lightning and thunder, awakening me around midnight. With the covers pulled up to my chin, I watched the storm from my windows overlooking the big oaks in the front yard. With the power in each strike of lightning, and every time the thunder rolled, the Big House seemed to groan and its old window sashes would rattle. With each bright strike, the limbs of the oaks looked like great arms stretching and reaching out. Watching the great show outside, with the lightning flashing and the thunder rolling, I imagined that the big oaks were reaching to calm the fear being placed upon the old King and his kingdom while his throne was being shaken. The old King knew, as I did, without a doubt, that after the storm passed and when daylight came, all would be okay on the dirt road. Sleepily, I laid back and closed my eyes, while pulling the covers up to my chin.

There was little rain in the storm, and it didn't stop the cane cutting when morning came. Maybe if things went well the cutters would take Thanksgiving Day off.

I heard Mama calling from the bottom of the stairs, "Billy, get up and get ready for school! Hurry! And it's cold out." She sounded a little strange, maybe urgent, but I could tell something wasn't right in her voice.

I quickly slipped into my school clothes and hurried down to the bathroom at the back of the house, past the kitchen. This was our only bathroom, and I guessed at one time it had been a big larder before the house had been plumbed and electrified. Mama was in the kitchen, and through the tall window, toward the east, I could see the red morning sky growing brighter over the trees in Bunkie. I said hi to her and went on to the bathroom to pee and wash my face. We had only cold water in the bathroom, and this was a cold day already. I came out of the bathroom shivering a little, and sat at the table. Mama turned around and asked, "Did the storm wake you?" and before I could answer she continued, "Guess what the lightning did last night?"

I shrugged my shoulders, stretched, and said, "Uh, I don't know, Mama. What?"

She set a cup of coffee in front of me, "Mag's house was hit by lightning, and it burned to the ground. Isn't that something? Dad's there now, looking it over."

I jumped up, pleading "Well, take me down there. I wanna see it, Mama."

She shook her head and said, "Well, you'll have to wait till we go to school. The weather's turning colder, and I have to get back here as quickly as I can." Mickey walked into the kitchen, books in hand. Mama told us to put on our coats and to get in the car; she would be right out.

The dirt road was muddy with big ruts from the tractors and cane buggies. The Chevy would slip and slide from one rut to the other, and the rear wheels had to spin to keep us moving slowly through the mud. Mama handled it with ease. When we reached the graveled road, she pulled to the side, and we watched several men poking in the ashes and the charred wood of Mag's house. Light gray smoke bloomed through the ashes into the breeze coming from the west, while the chimney stood tall, alone and naked. It was a sad reminder of what had once been, and I hated it. Sadly, I looked at the fireplace hearth, and remembered how, just about a year earlier, sitting on the floor in front of it, Mag had pulled several sweet potatoes from the warm ashes, a treat for Papa and me. The tall bushes that surrounded the front yard had all burned, too, along with the side of the oak tree, but the little gate was still standing. I turned and faced the road in front of us, and commanded, "Let's go, Mama."

By the time we reached the paved road in town, we could see a snowflake every now and then. Mama asked, "Do you remember how red the sky was this morning when you came downstairs?" I nodded yes. "Well," she said, "Hoss, thinks that the weather's gonna get a lot colder and bad today, maybe even a little snow. I hope you two have on enough clothes," and she glanced toward Mickey sitting in the back seat. Nearing the school, she dropped us off at the corner and we walked the rest of the way, looking for every little snowflake that fell.

At recess that morning, you could see more flakes, some a little bigger than others, and word got around that school was going to let out early because of the cold and the possibility of snow, giving us half a day more for the Thanksgiving holidays. That was really good news. I think Mrs. Gilroy was happy about it, too, but looking at her pretty pink blouse and sweater she wore over it made me remember the day she was hit in the back by the softball, just a couple of months earlier. She had never said anything about it, and I figured she never knew that Eddie had thrown the ball that nearly killed her, or worst yet, that Harold had called her an old battle-axe. Everybody on the playground laughed about it whenever someone mentioned it, and we teased Eddie that he had tried to kill our poor ole teacher.

Sure enough, when the bell rang, ending recess, and we went back to our classroom, Mrs. Gilroy stood up at her desk and announced, "Okay, everybody, listen to me. The buses will be here after your lunch period. So whatever you're taking home with you, take it when you go to the lunchroom, and be sure to get your coats from the cloakroom. Now listen to me! Quiet everybody!" She hesitated, then held her hand high in the air, announcing, "Over the holidays," and she hesitated again, "No homework!" Pandemonium broke out! Mrs. Gilroy hid her smile and tapped loudly on her desk with her spanking paddle, and called out, "Quiet, now, quiet!" Two of the teacher's pets helped her grade papers until the lunch bell rang. I figured they would probably be teachers like Mrs. Gilroy some day, and they would have teacher's pets, too.

Mister Armand drove the old bus at a snail's pace—in fact, I could have walked along the side in the snow and kept up with it—and he kept mumbling something in French. Every now and then, he would cough like he had a bad cold, then mumble some more. It was drafty around the windows, letting the cold air seep through, and it chilled my face while I pressed my forehead against the glass to watch the snow. The wipers squeaked across the windshield just every now and then, making the snow accumulate around the edges of the wide glass. Whiteness was beginning to show on the grass along the sides of the road, and the kids were overly loud and excited about the holiday, and especially about the snow. Somebody must have farted because a couple of the older girls started yucking and moved to another seat. One of them looked at me with a question in her eyebrows, but I just raised my hands and shook my head *no*. I laughed to myself, and turned to press my face against the window, while hoping the snow would come down harder, and quickly cover the ground.

I remembered just two times in my life that we had snow, at least enough to play in for a little while. Maybe today would be different, and it would be deep enough for us to play in for a day or two. The bus squeaked to a stop in the gravel, and ole man Armand yelled something at Mickey and me in French, then he sneezed just as we passed by his driver's seat. We quickly got off and crossed the gravel road, beginning our walk home. I glanced to where Mag's house once stood, while tiny plumes of gray smoke quickly disappeared in the cold wind, but no one was around. The snow melted almost as quickly as it hit the ground, but a little white began to show in the grass and on the limbs and leaves of the live oaks. My little brother and I walked down the side of the dirt road as fast as we could, facing a strong west wind and trying not to get our shoes too muddy. It seemed to me that the snow *was* falling faster and the flakes *were* bigger. My cheeks were stinging, and my lips were dry, while my heart pounded inside with excitement, and I felt really good.

Mama met us at the kitchen door and made us take our shoes off and leave them on the porch. We ran to the dining room and stood in front of the fire, trying to warm our hands and faces. Mama came to the fireplace, put her arms around us both and smiled, saying, "Well, maybe we'll get enough for y'all to play in tomorrow. I hope we do. Wouldn't that be nice, boys?"

She had gotten our rubber boots out of the porch closet and had them by the fireplace. I put on mine and went outside, feeling that the boots were a little tight. I guessed that my feet had grown a little, and I might have to wear them without socks. That wouldn't be much fun. My leather aviator's cap fit tight on my head, and had long ears that snapped beneath my chin. I liked it a lot. It was warm. I was hoping that someone would come to play, but I figured that most everyone in the Quarters would stay close to home, waiting to see what would happen with the snow. The field hands had knocked off a little before the school bus dropped us off, so they were probably hauling in wood for their stoves and fireplaces and getting ready for the cold. Hoss had hauled in plenty of wood for our fireplaces, and had already placed fresh kindling at each fireplace for the next morning. The snow was coming down faster, and the flakes seemed bigger. A thin white blanket was beginning to cover the green grass and the tin roof of the Big House. I stood at the corner of the screened porch, barely able to see through the falling snow to the end of the hedgerow where the driveway turned going into the Quarters. The sky was white and seemed to have broken into billions of pieces, all falling onto everything around us, and the wind began to sing through the big oaks and down the galleries that surrounded the Big House. The tops of the tall pecan trees were gently swaying in the wind, but still showing a few black specks on the tips of the high limbs—the shells left from their fall crop. Mama, Rosa, Papa and I had picked up the entire crop of pecans. Mama had hidden her cash in her room somewhere to buy Christmas gifts later.

My hands were wet and cold. I went back inside, held out my hands so she could see them, and asked Mama if we had some gloves I could use. She said in a very matter of fact tone, "Nope! Sure don't! But Santa might bring you some for Christmas."

"Mama, you know I know there's no Santa Claus," I said. She frowned and pointed to my little brother, who was warming himself at the end of the kitchen stove. She didn't know that I had already told him that Dad had beat the devil out of Santa last Christmas, and he wouldn't be coming back to our house anymore, but he didn't believe me, and anyway, he called me a liar. But I didn't know why I didn't have any gloves. Dad had four pairs.

My sister, Jerry, was living with Margie in Alexandria, a good-sized city about thirty miles north of Bunkie. No one had told me, but I knew that Margie would have a baby soon. It was like everybody could know except me. I stood warming in front of the fireplace in the dining room and remembered that Jerry had some leather gloves that would probably fit me, and I could easily find them in her room. I walked quietly through the family room, and went into her bedroom. The wood heater was unlit, and her room was cold, but I closed the door behind me in case Mama came into the family room. The first drawer I opened I found the pretty brown gloves. Dad had fussed about her having spent so much money for them that I remembered her buying them last winter at Weil's Department Store. Pulling them on, they were a little tight, but I could manage that. I hid them in the side pocket of my coat and went back to the dining room.

THE LAST WITNESS FROM A DIRT ROAD

In the winter, we used the dining room because it was closer to the kitchen, where the cooking stove stayed lit most of the time, keeping both the kitchen and dining room warm. Three big chairs sat facing the fireplace. The dining room was big, with the fireplace at the end farthest from the kitchen. I warmed up really well, then headed out to play in the snow, but when I opened the kitchen door onto the porch, Dad was standing at the screen, watching the snow come down. He turned to me, ordering, "Son, go open the gate past the airplane, so the cows can get under the trees for shelter. It's gonna be awfully cold tonight!" At the same time, he was pointing in the direction I had to go.

CHAPTER 13

That was great. I had a good reason to go out into the snow, since I was doing a job for Dad, so I really *needed* my sister's gloves—or at least that's the way I figured it. I ran around to the front of the house, carefully crossed the cattle guard, and continued to run till I reached the tall wooden gate onto the bank of the bayou. I climbed to the top of it and jumped to the ground. Pal slid under it. We ran toward the gate to the bayou pasture and toward the two oaks where the airplane lay. The snow was falling faster, and I could barely see the big trees through the whiteness of the snow in the fading light. A few seconds later, I came upon the silver plane and stopped. As the cold wind whistled about me, I crept slowly toward it, and with one hand shading my eyes from the wind, I peered at the silver ghost. Trying to hide under a thin layer of whiteness, it glared back at me, waiting, I imagined, for my next move, to see what I might do. I leaned forward to look into the front cockpit where the snow was already covering the instrument panel, and was settling onto the seat. Facing into the snow and wind, my eyes began to water and burn. My heart was pounding hard, and my stomach started moving about, feeling sick as the starburst began to spin in my eyes. This was a sad place, a place of death that I knew well, and suddenly, the cold reached deep inside of me, taking my breath away. I swallowed hard. Remembering the loneliness, the flooding tears, broken hearts, and the depth of despair months ago at the crash site made me groan, as though a fist had hit me very hard in my back, knocking the breath out of me. I had felt that way before, many times, when I would sit in the cockpit and imagine myself as the pilot; but on that cold, white evening I felt as though I were floating inside of a big cloud, where a great silver bird with no wings was going to devour me and take me away forever. I could feel the cold wind stinging my face, and it seemed to move me from where I stood, while whispering over and over, "Come closer, come....closer!" Thrusting my hands in front of me to push away from the cockpit, I screamed into the wind as my sister's gloves began turning red. Without thinking, I quickly put them to my face, covering my eyes, and I screamed again, realizing no one would help me. There was no one, again, who would help me, while this cold silver demon tugged harder and harder, trying to pull me into its broken body.

Pal barked twice and grabbed the bottom of my coat with his mouth. I jumped back from the plane and we both started running past the big trees toward the gate that I had to open. Stumbling on a fallen limb, my hands and face went into the snow. Pal jumped on me and started licking at my lips, but I pushed him away and jumped to my feet. The cows were standing all together facing away from the howling wind, and when I opened the gate they hurried through to reach the shelter of the trees. Leaving the gate open, I ran all the way back to the house, never glancing toward the airplane as I passed beneath the trees. Pal was close at my side as we ran, and he kept jumping to catch my hand, barking at the snow. In the cold, blistering wind, and with the white blanket of snow getting deeper, it seemed I had awakened a sleeping demon under the two big oaks, and it had torn into my mind, churning the memories I had buried deep inside.

When Pal and I reached the corner of the screened porch, the snow was blowing harder, but through the dim light and whiteness, I could see someone standing on the steps. It was Papa, and he was shaking from the cold. "Where's ya been, Billy?" he asked. I told him about opening the gate for the cows and he asked, "Ya got a coat fer me?" I told him to come on in when I remembered telling him that I would try to find a coat for him. We took off our boots on the porch and walked into the kitchen. Mickey was already sitting at the table, while Mama was placing the knives and forks at each place.

She glanced at Papa and said, "Well, Papa, you *do* need a coat, and I've got a good one for you. Go stand over there by the stove and warm up a little." She turned and went into the bathroom off the kitchen and came out with a heavy, faded jacket that Dad had worn for several seasons. She held it up, explaining, "I just took it up a little on the sides and it ought to fit you. You'll have to wear a couple of shirts under it to help keep the cold out."

Papa grinned big and said, "Oh, thanks you, Miz Florence. It sho is nice."

"You're welcome, Papa." Then she ordered, "You better go on home or your Mama will be looking for you. The weather's awfully bad for you to be out this late."

I couldn't believe Papa said "Thank you" without being told to do so. I studied him very closely in Dad's old jacket, and when the door closed behind him I thought, "That rascal knows a lot more than anyone thinks or that he lets on."

My hands were freezing, and my sister's leather gloves were soaked all the way to my wrist. I pulled them off and looked at my hands again, seeing the redness from being so cold. I took the wet gloves to the fireplace in the dining room and placed them on the hearth to dry, where the fire was warm and big, making my shadow dance happily around the walls of the big room. I held my hands toward the fire and raised my eyes to the mantle mirror. The flames in the fireplace were reflecting from the glass doors of the tall china cabinet, filling the mirror in front of me with flashing colors of fire. Glancing about the big room, I thought again about the airplane and how all of my memories from Juneteenth were painted in shades of red.

THE LAST WITNESS FROM A DIRT ROAD

The spell I was under at the moment was broken when Mama called from the kitchen.

"Y'all come on. Supper's ready!"

CHAPTER 14

For much of the evening, I watched through the dining room window. The snow was bright and still falling heavily, but the night was too dark to see beyond a few feet from the window. I put on my jacket and went to the front door. When I opened the door, the wind blew in, bringing some snow with it. The great hall had no fireplace or wood heater, and was always cold in the winter. Glimpsing through a small opening in the door, it looked as though the snow was about four inches deep on the front porch floor. I jumped when the phone rang right behind me. We had only one phone, and it was all the way in the front of the house, near the front door. Not many people had phones, and we didn't get many calls. We also shared the phone line with three or four other families down the road, but this time it was for us, two short rings.

"Shirley Plantation," I answered in my best voice.

"I am sorry, sir. This call has been delayed because of weather. Will you accept the charges, please?" and the lady on the other end of the line waited for me to answer. And she called me "Sir."

"Yes, Ma'am," I hesitated, since I didn't know what she meant, but I was anxious to talk to anyone, especially if the person on the other end wanted to talk about the snow.

Very nicely, the lady said, "Thank you, Sir."

Then, my sister Jerry asked in a disgusted tone, "Billy, what are you doing answering the phone? Where's Daddy or Mama?"

"I'll get 'um," and I called to Mama, who was already halfway down the great hall, with her arm reaching out for the phone.

Mama seemed anxious and jumpy, but quickly took the receiver, saying *hello* before she had it to her mouth. I could see her expression changing as she listened; she placed her hand on her forehead, then a pretty smile came out. Her eyes seemed focused on a little bouquet of red and pink roses, which repeated itself throughout the wallpaper in the long hall. As her focus changed, a big smile lit her face. She glanced passed me standing there, replying, "Oh, that's wonderful. I wish we were there, but you know how bad the weather is. I can hardly wait." She listened again for a few seconds and replied again, "Well, I doubt that we can come tomorrow either. The snow is going to be more than we've seen in a long time, but you know we'll come as soon as we can. Maybe Friday if the snow melts, but maybe not till Saturday." She listened again for a few seconds, then, said, "I just can't believe it. Tell Margie we'll be there as soon as we can, and we love her." She listened again then said, "Okay, bye, dear." She raised her hand to her eyes and wiped the tears away.

"What, Mama? What's the matter?" I pleaded, wanting to know what was going on. She pulled her sweater tight around her and hurried toward the other end of the great hall to the family room door.

Never looking at me, she sang over and over, "Oh, I have to tell your daddy. I have to tell your daddy!"

I followed closely, closed the door from the hall, and wondered if Jerry ever mentioned the snow to Mama, or how much they had up in Alexandria.

"Guess who that was," Mama said in a happy tone. "Jerry! Margie had a little boy early yesterday morning! They've been trying to call, but I guess the phone lines were down somewhere!"

I knew the weather had been bad all day Tuesday, and Tuesday night we had the lightening storm, then today the bad cold, with snow and wind. Daddy stood up and hugged Mama right in front of me and my little brother. They just stood holding each other, and looking into the roaring fire, then Mama started to cry again. The curtains, hanging limp over the two big windows in the family room, were slowly moving from the air seeping through the cracks around each sash, and the windows every now and then would rattle when the wind gusted.

"Margie had a baby?" I asked and looked over to where my little brother was dozing on the divan.

Mama looked my way, commanding sharply, "I'll tell you about it tomorrow, Billy. Wake Mickey, and y'all go to bed."

Under a mountain of quilts on my bed, I could hear the old King moan each time a gust of cold wind blew against his walls, making him as cold as I was, and making the windows rattle again and again. Never having been told that my sister was going to have a baby hurt my feelings, and made me sad at the same time, but I was angry, too.

I wiped my eyes on my pillowcase, and slept in my clothes that night.

CHAPTER 15

Hearing the birds chirping, I slowly raised my head and looked over the windowsill at the front yard. I was warm under the covers as I looked at the snow clinging to the limbs and the green leaves of the big oaks. It was so deep in the yard that I could see only the green tops of the rows of narcissus that connected the four big trees to each other. Paw Paw would have said, "We had a *good one* this time!" I quickly slid out of my bed, grabbed my socks, and ran all the way to the dining room before I would get cold. Dad was drinking his first cup of coffee, and Mama had started breakfast.

I asked Mama to pour me a cup of coffee. She said she didn't have any biscuits left, so I fixed my coffee with cream and sugar, and went back to the dining room to sit in front of the fire with Dad. The wind wasn't blowing anymore, and the sun was blinding when I glanced through the dining room window, and figuring that Papa would be around before long.

Dad looked at me, announcing, "They named him after his daddy, but they're gonna call him Spike." I figured he was talking about Margie's baby. "Spike!" he said again, like he had a question inside of him. I just kept looking into the fire and sipping my coffee with both hands wrapped around the warm cup.

Every time I thought about *Spike* I saw a big rusty nail, but he wasn't my baby, so I figured they could call him whatever they wanted. Dad put his hand on my arm, and with his other hand he held toward me two little pieces of what looked like roasted pigskin, with a stiff little hand cupped at the end of each piece. He chuckled, shook his head as though he couldn't believe what he was holding, then said, "Look at what's left of Jerry's new gloves!" I swallowed my coffee hard, and just looked at him, waiting for him to get onto me. He continued to smile and said, "She's sure gonna get you this time, boy! You oughta know better than to dry wet leather in front of a hot fire," and he laid them in my lap, while still chuckling.

Not touching them, I looked closely at the small, cupped hands, reminding me of the story that Mrs. Gilroy had read to the class a few weeks before called "The Raven and the Monkey's Paw," thinking, "I bet Mister Edgar Allan Poe would think that this is what a monkey's paw really looks like, hard and stiff." Then I thought again, "They're too little to fit even on Pal's feet." Dad chuckled, shook his head again, and set his gaze onto the fire in front of him, my not knowing if I should laugh or what.

"You oughta know better than that! What are you gonna do now?" he grumbled to me, making me glad that I hadn't laughed about the gloves.

My eyes stayed locked on the shrunken little gloves, hard and stiff, while I shook my head, answering, "I don't know. I'll figure out something, I guess," and I looked at him directly in the face.

He chuckled again and said, "I keep wondering why you fool around in her room. She's told you to stay outta there! You're just asking for trouble, boy."

"Yes Sir," and I quickly gulped the rest of my coffee.

Jerry wouldn't be home for a couple of weeks, so I figured that by then, if she missed her gloves and asked me about them, I could have several reasons why her new gloves had disappeared, like when I tried them on, I took them outside, laid them down on the steps, and Pal took them. He did things like that anyway. Or better, yet—I had to do a job for Dad during the snow and I needed her gloves. That was a good reason, but I figured she wouldn't believe that one either. In fact, whatever reason I would give, she wouldn't believe it. But, I had a few days to think about it before I would have to start worrying. Besides, we had the snow to think about, and that was much more fun than thinking about those crummy gloves.

The kitchen door sounded with a special knock, which I quickly recognized. Thank goodness, Papa had come at the right time, and I hurried through the kitchen to the door.

He had on his coat Mama had given him, and both shirts. The shirts sleeves were dangling from the coat's sleeves, well below his wrists, and his pants legs were tucked into his rubber boots. I asked him, "Papa, did you put on some socks?"

He looked down at his boots and said, "I sho did, jist lak ya said. I's put two socks on evy foot, Billy! I's good and warm. Ain't dis nice?" And he looked at me with a big grin crossing his face, waiting for me to compliment him more. I figured he would be warm.

Last winter I had given him my knit cap when Mama had bought my leather aviator's cap. He had the knit cap on, too, and it looked awfully dirty, so I asked, "Papa, has your mama ever washed your cap? It sure looks dirty to me."

He snatched it from his head, glanced at it and held it out toward me. Frowning, he growled to me, "Billy, ya blind or som'um. Dis cap ain't got dirty yet! Yo ole leather cap is a lot worse off dan diss'un! Look at how brown it done turned."

I put on my coat and boots, and we pranced our way across the yard to the fishponds. Both ponds had a thin layer of ice on top, and I wished that they had frozen solid so we could slide around on them.

"Step on that ice, and see if it'll hold you up, Papa." He started to step into the pond; but I stopped him, commanding, "Ah, come on, Papa, I'm gonna write your name in the snow."

With a small stick, I wrote "I-S-A-A-C." Papa stood back, shook his finger at me, complaining, "Billy, now ya know dat ain'ts ma name. Ya tryin' to fool me, ain't ya?"

"Yes it is, Papa! That's your real name. Isaac *is* your name!"

He looked at it again, crooked his head to the side and said, "Well, it sho ain't got no 'Ps' in it," and he was reaching over to mess it up.

I grabbed his arm and said to him, "Papa is your *nickname*, not your real name."

He looked puzzled again and said, "Nick, like mean old Uncle Nick?" Before I could explain it to him, he yelled at me, "Uncle Nick mean to me and I don likes Uncle Nick, Billy, an ya ain't gon make me no Nick! I don wants to be no Nick. So ya jist fergit dat!" I could tell that he was upset and mad at me for his not understanding that *Papa* was merely his nickname.

Uncle Nick, Nick Searcy, worked in the yard, raised and took care of the chickens, turkeys, and guineas. He was older than Hoss, and spoke in French as much as English, making it very hard for me to understand him when he fussed at Papa and me. He had trained Pal to round up the chickens every evening about five, and Pal would drive them into the chicken pen. Anytime I told Mama that Uncle Nick had threatened to whip Papa or me, she always took his side.

Papa looked down again at the letters in the snow, fussing, "Billy, I ain't gon be no Nick," and he stepped into the letters, kicking the snow about.

"Well, let's go, Papa, but I'm gonna tell Uncle Nick what you said."

He stopped in his tracks and yelled at me, "Ya betta not! Billy, is ya gon tell'm? I's gon sho kill ya if ya do! Ya hear me?" and he reached down, then threw a handful of snow at me.

He looked as though he was about to cry, with his big lips turned down and fire in his big eyes. "Nah, Papa! You know I wouldn't tell him that. Come on. Let's go, buddy, before we get cold!"

I wondered again if I could ever get Papa past the alphabet or teach him to sign his name, his real name—Issac Vead.

The snow was up about eight inches on my boots, and my feet were already cold.

We slowly walked to the end of the hedgerow, where I stopped and turned around to look back at the Big House and the yard. The dark smoke from the chimneys was meandering upward and disappearing into a blue sky. The tall, old house with the big yard and big green oaks, in just one snowy night, had been turned into a wonderland of majestic beauty, a real King with a beautiful throne all around him. My King. I had believed, for a long time, that the Big House was almost royalty, and that Shirley was the king of the plantations around Bunkie.

Looking all around me, I smiled and wondered how long it would be before I would see the King all dressed up in shiny white snow again. Pal barked once.

Papa pulled on my coat sleeve and whined to me, "Ah, com'on, Billy! I's gittin cold."

With the whites of his eyes gleaming like two big bulbs, he shook his finger at me, commanding, "And ya betta not go tell Uncle Nick what I don said."

CHAPTER 16

We walked slowly down the graveled driveway, kicking the snow with every step. Pal was jumping above the snow, and ran a little bit ahead of us. When we reached the tool shed, we could see all the way to the far end of the dirt road. Though still a little early, I was surprised there was no one playing in the road or in the yards of the houses in the Quarters.

I looked at Papa and wondered out loud, "Where's everybody? No one's out playing in the snow!"

Papa stopped and picked up a hand full of snow and threw it at me, then announced, "Dey gon stay by da fire! Billy, you know don evybody gots no coat and boots like me and you."

When we reached the Gaspard house, I could smell coffee roasting and, I thought, the smell of fresh baked bread. "Papa, let's go see if Cathrine wants to come out and we'll make a big snowman," and I turned to go up their walk to the front porch.

Papa said, "I ain't gon go up dare. Miz Mazie don' likes me."

I frowned at him and said, "Ah, come on Papa, maybe she'll give us a hot roll."

He shook his head *no* and said, "I'sll wait here fer ya, Billy." He reached down to hold Pal's collar, then rubbed his ears, and as I walked away I thought— my two best friends Pal and Papa.

I had to knock twice, and finally Cathrine, with her bright blue eyes smiling, opened the door just a little. She still had on her robe, and offered, "Come around to the back, Billy. It's too cold in here!"

I ran around to the back porch and knocked on the kitchen door, and then Mister Alfonse called for me to come in. I walked into the kitchen and saw the big black pan full of hot rolls sitting on top of the stove's warmer, while little clouds of heat moved toward the ceiling. My timing was perferct, and my mouth began to water quickly.

Mrs. Mazie looked at me, but never smiling, and said, "I bet ya want a piece of my bread!" While taking some coffee beans out of the oven, she said directly to me, "If ya want a piece of bread, you gotta turn the grinder fer me!" I must have looked a little disappointed, and she continued, "Com' on, it want take long. Papa can wait!" I wondered how Mrs. Mazie knew that Papa was waiting out front.

Cathrine had come into the kitchen barefooted and still in her robe, and I knew then that she wasn't planning to play in the snow. She had my two *Superman* comics, holding them in one hand, and complimented, "These are good. I read them twice," her blue eyes shinning while she smiled at me.

"What about Caroline, Cathrine, do you reckon she'll want to read them?"

"I don't guess Caroline'll want them. I haven't seen her for a day or so. Thanks, anyway," and she handed the comics to me.

I tucked the comics into my coat so Papa wouldn't see them, or I would have to read them to him again.

Mrs. Mazie, with one hand planted on her hip, looked at me and said, "Okay, Billy, Cathrine can grind my coffee. Ya still want a piece of bread?"

"Yes, Ma'am!"

She tore a piece from a brown paper bag, and put the roll on it. I turned to go to the door, "Thanks Miz Mazie. I'll see you Cathrine, Mister Alfonse!" I closed the door behind me, jumped off the porch, and ran to the front where Papa and Pal were waiting.

I tore the roll in half and gave one piece to Papa. Pal kept looking up at me and wagging his tail, so I broke off a piece and gave it to him. He gulped it down as usual. Mrs. Mazie didn't put any butter on it, but Pal kept begging for another bite.

A breeze had started blowing from the south, feeling a little bit warm, especially compared to my feet and the deep snow covering the dirt road. The sun was bright, and it seemed to me that the snow was starting to melt a little. As we walked and nibbled on our bread, I started thinking about Margie's little baby, Spike. I wondered how that was going to work. Would it be a problem like the name "Papa"? Spike was his nickname. What would people call him when he got a lot older?

My mind was quickly jumping from one thing to another, and suddenly I remembered the visit to the silver plane the night before, and I became angry when I wondered why I let the monster play in my mind and dig itself out of my memory.

I felt anxious, too, suddenly, in a hurry, like I wanted to run away from something, or climb high into a tree, or even sit in the cockpit of the silver plane and cry—no, not cry, but curse and yell and scream. Yell, and scream as loud as I could, over and over. I looked all the way to the end of the dirt road while it layed calmly covered with a clean blanket of snow. There was no one in sight on that cold, white day. Where were they? Where were my friends? That's where we grew to know each other, right there on the dirt road and in the rows of houses on each side. And my heart pounded harder. We never had this much snow to play in, at least that I could remember. Where were they? Why didn't they come out and play, or, at least, come out and talk about the snow? Then, I remembered what Papa had said a few minutes earlier: "Don't evybody gots no coat and boots like me and you, Billy."

I gritted my teeth and balled up my fist just as the silver plane, again, came into my mind, and I could see the ever-present color of *red*. Papa was walking with his hands in his pockets, about three steps in front of me, humming one of his stupid little songs as he watched the snow scatter in front of him with each step. I lunged toward him, and pushed him from the back as hard as I could. He fell face first into the deep snow, his hands still in his pockets, and not knowing what had hit him.

"Go home, Papa! Go on home and wash your dirty old cap! You stink, old Nick Searcy!" I turned, and started running as fast as I could toward home.

Pal kept barking and trying to catch my hand in his mouth, and I kicked at him and yelled for him to leave me alone.

I was tired of Papa, tired of Cathrine and Mrs. Mazie, tired of the snow, tired of Superman comics, tired of Pal, tired of this old plantation, this dirt road, and I hated the silver plane. With all my heart and mind, I hated it. But I knew I would keep going to it: crying in its cockpit, I would fly it, and sometimes I would crash it. Over and over, I would return to it, and it would continue to haunt my memory.

***

That day was Thanksgiving, and everything should have been right. The snow was beautiful and deep, a winter scene seldom coming to Central Louisiana, and a *treat* the memory of which would have to last a long, long time before it would come again. The road through the Quarters should have been roaring with kids, laughing and playing in the snow, throwing snowballs and making snowmen. But something was wrong on our dirt road, and I could feel it. In every direction I looked, the houses in the Quarters, the big oaks, the little bushes, and the road itself were covered with a clean white blanket, undisturbed except for a trail of our footsteps. It was too quiet. It was too still and cold, and nothing was moving except the smoke from the fireplaces in the little houses on both sides of the dirt road. It drifted straight and high, disappearing quickly into a blue sky, leaving the Quarters, leaving all of us on the dirt road, locked inside, leaving me cold, empty, lonely and heartbroken.

My stomach turned over while I cried inside. On that snowy white day with undisturbed beauty in every direction, for the first time in my life I felt the *whip* of the dirt road, slashing across my heart, knowing that my friends were held captive in their own houses, simply because they had no coats and boots. Papa was right: "No coats and boots like ours."

Only Papa and I had been so lucky.

My stomach stirred again, and colored circles began to move about and gather in the wetness of my eyes, some green, but most were shades of red, again.

Coats and boots! I knew that I could never find enough coats and boots for my friends.

The snow, clean, pure, and beautiful, was unable to hide the dirt of our road beneath it. On Thanksgiving Day in 1946, a picture of our dirt road, a changing picture, began to develop right in front of me.

It was ugly.

And it was vile.

CHAPTER 17

I ran as fast as I could in the deep snow. Breathing hard by the time I reached the hedgerow, and feeling my heart beating rapidly, I stopped to catch my breath and to look again at the Big House. Its beauty had gone. It had turned old, and ugly too, even with its rusting tin roof being hidden by the snow, while the green yard around it was buried beneath the clean whiteness. "A King on his throne," I thought. "No, an old tyrant, mean and selfish, who has been witness to more than a hundred years of pain to thousands of people who worked his lands and cared for him, while he gave back only enough to hold them in his tight grip for all of their lives." I recognized he was weary, very sad, and very different from the way Papa and I had seen him only a little while before. *And I figured his feet were as cold as mine, and like me, he seemed to be gasping for breath, or maybe he was tired of being who he was. Maybe the King was afraid, too—afraid of not understanding what was happening around him, not knowing about changes, or how to change, or what one-day he might become. Maybe he was just plain scared of what was happening in his life, in the little world he thought he knew so well, and he didn't know what to do. It was so cold on the dirt road, so white, and so silent. And no one had any coats and boots, and he knew he could never find enough for all of his friends.*

With every slow step I took, Pal was beside me, looking up at my face, reading it and waiting for me to make a gesture or a move that involved him. I walked slowly down the driveway and finally stepped onto the porch. Struggling to get my boots off my cold feet, I looked to the other end of the porch and saw my dad's boots parked next to the screened door. They were partially coated with manure, and I could smell the faint, sweet odor, all the way from where they stood. I hated that, too. I guessed that he had been helping at the barns so Hoss could go home and have his own Thanksgiving Dinner with Helen and Papa. Hoss would have to come back to do the evening chores, but Dad would help him again, and I would help them, too.

I opened the kitchen door, and Mama was standing at the stove, stirring in a small skillet. Little clouds of steam burst out of other pots and pans as our Thanksgiving dinner bubbled inside each one. The aroma of a fine Thanksgiving dinner quickly filled every corner of my mind and crowded the thoughts that had held me captive just a few minutes before, when I had left the dirt road. The sight and smell of a fresh cooked turkey cooling on the kitchen table upset me further, because I knew that my friends wouldn't even have a Thanksgiving turkey, for the same reasons they had no coats and boots.

Mama glanced toward me, commanding, "Billy, go get a few sticks of stove wood. It won't take much." I said nothing but went back on to the porch, put on my boots, and headed to the woodpile. Brushing the snow off the short sticks of wood, I picked up an armload, and struggled back to the kitchen door.

Dad had heard me coming and held the door open for me. I dropped the wood into the wood box in back of the big iron stove.

Mama spoke softly, almost to herself, "Well, I guess it will just be the four of us for Thanksgiving dinner. The roads are too bad for anybody to drive in this snow."

Dad watched while I brushed the snow from my arms, then, said, "Billy, I talked to Hoss about Papa, and he says that he has to whip Papa every now and then. I guess Papa's gonna have to learn to mind better."

I looked directly into his face, and said angrily, "But, Dad, Papa doesn't understand everything. You know how he is, but he's a *good* boy. Hoss is mean to him and so's his mama, and you could stop it, if you wanted to!"

Dad shook his head and raised his voice, "I've said all that I can to him. Papa belongs to them, and they have to raise him the best way they know how," and he shook his finger in my face, continuing, "and don't you be putting crazy things in Papa's head! Hoss has told me about some of the things you're telling Papa."

I knew the law was being laid down to me right then, so I said nothing, but he saw me clinching my teeth, and my right hand made into a fist. My lips began to quiver.

He continued in his angry voice, "Don't you show your temper to me, boy, so just calm down before you get yourself in some really bad trouble. And I want to tell you this: you're spending too damn much time in the Quarters! You're not a child anymore, and you can't be running in and out the houses like a little kid. I'm telling you now, keep your butt out of there. Do you understand me?" And he stood ready for me to make a move.

"Yes, sir, I understand you!" and I stood waiting for another outbreak while looking directly into his eyes, wanting to hit him squarely in the mouth with my fist. He stood glaring at me, waiting still for me to make a move, or say the wrong thing. I knew then that he had heard me Sunday night on our way home from church, but worse yet, he knew before I said it that Hoss and Helen were mean to Papa. Hoss and Helen did whip Papa, and they whipped him a lot, only because Papa was there, was handy. I gritted my teeth again, holding down my anger, knowing Dad would try to give me a whipping if I made a wrong move, and I knew I would not stand for a whipping, ever.

I took my boots off in the kitchen, and Mama told me to put them on the porch. I followed Dad into the dining room where a big fire was burning in the fireplace. He knew that I was still angry about what was said in the kitchen.

Quickly, I dropped into one of the big chairs, and before he sat down, I tried once more, "Papa's a good kid, and you ought not let them beat up on him the way they do. They're taking out their meaness and anger on..."

Before I could finish my sentence, he stood over me and growled again, "I told you, Billy, that I've done all that I can, and don't you bother me with that foolishness again! This conversation is over, and I mean *over for good!* Do you hear me, Billy? Do-you-hear-me?"

I hesitated a moment, then, said emphatically, "Yes, sir, I hear you!"

Never moving from his spot, and pretending he heard nothing, Mickey was playing with a little toy tractor on the floor in front of the fireplace, humming like a motor while he rolled it about. I looked down at him and remembered doing the same thing in the same spot, and thought to myself, "I wish that was me," and I glared into the big fire, anger surging inside me while I felt my heart beating in the tips of my fingers.

Dad sat in one of the big chairs, looked into the fire and mumbled, "It looks like there'll be a warm rain this evening. That'll melt the snow. Maybe by Saturday we can get back in the cane fields if it's not too muddy." And he sighed deeply, while slowly brushing his forehead back and forth, with his hand.

He kept thinking out loud, but seemed to be waiting for me to comment. I didn't care if it rained or not, or about the fields. I left the fire in the dining room and ran through the cold family room, crossed the great hall and in only six jumps, I was at the top of the long stairway. My room was colder than the outside. I crawled under the quilts, covered my head and began to shiver. The bed was cold, but it would warm quickly. Dissapointed and angry, I didn't understand why so many bad things were happening around me. I felt as though I had been given a hard whipping, beaten down to the ground, yet I wasn't told why, and I couldn't get up. My mind was jumping from one thing to another; I thought about Mag and why she had to leave the plantation, when she didn't want to, and about Papa. Never had I thought that Hoss and Helen were mean people, but I believed that day that I had been wrong. They were laying out years of anger that had turned into meanness on my friend Papa. I banged my fist into the pillow as hard as I could.

Alone in the quietness of my room, I cried softly, not for me, but for the world around me, my little world on the dirt road, which seemed to be changing so fast. I was changing, too, and I could feel it, but I was lost in all of it, not knowing what was happening to me or to my friends. But one thing I had decided, for sure, was that I would spend as much time in the Quarters as I wanted. The Quarters and my friends on the plantation were the biggest part of my life, but they were also the part that puzzled me and confused me the most, often tearing holes in my heart and clouding my mind.

I must have dozed off, because when Dad called to me I didn't know where I was in the darkness under the covers. I threw the quilts back, jumped out of bed, and looked around for just a second to regain my bearings. It was cold, and the bright sun was gone. The clouds had come, and it looked like Dad would be right about the rain coming in.

I went to the kitchen where Mama was serving the food into the dishes to take to the dining room table. Very soon the four of us sat at our places. Dad said the blessing and started carving the Thanksgiving turkey when a familiar knock on the kitchen door told me that Papa had come, right at dinnertime. I looked at Dad but said nothing, and waited for a quick comment. Nothing came, so I excused myself and went to the kitchen door leading onto the porch. I did the same familiar knock, opened the door, and Papa was standing there, wiping his eyes. He stepped into the kitchen closing the door behind him. He had been crying.

"What's the matter, Papa?"

With his chin still quivering, he asked, "Is you mad at me, Billy?" He smelled like their smoky house, and I could see a few naps in his tight black hair.

"No, I'm not mad at you, Papa. Wait here for just a minute!" and I held up my finger toward him. I turned and ran all the way up to my room, picked out five Superman comics and ran back to the kitchen door. He was still standing where I had left him, shuffling his dirty knit cap from hand to hand.

"I'm glad you came. I wanted to give you these comics. You can keep them, forever. They're yours." He looked at the comics and smiled. Then I told him, "I'm sorry I pushed you down in the snow this morning, Papa. I was mad about something."

He again glanced at the comics, then at me, and said, "Ah, dats awright; I wudden hurt, no nothin." He smiled a little and sniffed.

"Okay, we're ready to eat dinner, and I'll see you later. In fact," I whispered to him, "I'll come down to your house, and we'll read Superman. Okay?" and I reached for the doorknob.

Before I could open the door, he sniffed again, blurting out, "Mama don sent me to tells yo daddy dat ma daddy is sick, an' fo yo daddy to come down to da house righta way."

Dad must have heard what Papa said because he came quickly into the kitchen. His forehead was creased and his eyebrows were tightly fixed. He went close to Papa and, with his hand on Papa's shoulder, asked, "What's the matter with your daddy, Papa?"

Papa started crying again, and mumbled softly, "Ma Mama say he gon die if ya don come real fass, Mista Carl."

Dad quickly opened the door, grabbed his coat from the hooks on the back porch, and put on his boots. By then, Mama was standing on the porch by Papa, holding her napkin to her lips. The frown on Mama's face was really bad, and her eyes began to tear. I grabbed my jacket off the hooks and put on my boots. Dad,

Papa, and I ran to his truck in the garage, where Papa and I jumped in the back. Dad backed out, and then drove fast down the driveway, and into the Quarters.

Much of the snow had vanished, and the truck slid to a stop in the mud in front of Papa's house. We jumped from the truck, and Dad ran to the front door. He didn't stop to knock, but Helen met him just inside the front room.

She had the hem of her white apron up to her eyes, and while slowly shaking her head, she whispered, "He done gone, Mista Carl. He done gone!" Dad put his arms around her shoulders. Crying softly, Helen reached up and took off her head wrap and wiped the tears from her eyes. Her white hair, cut tight to her head and as white as the snow outside, made me realize that she was as old as Hoss, and was much too old to have a kid as young as my friend Papa.

I was in back of Dad and turned around toward Papa when he started crying again. He knew what his Mama meant. I took his arm, led him onto the porch, and we sat in the swing. The air felt cold to me again; the beauty of the snow was gone, and the dirt road was turning quickly into a heavy brown mud. And Hoss had died.

"Give me those comics, Papa! Let's read *Superman!*" and I took them from his shaking hand. Reading Superman didn't work that time. He put both hands over his face, leaned forward, and put his elbows on his knees, crying like I had never seen him cry before.

He mumbled through his hands and tears, "Ma daddy don died. Wats Mama gon do, Billy?" He raised his face to look at me directly and muttered softly, "We gon hav ta leave da plantation." I could only hold on to Papa's arm while I hammered down my own tears.

✧✧✧

I knew Papa was right, and I knew I didn't have a long time to teach him to just sign his name, or maybe even be able to read a simple funny book. I wondered what was going to happen to Helen and Papa, not next week or next year, but a long time from that Thanksgiving. Dad, I felt, wouldn't know either. Along with the holidays and the beautiful snow came a lot of bad things to Shirley Plantation. Twice on Thanksgiving Day in 1946 our dirt road had become longer, meaner, and dirtier. While we sat quietly in the swing on Papa's front porch, a gust of cold wind blew across us and I shivered, thinking that the dirt road had whipped us, and me, two times on one snow-white day, and my heart was broken twice.

CHAPTER 18

It did rain that night and the next morning's weather was back to a cool and balmy November day. The cane fields were too muddy to work in, and the entire plantation was amiss about Hoss's death. Hoss had lived and worked on Shirley Plantation for almost his entire life. Papa was the last of his and Helen's five children. The others had gone to school a little, and had left the plantation a long time ago, probably before I was born. I didn't know any of them, only my friend, Papa. Dad took Helen to town, met with the funeral home director, and worked out the cost of taking care of Hoss's burial. For the next two days, everybody on the plantation pitched in with food and as much money as they could get together. The funeral director wanted three hundred dollars. Whatever wasn't paid, I knew my Dad would get the Company to pay the rest, or he would pay it himself. He would make sure that Israel Vead had a proper burial.

***

Sunday was bright and sunny, and Dad let me drive our new Chevy all the way from Church. Right before we got to the Prosser's house, he pointed across the steering wheel of the car toward the little white church that I had seen a thousand times, and said, "That's where we're gonna lay Hoss to rest today!"

"What time?" I questioned him.

He said, "Well, I'm not really sure yet. I have to see Helen and her family in a few minutes. Stop at their house."

I slowly pulled to a stop in front of Helen's house. There were two cars already parked on the side of the road, and about twenty-five or thirty people were there, on the porch and standing around in the front yard. Dad left the car and walked through the crowd, nodding and saying *hello* as he went. Some of the people had been crying, and others were hugging or patting each other on their backs. We knew just about all of them, as most of them lived on the plantation. J.B. strutted over to the car and I rolled the window down.

"Look at chu, Billy, drivin dat new cah like you knows what chu doin." As he leaned over, he glanced into the back at my mother and little brother, "Hello, Miz Florence, Mickey," and he tipped his hat.

"Hi, J.B.," Mama smiled and continued, "You look mighty nice today."

J.B. was all dressed up in a new suit. I looked him up and down, teasing him, "Shine's letting you wear one of his old suits, huh?" He reached through the window, tapped me on the back of my head with his hand, while tucking his bottom lip under his upper lip, and then chuckled. Before he would do anything else, I brought some spit to the front of my lips, ready to spit at him, and he quickly jumped back, laughing.

About that time, Dad came back to the car, sat down, closed the door announcing, "Well, the funeral's at two, but they're gonna start at the gravel road in just a little while and walk to the church."

I looked to the porch where Papa was leaning against a post with one arm wrapped around it. He motioned to me to come. "J.B., tell Papa I'll be back in a little while," and I let out on the clutch to make the wheels spin, hoping some mud might splatter on J.B.'s new suit, but he stepped back again, clapped his hands together, bent over a little and started laughing.

Dad frowned at me, shook his head and said, "I don't know about you!" then asked, "Son, aren't you almost twelve, now?" and continued to shake his head with a disgusted look on his face. I really didn't care what he thought, and ignored his question.

CHAPTER 19

Mama fixed us some left over turkey and dressing, and we ate Thanksgiving dinner all over again. I wasn't very hungry, and I kept my Sunday clothes on to go to the funeral. At about one thirty, we quietly loaded into the Chevy and left. I told Dad to let me out at Papa's house, that I wanted to walk to the church with everybody. He stopped the car, and while I crawled out of the back, Papa came from the porch to meet me. We walked to the front door where his Mama was sitting in a little chair on the porch, with three or four women standing by her. They were all dressed in white, and each had a white cloth on their head, tied in a big bow at the top. Aunt Colleen was dressed that way at Gilbert Frank's and Emma's wedding just a few days before, and Aunt Colleen was seated in a chair next to Helen, dressed the same way again.

Papa whispered to me, "Mama's Soci'ty ladies is here," while holding on to the back of my jacket with one hand. I turned around and told him not to hold on to me. He dropped his head a little, pouting, and announcing, "We's gon start down to da end of da road and walk to da church, Billy."

"Yeah, I know, and I'm gonna walk with you, Papa, but you can't hold on to me."

"I ain't gon hold to ya, Billy," and I felt his hand pat me on my back as I slowly moved away.

About twenty-five people were waiting at the end of the dirt road when we started from Papa's house. By the time we reached the gravel road, I figured there were at least fifty people to walk the short distance to the church. Many of the women had on white from head to toe. Some men were dressed in their Sunday clothes, and others wore their work clothes. I thought I was the only white person there until I found Cathrine and Mister Alfonse, with Caroline and her little brother not far behind them. Helen, her four grown children with their families, and Papa and I, were at the front. After just a bit, everybody started singing as we walked very slowly.

"Swing low, sweet chariot, comin for to carry me home, Swing low, sweet chariot, comin..." I knew that song. We sang it in church sometimes, so I just sang along with everyone else. I turned to Papa, commanding, "Sing, Papa. Sing loud!"

He frowned at me and said, "Ya know I don't knows da words," and I felt his hand when he latched on to the sleeve of my jacket, right above my elbow.

I glanced toward him as he looked straight ahead, smiling, with his chin held high.

Papa was my friend, and he needed me.

I said nothing.

CHAPTER 19

My feet were hurting from the rocks, and I guessed that everybody's feet were hurting, too. When we entered the front door of the little church I saw Mama, Daddy and Mickey sitting about five rows from the front. Going down the center aisle, I stopped at their pew to sit with them, but Papa pulled at my jacket to lead me to the front. I looked at Dad, and he nodded his approval, so I went on.

Papa didn't know his older brothers and sisters very well, and I guessed that he would rather have me there with him, sitting between him and his mother. Helen never stopped crying, slow, but with no tears that I could see. Hoss's coffin was just a few feet from where we sat, and I could smell the small bouquet of red and white flowers that lay on top. Staring at the brown wooden casket, I sighed deeply, and thought about Hoss being closed tightly inside. My stomach started churning, and I hoped that Papa wouldn't think about his dad being laid out inside the long, brown box, and possibly his nose being pushed into the lining of the casket top. That was bad. At that very moment, I decided that I never wanted to be put in a box like that and buried in the ground. That's what they did to my grandfathers and to my brother, but I quickly realized that I should think about something else before the bright colored circles started coming in my eyes and my stomach started turning over. "Teach Papa to sign his name. Yeah, that was a better thought, maybe to read, too. Yeah."

We sat quietly in our places while the choir sang a slow, sad song about crossing over Jordan, or something, but every now and then a choir member would sing out really loud and maybe even start to cry. Others would have to hold her, or fan her, when her eyes sort of rolled back and she looked like she was going to pass out. After a short while, a tall but heavyset man in a white robe with tiny gold stripes around the sleeves stepped from behind the choir and stood on the podium behind a wide pulpit, which overlooked the casket. Little beads of sweat sparkled on his brown forehead; his eyes wandered across the congregation, finally settling on Helen, Papa, and me. His mouth twitched a little to his right side; at the same time, his right eye closed slowly, then reopened slowly, then he swallowed hard. Raising his hand high with his long, fat fingers spread wide apart, the choir became silent and the congregation began clearing their throats. I coughed, but not knowing why. With a big white handkerchief, the man in the white robe slowly wiped the beads of sweat from his forehead; then, he pulled the sleeves of his robe up to his elbows, showing his blue suit and stiff white shirt cuffs and gold cuff links. His pompadour was tall and wide, and his thick black hair glistened. I suddenly caught the aroma of fresh pomade.

With a strong and deep voice, the preacher broke the silence as he began very softly, "My deah brothas and sistu's, thank ya for commin' heah today. We'ah gathaed t'day to lay t'rest the tired body of our brotha, Mista Israel Vead. Ma good friend, knowed foreva' for his strength and his power, by the name given to him when he wuz jist a young boy, by his boss man, Mista Hilliary Vead. Mista Vead called him 'Hoss.' Hoss, watta name that wuz and watta man this fella wuz, even up till the very day he left us, to go meet his maka. I loved this powerful man, almost lak'a daddy, he wuz to me." The preacher cleared his throat with a little cough, swallowed, and his mouth twitched again, but his eye didn't close like before. He continued, "Fer twenty five yeahs or mo, we's would sit on his poach, or in his and Miz Helen's house, and he would tell me bout his boyhood days, bout when he was jist a little kid."

My ears perked up because Hoss would often tell Papa and me about his boyhood days, and the preacher made it sound really interesting. The preacher wiped his head again, took a sip of water from a glass on the podium, and continued, but in a louder and bigger voice. He appeared to get taller, and his chest got bigger, too. He took a deep breath, while everyone waited, very still, and in total silence.

"Hoss was born a little bit mo than eighty-some yeahs ago, the first son of a young slave girl by the name of Winnie. He wuz born on the old Dallas Plantation down below heah, near bout to Gold Dust." The preacher straightened the sleeves of his robe, and wiped the handkerchief across his forehead again, continuing, "A few yeahs ago, me and Hoss rode down to da ole Dallas Plantation, and sat in da little brick cabin where he was born, and where he grew to be a strong young man. Almost nothin' wuz left of dat lit'le house, but part of da brick walls and part of da lit'le fireplace where he said his Mama cooked da food." The preacher hesitated for a second, looked up to the ceiling, holding his gaze there, then continued, "Big tears came to Hoss's eyes, and he told me 'bout the hard times, the awful times when there weren't no food, 'bout his two lit'le brothas, and how they died, right in dat cabin. An da days when he thought theah would be no tomorra', no sunshine for him or his mama, ever in their life, and their life would be fer nothin." The preacher looked toward the high ceilings again, then toward Helen, Papa and me, and announced, "Hoss wuzz'a Godly man. He wuzz'a strong but a gentle man." Then he raised his fist toward the congregation, leaned forward a little and glared as though he was looking straight into the eyes of everyone there. He suddenly raised his gaze toward the ceiling again, stretched his arm as high as he could, and yelled out, "Thank the Lawd above, the old Dallas died, and wuz buried ova sixty yeahs ago!" *Amens* flooded the church from all directions. He shook his head, and raised his handkerchief to wipe away the droplets of sweat, adding, "Jist the name," and his mouth twitched several times in a row. Speaking very slowly while leaning over the pulpit, his bad eye completely closed, and he continued, "Yes, jist the name, my brothas an sistas, *Dallas Plantation*, it broke the hearts and smothered the souls of thousands of our brothas and sistas." Amens again flooded the church, and I waited for more. His eye slowly opened again, and he blinked it two or three times in a row.

Several women were in the choir, and only two men, and I knew some of the singers. The preacher rumbled out a few more words before Papa grabbed my arm, breaking my stare at the preacher: "What, Papa? What's the matter?"

"I needs to go pee, Billy! Real bad," he whined to me.

I did, too, but I didn't know where the bathroom was. Other people had started going out and coming back in, so I leaned over and whispered to Helen that we were going out for a minute. She was still crying and had started to fan a little with a cardboard fan from a funeral home in Bunkie. It wasn't hot outside, but the little church was full of people, and it had started to get really warm. A lot of other folks were slowly fanning, too. I didn't have a fan, but I sure wanted one. I wanted one to take home with me, to keep in my bedroom.

I leaned toward Papa and whispered, "Let's go Papa!"

He looked at me and copied, "Let's go, Billy!"

We tiptoed out of the side door, around to the back of the church, and found our way through a maze of headstones and graves. Suddenly we came upon a pile of fresh dirt and the deep hole that was ready for Israel Vead's casket. We stopped abruptly, slowly stepped closer, and looked down into the hole, then, I glanced at Papa. He looked up at me with his eyes open as wide as I had ever seen them. He pulled at my sleeve, and we headed toward the outhouse about twenty yards away. I pulled on the door. It wouldn't open, so I pulled harder, just before a familiar sounding voice from inside yelled real mad-like, "Y'all git away from heah, right now! Ya heah me!" Papa looked at me and grinned, and we both quickly leaned against the door and peered through a wide crack in the boards to see who was inside. The voice yelled again, "I sho gon tell Mista Carl bout yo sneakin' up on me like dis, Billy. Y'all git away fo I come out dare. Git, now, and leaves me 'lone. Git away!" and I finally recognized the voice. It was ugly ole Kaiser, and I knew she would blabber the whole thing to Dad, and she would get all over Papa's mama, too. Papa pulled my sleeve again, and we headed toward a big tree about thirty yards behind the church.

We tiptoed back into the church and sat down. The preacher was naming Hoss and Helen's children. He named four, and I kept waiting for him to say, "Isaac Vead." He kept on talking about something or other but never named Papa.

Then, all of sudden, with a crooked little smile on his big, round face, and lightly bouncing with big chuckles, he announced, "An'of cose, there's Isaac heah," and pointed to Papa on the front row. Still grinning from ear to ear, he wiped his brow again, and continued, "Evybody knows po 'Papa'. Thank the Lawd for good folks like Miz Helen and po ole Hoss, who would take in a boy like po little Papa, who wuz jist a little baby, when nobody wanted him."

There were five or six *amens* again, as I glanced at Papa. His eyes were big, his jaw had dropped, and his lips were starting to quiver. The tears were coming fast.

He wrapped his hand around my coat sleeve and arm right above my wrist, and started crying softly. As he let his head drop, two big tears splattered on his brown pants. My whole body twitched, and I nearly jumped up, wanting to yell back at the preacher, "You son of a bitch! Look at what you did to my friend!" "When nobody wanted him!" "When nobody wanted him!" How could he say that right in front of Papa, and the whole world, too?

While the preacher continued, I stood up, turned and glanced at my Dad. He had a frown on his face, and nodded to me that they were leaving, so I whispered to Papa, "I have to go, Papa. I'll see you later," and I felt his hand grasp harder on my arm. I yanked it free, and pointed for him to slide over next to his mother. Helen looked at me standing there, so I pointed to Papa, my wondering if the preacher's words had even entered her mind. She never moved and kept her hands lying in her lap, holding her little white handkerchief and the fan. I walked quickly out of the side door.

I couldn't remember anything the preacher had said, except "When nobody wanted him!" The words kept ringing in my ears, over and over, faster and faster, "When nobody wanted him." "When nobody wanted him." Running to the front of the church where a few cars were parked, I waited on the back seat of the Chevy for my family to come. "When nobody wanted him!" Papa knew very well what those words meant.

I rolled the window down and spit as hard as I could at the preacher, hoping his bad eye would close and never open again.

School would get off to a fast start the next morning, and I planned to ask Mrs. Gilroy how I could teach Papa to read and write. He had to learn, at least, to sign his name.

And I was ready to go to town.

CHAPTER 20

The ride home from the church was short and quiet. The car quickly filled with the aromas of perfumes and pomade, all smells that were part of the crowd in the church, and very familiar to me. Papa put pomade in his hair, and every now and then he would give some to me to use in my hair. I couldn't use much, or Mama would make me wash it out.

Mama knew that I didn't like what the preacher had said about Papa, and I could see she was upset about it, but said nothing. I wanted to ask Dad what was going to happen to Helen and Papa, but I didn't want to hear more bad news. When things weren't good or to her liking, Mama most often remained silent, and that day I remained silent, too.

My little brother, Mickey, was kneeling on the seat beside me, leaning against the back, and poking his finger into my ribs, even onto my cheeks. I figured he could tell that I was upset about something. Before I could punch him in the tummy to make him stop pestering me, he looked straight into my face and asked, with his head leaning to one side, "What's the matter, Billy? You mad at me?" Puzzled at his questions, I creased my forehead, looked closely at him, and realized how beautiful he was.

I shook my head, answering, "No, I'm not mad at you, Mickey," and I reached up and touched his blond curls. I knew that I loved my little brother very much, but I wondered, "Where would he be if Mama and Daddy hadn't wanted him, or where would I be if they hadn't wanted me?" The preacher was wrong! There's always somebody who wants a little baby, even little babies like Papa. I reached over; and, to his surprise, I pulled my little brother to me and hugged him. Looking at his big blue eyes, like our mother's, I wondered if he would ever forgive me for all the teasing I had laid on him.

Our Thanksgiving holidays were supposed to be good, especially with the big snow, but I was glad they were almost over. We didn't go to church that night. Dad and I helped Wesley with the chores in the horse barn and the milk cows, and we all moved about with silence and heavy hearts, knowing that the familiar, everyday scenes at the Big House—from the barn, the yard, and into the Big House itself—would forever be changed. Hoss, with his snow-white hair and his floppy old hat, had suddenly been taken away, painted out of our picture. Israel Vead was gone. Was gone forever.

The class was loud on Monday morning. I guessed that there was a lot of "doing" left in some of my friends, and we were glad to see each other, too. Mrs.

Gilroy had to yell and scream a lot to keep everyone in line. By Wednesday, things were a good deal better, but it was cool and damp, and Mrs. Gilroy announced that we wouldn't be going out for play period. The racket started again.

"This can be your study period today, so get out whatever you want and start your homework!" She motioned for Marilyn to sit down and be quiet. I think Marilyn was pretty close to being a teacher's pet.

"Now's the time," I figured, so I walked up to the front and stood at the end of her desk. Mrs. Gilroy turned a paper over and looked up at me through her gold-rimmed glasses.

"What is it, Billy?"

Bouncing my pencil in the palm of my hand, I answered, "Miz Gilroy, I have a bad problem, and I want to ask you something."

She looked a little puzzled, replying, "Tell me about it," and she turned to face me directly, and crossed her long legs while leaning onto the back of her chair.

I turned my back toward the class, and told her about my friend Papa and his problem of not being able to read or write. She asked me how old he was and why he didn't go to school. I explained that Papa couldn't learn very easily, and, when he was just a little baby, he had been *taken in,* by Hoss and Helen. I told her that I had taught him his ABCs, and he liked for me to read Superman comics to him. When I had almost finished my long story about Papa, she leaned back in her chair again and sighed; she looked across the class at Janet, who was laughing while Eddie pulled on Marilyn's long pigtails. I wished they would calm down so Mrs. Gilroy would have enough time to think and figure out what I had to do to help Papa.

She looked back into my face, explaining, "Billy, there are no schools for children with your friend's problems, none around here anyway. The only thing you can do is to try to help him as much as you can. You can teach him a little. It sounds to me as though he can learn to at least read a little and sign his name." She sighed again, hesitated, and said, "I can tell you want me to do something, so tell me what it is!" She didn't smile, but I did, especially when I heard Marilyn squeal, and Janet burst out laughing really loud. Mrs. Gilroy turned quickly toward the class, but everybody was in their places, and she sighed very heavily, again.

Standing straight and as tall as I could, I looked directly into her glasses and commanded, "I want you to show *me* how I can teach him to read and write."

She sighed a third time, turned and looked down at the papers on her desk, sort of rubbed her chin, then looked back at me, asking, "Billy, are you really serious about that?"

My eyes had moved to a small mole on her cheek, and it seemed to get bigger and moving a little, but I quickly looked back into her glasses, answering,

"Yes, Ma'am, I *am* serious. He has to learn something! He can't stay like he is all of his life. Who's going to take care of him?"

She put her hand to her forehead, cleared her throat, and said, "I'll make a short outline for you tonight and bring it to school tomorrow. Is that okay?"

"Yes, Ma'am. That'll do good," and I smiled.

She shook her head and said, "You know better than that, Billy! It isn't *good*. It's *well*," and she smiled a tiny bit. The little mole on her cheek looked smaller.

"Yes, Ma'am," and I started moving toward my seat. I looked toward Eddie, and he was mouthing, "Teacher's pet, teacher's pet!" and laughing. I stuck my tongue out at him, raised my hand to my chest, and gave him the *finger*, then mouthed back to him, "Shut your damn mouth."

CHAPTER 21

As usual on Wednesday evening, we loaded into the car and went to prayer meeting at the church in Eola. I drove all the way there and all the way back home. Dad sat in the front with me, watching every move I made, and was ready to complain if I made a mistake.

He kept saying things like, "Slow down," "That's a hard curve, there," "You're going too fast," and "There's a red light." He was really enjoying himself, bossing me every chance he got, so I said nothing.

Where the gravel ended and the car moved on to the softness of the dirt road, I sighed feeling a sudden calmness around me, a quiet feeling that was nice; I was safe, and I was home. The oak trees and the rows of small weathered houses on both sides of the dirt road were very familiar to me. I had a friend almost in every house. The bright headlights of the car cast broken shadows onto the little houses while the car quietly moved through the dark Quarters. I could feel myself smiling and thinking, "We just crossed a line back there, where everything changes, where everything is different from anywhere else I go, and I feel good here. This is where I belong. And this is my home." I had had those feelings before, and just as before, it seemed I had to gather all of my thoughts and figure out why they were suddenly coming into my mind so often, sometimes confusing me, sometimes fearful. But that night they were happy.

What about Papa and his mama? I needed to know what was going to happen with my friends, so I asked my dad if they would have to move from Shirley.

He looked at me and said, "Yeah. You know they'll have to move. Helen's too old to work in the fields, and Papa can't work. That's the way things are."

"That's not fair, Dad! Hoss and Helen lived here just about all of their lives." Before he could reply, I asked, "When are they gonna move?"

He sighed, shook his head and answered, "Well, I'm trying to work out something so they can stay till Helen can find a place in town, maybe with her sister. It'll be a month or two." I said nothing more, but then I heard him mumble softly, "It isn't fair? Not fair? No, I guess not," and he shook his head again, just as I pulled the new Chevy into the garage.

As the car doors opened, Mama said to Mickey and me, "I guess y'all know that Jerry, Margie and Spike are coming Friday evening after Jerry gets out of class!" Besides helping Margie with her baby, Jerry was going to school in Alexandria.

I said, "Good!" then I thought to myself, "Is it *good*, or *well*?" It was too late in the evening to worry about that.

The next day, a little before the bell rang to go home, Mrs. Gilroy called me to her desk. I knew that Eddie and everybody else would be teasing me now about being the teacher's pet, but I figured that she was going to give me the outline I needed in order to help Papa.

"Yes, Ma'am?" and I waited at the end of her desk.

Looking straight at me, she said, "Billy, I just didn't have time to finish the outline, but I promise, I'll have it for you tomorrow before we go home." Disappointment must have shown on my face because she quickly added, "Oh, don't worry. I'll have it for you! This must be really important! Now don't look so down, it's just one more day," and she patted my arm. I jumped back when she touched me. I sure didn't want my buddies to see her do *that*, or I would never hear the end of it.

Mrs. Gilroy didn't know that my days with Papa were numbered and I had to get on with the job. A month or two wasn't a long time.

The day went fast on Friday, and right before the lunch bell rang, Mrs. Gilroy handed me an envelope and told me to look at the outline at lunchtime. But I wasn't about to pull it out on the playground in front of my friends. They would never believe or understand my other life down a dirt road on Shirley Plantation. Sometimes I didn't understand it either, but it was part of me, part of who I was, and it had always been that way. I liked it, and I didn't want anyone making fun of it.

I ate lunch quickly, went back up to the classroom, sat at my desk, and opened the envelope. The outline was awful. I didn't know much about outlines, but figured that Mama could help me. We could go over it early Saturday morning so I could get started with Papa. Folding the papers, I put them back in the envelope and slid the envelope into my history book, knowing that it was going home with me. My mind wandered happily to the thought that my sisters were coming home that evening with Spike.

As I walked fast down the dirt road toward home, Mickey complained because he was left behind, and he would have to trot every now and then to catch up. I never said anything to make him worse. Rounding the turn at the end of the hedgerow, I recognized the blue Oldsmobile parked near the front steps. They had arrived early. I ran down the side of the house, noticing that Mama's car was not in the garage. Jumping up the steps, I crossed the porch and opened the kitchen door. The Big House was cold and unlit, and the sky was turning a bright orange, lighting the kitchen through the wide windows that ran almost the length of the cabinets. My sister Jerry was getting an iron skillet out of the bottom cabinet. I wondered if I should tell her right then about what happened to her leather gloves, but instead I quickly asked, "Where's little Spike?"

"In there with Margie," Jerry replied, then, "She's trying to light a fire. It's so cold in here." And she sort of wrapped her arms around herself and shook.

I went into the dining room and Margie was kneeling on the hearth with a lighted match, trying to light the kindling. In a deep voice, I scolded, "Hey, lady, that's my job!"

She blew the match out, turned around and smiled at me and said, "Hi! What are you up to, Bill Beau?" We hugged, and she pointed to a bundle of clothes on the dining table.

I asked, "What? What's that?" She walked over and opened the blanket a little, and there was my new—I think—nephew. I didn't know exactly what a nephew was, but Mama had said that I was going to get one. That was when I first guessed last summer that Margie was going to have a baby. Mickey just stood there, looking and smiling at our new nephew.

Margie kissed us both and called toward the kitchen, "Jerry, the fire'll be ready in just a minute."

With a little coal oil poured on it, the kindling had caught, and the flames were beginning to grow. Jerry brought the skillet with some water in it. I kept looking at my new nephew and thinking, "His hands sure are big, maybe he'll be big like his dad, and a boxer." His dad had been the boxing champion on the Saratoga when he was in the Marines. Or maybe Spike would be another Joe Louis.

Jerry carefully placed the iron skillet over the logs in the fireplace. We laughed and talked and I thought now would be a good time to tell her about Pal having taken her gloves, but she was in a good mood, so I decided I would rather keep it like it was. She would find out soon enough, but I was anxious to get it over with. I looked again at Spike's hands. Those darn gloves were too little to fit even Spike. Thinking that would be a good line for me to start with, I opened my mouth to begin the confession when the water in the skillet began to boil. Jerry took it to the kitchen, and I thought again, "I'm going to tell her as soon as she gets back in the dining room." She walked in with three cups of hot tea, announcing, "I've put a little sugar and cream in it. I hope it's okay," and she smiled at me.

"Hot tea," I thought, "we don't drink hot tea here; we drink coffee. It must be some city stuff she and Margie learned." But I figured I should wait to tell her about those damned ole gloves.

The way she smiled, I figured she probably already knew about the gloves and was waiting to see how long it would take for me to confess.

The flames grew taller and warmed us as we faced the fireplace, sitting in the big chairs and watching Mickey play with Spike's hands. We talked and laughed about everything—the snow, school, and especially Spike. Our shadows moved about like dancers, playing onto the walls and all the way to the tall ceilings. I could feel my heart beating in the tips of my fingers; and, in a little while, the setting sun cast its bright orange glow through the tall windows. Magically, the old dining room became a grand palace, full of color, full of laughter, love and happiness, where a little country boy, with a beautiful sister on each side of him, sipped his very first cup of hot tea. I smiled, and almost in a trance I set my eyes toward the tall flames in the fireplace as they cast a warm *spell* on me and all over the big room.

Jerry didn't know that she would never see her gloves again, and neither she nor Margie knew that we had buried Hoss last Sunday.

CHAPTER 22

Margie was holding Spike on her lap when we heard the kitchen door open, and Mama called out, "You-hooh! Where's everybody?" We all headed into the kitchen.

Mama was setting the groceries on the cabinet, and anxiously begged, "Oh, let me see that boy!" Margie carefully handed Spike to her, and she cradled him in her arms. She smiled, "Look at that! I think he's grown since Tuesday!"

As usual, I had not known that she and Dad had driven to Alexandria to see their first grandchild. Mama looked at Mickey and me, asking, "Well, what do you think? Isn't he something?" I nodded and smiled, and then she said, "Son, please light a fire in the stove for me, and I'll make some pancakes and ham for supper."

Mama was good with words. When she wanted something, she called me "son" and when she wanted to tell me something, she called me "Billy," but when she was mad at me, she called me "boy." This was a "son" thing, and I was glad.

Margie commanded, "Come on, I'll help you. We have to hurry. Jerry and I are going back right after supper," and she hugged me again.

Mama held Spike the whole time. Margie and Jerry made supper, and at the perfect time, Dad had come in from the fields. He hugged them both and went to the bathroom to clean up. Afterward, he and Mama played with Spike in front of the fireplace till supper was ready. We all sat around the table in the kitchen for almost an hour, with Spike in Mama's lap. Looking at my little brother and my two older sisters, and how Mama and Daddy played with Spike, I wondered what was going through their minds: maybe thoughts about my older brother, who had died about a year and half before? I thought about Freddie a lot. He died from a ruptured appendix when he was about fourteen, but now that we had Spike, maybe he would sort of take Freddie's place. I missed Freddie.

Jerry asked Dad how the cane cutting was going. He told her that in about two or three days they would be finished, if it didn't rain over the weekend. Dad told us that he was going to have the big barbeque next Friday for everybody on the plantation. He had done that every year when the sugarcane was all in. Everybody liked the big barbeque.

Directed mostly to my sisters, he explained, "Everybody's worked extra hard to get the cane out. Big crop this year. Even with Hoss dying and his funeral, they all got right back to work." I could tell by the look on Margie's face and Jerry's when they looked at each other that they had not been told about Hoss. I guessed that Mama and Daddy, with all of the other things going on at this time of the year, with Thanksgiving, the big snow, and especially with Spike having been born, they had just forgotten. Margie's eyes started to tear up a little, while Jerry shook her head and looked straight at me as though I should have already told them. I looked away.

Their visit home ended after Dad told them about Hoss's funeral. After a little while, Margie and Jerry picked up the bundles of things they had brought with them, and we all moved to the front of the house. Mama, Dad, Mickey, and I stood at the top of the porch steps in the dim light of the single bulb high on the porch ceiling as Jerry started the Oldsmobile. The car slowly moved on the driveway around the four big oaks in the front yard, heading to Alexandria. From the tears that Mama wiped from her cheeks and the way Dad's eyes followed the car's tail lights all the way to the hedgerow, I knew that little baby would be taking over their hearts in just a short while.

CHAPTER 23

Waking up early the next morning, I hurried down to the kitchen. Wesley had already lit the fireplaces in the dining room and the family room, and was drinking his coffee. I liked Wesley. He was tall and stout, a strong man like one you knew could do anything you wanted him to do, and he was kind to everyone, especially to me. On rainy days, Papa and I would often help him shuck corn in the barn crib, where we joked around a lot and picked at each other.

He poured a cup of coffee for me while I went to the bathroom.

Sipping our hot coffee while we sat at the kitchen table, he asked, "You wants a biscuit in 'ya coffee?" Hoss seldom asked anymore.

"Yeah. Do we have any?" Wesley brought a biscuit that must have been two or three days old, and was as hard as a rock. I laughed and said, "Wesley, I can't even break up this thing!"

He laughed, "I knows it. I jist wanna see wat chu'd say. Rosa gon trow 'um away when she come today." We sipped our coffee, then he looked directly into my face, and asked, "Do ya recon Mista Carl's gon let me take ova heah at da yard and da Big House, now dat po ole Hoss is gone?"

I figured that Wesley *would* get the job, but I answered, "Well, I don't know, but you're the only one who's helped Hoss for a long time now, so I guess he'll let you have the job."

He smiled a little and said, "I sho hope he do," then added, "Well, time to ring da bell!" The booming sounds of the big bell shattered the morning stillness, and at that very moment the first rays of the sun shot through the big window, making the entire kitchen glow in pink and orange. Seeing the colors flood the room, I felt sure the old *King* knew that Wesley would get the job to take care of him, replacing Hoss as the caretaker and *the man* around the yard. My smile grew bigger, and the kitchen glowed brighter.

Wesley rang the big bell for two or three minutes, and I knew that Dad would be coming into the kitchen soon. If I were up early enough, Hoss would let me ring the big bell that boomed the field hands awake each morning when the sun came up. Hanging onto the long rope from the bell to the ground below, I would be pulled into the air each time the bell tolled in its backward motion. On a clear day from the top of the bell tower I could see the steeple on the Baptist church in town. Dad always said that he would whip me if I climbed the bell tower to the top. I climbed it many times, but he never knew it.

Wesley came back in and was pouring a cup of coffee just when Dad entered the kitchen and sat at the table to put his boots on.

He took a sip of coffee, mumbling, "Ummh, that's good, Wesley, thanks." Wesley was standing in front of the stove when Dad asked, "Well, Wesley, do you think you can handle all of the work at the yard and the Big House by yourself?"

"I sho do. Jist evy now and den I mights has to have a lit'le hep."

"Well, you can count on it. The job's yours," and he finished tying his second boot.

Wesley was smiling big when he looked my way, announcing, "I gots ta go git the cows and start da milkin. Mista Carl, do ya wants Bessie t'day?"

"Yeah. Bring her to the saddle room for me." Knowing that the fields were too muddy for the truck, Wesley knew that Dad would have to go on horseback to reach the cane fields, and Bessie was his favorite riding horse. I figured that Mickey and I would likely ride our horses out to the cane fields, too.

We missed Hoss very much and thought often about him, but Wesley quickly fit into the job at the yard and in the Big House. He was about fifty years younger than Hoss; he thought differently and with much more energy and determination. He was good, and I was glad he would run the yard and the barns at the Big House.

CHAPTER 24

While I waited for Mama to come to the kitchen I glanced through the outline that Mrs. Gilroy had given me the day before. I didn't know what it all meant, but I was hoping that she could help me. After a short while, she walked in with her housedress on and an apron over it, ready to start the day.

She poured a cup of coffee and sat at the table with me, asking, "What's that you've got?" I told her about it and what I wanted it for, but I didn't understand it. She reached for the outline and laid it in front of her on the table while she sipped her coffee. After a little while, she looked up and said, "I just don't think you can do all of this. This is what a teacher would use in her classroom in the first or second grade. I don't think poor Papa is ready for this kind of work." She could tell that I was disappointed at her comment. Hesitating a few seconds, she added, "You're taking on a really big job with Papa, Son, and I hope you can do it. There is one thing I see here that would probably work for you and maybe for Papa," and she read directly from the bottom of the paper: "You may have to make your friend read out loud to you, with your pointing and helping him say each word. Eventually, he will learn to recognize a few words. This will be a long and *tedious process*, but it may work well for your friend."

"But, Mama, I don't have a long time," I whined.

Mama sipped her coffee again, and looking at me, she replied, "You'll just have to do the best that you can in the time you've got. If you just teach him to recognize a few words, and he can sign his name, you will have done a day's work. Give it a try, Billy!" There was that "Billy" word, and I wondered what a *tedious process* was. I didn't ask her, figuring that I should have known, but I would ask Marilyn at school on Monday. She would know.

I felt good. I ran upstairs to my bedroom desk and found a writing pad and a pencil with a broken point. I threw it back into the box and found one with a pretty good point. I knew that Papa had five of my old Superman comics and we could use them to start with. I grabbed my jacket from the hook on the back porch and headed out to the Quarters with Pal beside me. When we reached the end of our gravel driveway, I could see a few people walking in my direction, getting a ride out to the fields on the cane buggies. J.B. stopped me.

"Where ya goin' so early, Billy?" I had tucked the pad and pencil into my jacket, and told him that I was going to see Papa, but I could tell he wasn't interested in that. He leaned over and spoke softly into my ear, "Me and Bernice don got togetha."

"You're lying, J.B. I know Bernice wouldn't marry you."

He chuckled, and with a smirk on his ugly face, he conintued, "I ain't talkin' bout no marryin. I's talkin bout a little poon-tang, boy!" I couldn't believe he was telling *me* about it, but he always bragged about some of his doings.

Frowning, I quickly replied, "Boy, you're crazy. You're gonna get yourself cut up or maybe killed, talking like that about Bernice."

He started leaning toward my ear, speaking very low, and said, "Nah, don nobody knows but me and her, now yous, too. In da cane field yestiddy, Billy! We's don met in da cane. Right bouts noon time." And he opened his mouth and wiggled his tongue.

"If Alex finds out, he'll kill you. I'm telling you, you better keep your big mouth shut!"

"I ain't tolds nobody but 'chu, Billy, and don'chu go tell nobody."

I frowned at him again and said, "You're crazy, you know that, and somebody ought to beat the hell out of you. I hope Alex finds out. He'll cut your damn throat." He laughed again and strutted toward his water cart like a rooster in the chicken yard. Frozen where I stood, I watched him, and hated him, too.

Several workers were placing their lunch buckets in his water cart, and I thought to myself, "He's crazy, and one day somebody's going to give him a good whipping, or maybe kill him." I wished he hadn't told me, and I really wanted Alex or even Shine to know about it, but I wasn't going to be the one to tell either of them, and J.B. knew it.

Hurrying down the dirt road, I tried to forget what J.B. had told me, until I passed in front of Bernice's house and wondered again if J.B. was lying to me. Angry at the thought of J.B. making love to Bernice, my friend and Alex's daughter, caused me to shiver in the damp morning air, but I figured it really was no business of mine, and I had to lay it aside. I turned into the walkway going to Helen and Papa's house, and just when I stepped on the porch, the front door opened. Helen came out, closed the door, and began wiping her hands on her long apron. Looking into her face, I waited, knowing she had something on her mind, which she had to let go of.

With one hand on her hip, while the other held the hem of her apron, she looked at me with a mean frown on her face, demanding, "Billy, wat'chu gon tell Papa today? Evy day it's som'um else, and I's havin trouble 'nough with all that learnin stuff y'alls puttin in 'is haad. Ya sho ain't hepping me none." Feeling her anger toward me, I glanced to the floor, seeing the whiteness of the soles of her bare feet, and I knew I must ignore totally her comments and demands.

"Where's Papa, Helen? I want to talk to him," I asked calmly. I had already turned up the ears on my aviator's cap, hoping that my head wouldn't get hot, but it started to itch a little, so I reached up, pulled the cap off and stuffed it in the pocket of my jacket. Helen frowned at me for a second or two, pursed her lips, and shook her head in disgust. Placing both hands on her back at her waist, she stretched as though her back was in great pain, and she was desparate for a quick relief.

She turned, flung the door open wide, and announced, "Lawd, God 'amighty, I's sho tired! All dis 'bout to kill me! Papa's righ' chere!" and she never stopped her rush into the kitchen.

I walked in and closed the door behind me, darkening the little room. By her anger and her impatience, I figured that Helen must have been tired of me, Papa, and everything else that was happening around her. Beaten down by Hoss's dying, and left alone with the job of raising Papa, I figured she needed help, and she needed some peace in her life.

The room was dark except for the light from the little fire and a soft light filtering through the limp, white cloth covering the front window. Papa was sitting at the fireplace on a small, low stool, never looking up, and slowly rocking back and forth while rubbing his hand lightly over his pompadour. He slowly turned and glanced toward me, and I could tell that he had been crying.

"What's the matter, Papa? What's wrong?"

He turned, looked back into the fire, and slowly spoke, "Billy, I ain'ts neva gon learn to writes my name an read nothin, and yous jist wastin time foolin wis me." His big lips began to quiver.

Placing my hand on his shoulder, I gently shook him, "Yes, you are, and don't you let anybody stop you. I'm gonna help you, Papa." I took my jacket off, threw it onto Helen's rocker in the corner, and sat on the floor next to him. As always in winter, a strong smell of wood smoke had taken over as the primary smell in the little house, and the clothes they wore. A tiny, red flame in the middle of the dark fireplace was struggling to catch onto a fresh log just placed there.

Staring at the small flame, I said loud enough for Helen to hear in the kitchen, "Papa, get your comics, boy!" and the little flame suddenly burst into a big red fire, dancing about while it quickly filled the room with a warm, glowing light.

Papa and I glanced at each other and smiled.

Cupping his hands around his mouth, while leaning as far back as he could, Papa called out loud and clear so the whole world could hear it,

"Less read Superman, Billy..."

CHAPTER 25

It was just Helen and Papa in the little house on the dirt road, and they knew that they would have to leave the plantation now that Hoss was gone. Helen's sister lived in Bunkie and worked in the lunchroom at the White school. Often, when I saw Mary, she would ask about Helen and Papa, and she was hoping they would come to live with her in town. I figured that living with Mary would probably be good for them. Helen and Mary had grown up in town, and Mary could read and write a little. Helen was a lot older than Mary and probably had never gone to school, but Mary faced learning every day, and was reminded of the importance and the need for as much education as could be had. I knew she would help Papa, if he tried even just a little.

With a full-size bed covered in white sheets and white blankets standing in one corner, the small front room of Helen's and Papa's house began to warm from the growing flames in the fireplace. Papa opened one of the comics and I nervously pointed to the biggest word flashed across the page, *Superman*. "What's that word, Papa?" I asked.

"Superman!" and he looked at me and grinned. That was just a guess, and I shouldn't have asked him such a familiar word. Looking on the next page at all of the words that normally looked easy to me, they suddenly seemed to move about the page faster than I could see them. The fire became hotter, and I started to sweat.

I pointed to a word, and told Papa, "You're going to read to me from now on. What's this word? Say it!"

Papa looked at me, then back to the page and said, "Dat's befo."

I couldn't believe he knew the word, but I said, "No, Papa, it's 'before,' not 'befo'." Say it again. Before!" and I repeated it again. "Before!"

He quickly snapped at me, "Nah, I ain'ts gon do dat, Billy," and he shook his head.

Frowning, I asked, "Why not? You wanna learn, don't you?"

He frowned back at me, and announced in a high, whinny voice, "I can'ts talk like yous, Billy! Evybody gon laugh at me, if I talks dat a way. Ya jist tryin to gits me in mo trouble dan I's can fool wis."

"Does everybody laugh at me? That's crazy, Papa."

He smiled a crooked little smile, announcing, "Billy, yous a white boy. Ya can talk like dat. Ain't nobody gon laugh at chu!"

I glanced away from his face, and wondered about what Papa had said. I shook my head to get the cobwebs out, hoping also to throw out his crazy comment. "Do you know these books by heart?"

"Nah, but I don ah'ready learn some of dim words ya pointin to."

"How did you learn them?"

He smiled and said, "Cathrine heps me some, if I goes over to huh house. I been hepping Mista Alfonse clean out da stalls and Cathrine been hepping me learn. I likes Mista Alfonse, but I sho's don like Miz Mazie, no, I sho don," and he was shaking his head verifying his statement.

I looked at him and said, "Ah, enough of that Papa. You don't even know Miz Mazie. You have to get over being scared of people. Miz Mazie's okay." I wondered if I really believed myself.

Cathrine was smart and probably had a lot more patience with Papa than I had. She was a year ahead of me in school. I asked him, "Well, how much can you read?" and I pointed to another line, and he slowly spoke a few of the words. He knew all of the *ands, buts, goes, yeses,* and occasionally, a word with four or five letters, helping me believe this might work after all. Maybe! Just maybe. Then I wondered, is it worth it? It was going to take a long time, but yeah, it was probably worth it. And again, maybe! Just maybe. I knew, also, that I didn't know what I was doing, or what I had gotten myself into, and I needed help. Cathrine. I thought about Cathrine, realizing that she was already helping Papa. That was *good.*

We slowly went through several of the Superman comics, me having to say most of the words first. Papa was spoiled and didn't want to take this as anything other than fun and a game we were playing. I figured that most of his life he had to laugh off being picked on a lot, and people making fun of him. At the end of each comic, Papa became more excited, and I wanted to believe that he was beginning to really want to learn to read. Helen had come back into the room and draped my jacket onto the back of her rocker. Sitting quietly, she rocked back and forth; listening to us read the last two comics.

When Papa finished the last one, Helen looked at him, smiling, "Dat's real good Papa! Ya doin good, boy, and I's sho proud of ya! Yeah, dat's real good, and I betcha yo daddy sho would be proud to hear ya read like dat."

I was surprised at what Helen had said, and when she finished telling Papa how proud she was of him, I added, "Helen, Papa's going to have to work really hard to learn to read, and I want him to learn to write his name. He can do it."

She shook her head *yes* while announcing, "I sho do hopes ya right, Billy. Life's sho hawd if ya don knows nothen, like me, and po ole Hoss. Po ole fella, he don gone, but I sho wish he could heah Papa read dat-a-way," and she fixed her watery eyes onto the blazing fire.

I didn't know that Helen and Hoss didn't know anything. Like all of my friends on the plantation, they were who they were, and I loved them that way, but I was beginning to realize that very few could read or write except for the younger friends closer to my age. I started to tell her that she was wrong, that I thought she and Hoss were smart, but as a kid whom she had known since birth, she wouldn't have believed me. Like everyone else around, she didn't pay any attention to me. But come Hell or high water, I wanted my friend Papa to learn how to read and write, and that was the important thing for all three of us. Time was going to pass quickly, I knew, but he had to learn to write his name, and learn to read as best he could.

I left Helen and Papa's house, taking my five old comics with me. I told Papa that I would let him have five more, if he promised to read them to his mama. He was primed and ready, and I knew that I had to get the comics to him soon.

It was a little past dinnertime, and I figured that Mrs. Mazie probably had some fresh baked bread. Besides, I had decided to talk to Cathrine about helping Papa, that being a good reason to barge in. I turned into the walk at the Gaspard house, reached the front door, and knocked real hard. They usually stayed in the kitchen in the back when it was cold, but Cathrine came to the door. She glanced at my dirty boots, and said, "Billy, you'll have to come around to the back. Okay?"

I was glad. That way, I could get into Mrs. Mazie's kitchen, and maybe they would be eating their dinner. Cathrine met me at the kitchen door, and opened it for me. Mister Alfonse was eating, while Mrs. Mazie fixed her plate, and asked me, "Billy, you want enythang to eat, fo I set down?"

"Oh, just a roll, Miz Mazie, that's all." Cathrine giggled, sat down at the table and began to eat her dinner.

Mrs. Mazie asked, "You want some butter on it?" and I shook my head, "Yes."

In just a second, she handed me the roll, and I asked, "How's Papa doing in the barn, Mister Alfonse?"

He didn't stop chewing while he answered, "Aw, Papa's alright. You jist gotta stick with 'im and tell 'im what to do, but he can learn. He's jist spoiled real bad, poor little fella."

I looked at Cathrine, "You've been teaching him how to read a little. That's good!"

Cathrine giggled and said, "He's doing really well. He can count to a hundred and can add a little bit. I think he's catching on."

I asked her, "Can he sign his name yet?"

Giggling again, she replied, "He thought his real name was Papa, and you wanted to change it to 'Nick,' like Uncle Nick next door. He doesn't like Uncle Nick, you know." Even Mrs. Mazie laughed with us, while she handed me a fork and placed a plate of red beans and rice in front of me. Standing over me like a fox, she looked down at me; then, she smiled really big.

A little surprised at the way she treated me, I told her, "Oh, thanks, Miz Mazie. They sure do look good. I didn't mean to break in like this."

She knew I was lying, asking, "How bouts some vinegar fer dose beans, Billy?"

"Yes, Ma'am, just a little if you got some with peppers." Mister Alfonse reached over and handed me a little bottle with green peppers inside, while Cathrine giggled a little more. I figured that all three of them could read me like a book, especially Mrs. Mazie. Most of the time, she knew about things before they even happened.

After a little while Mrs. Mazie commanded, "Y'all git outta here, so's I can clean up," and she started sweeping the clumps of mud on the kitchen floor toward the door onto the porch.

Cathrine and I left the kitchen and went into the front room. It was cold. I told Cathrine what I wanted to do for Papa before he and Helen moved from Shirley Plantation. Cathrine became excited about teaching Papa his words and numbers, and we both knew we had to act quickly. Cathrine suggested, "Why don't we set a goal of getting him to read better, to say his numbers, and to sign his name by Christmas Day. That's a little over three weeks."

"Oh, I don't know. Papa's hardheaded sometime and won't do what you say. Besides, Helen can't help him and won't make him work at it."

"Yeah, I know, I know, but Daddy will make him come here every day when we get home from school. He'll do what Daddy says. Mama knows he's afraid of her, but she'll try to make it up to him some way."

"One of your mama's big rolls! That's what he needs, every day. That'll keep him coming," and I chuckled.

"Good idea. Mama'll do that," and she laughed.

We were proud about our little plan, and I knew it was going to work. All we needed was a lot of patience, plenty of good fresh rolls, and Papa.

I left the Gaspard house and walked toward home. Before I reached the toolshed, I could see the cutters coming in from the fields and wondered what might have happened for them to be coming in so early. J.B. had unhooked his water cart, and was crossing the road to take Josie into the barn lot. I stopped him and asked, "What's the matter? Why's everybody coming in?"

He took off his cap, hit me across the butt with it, and announced, "It's don over, boy. We don finished. The last load don went to da derrick bout uh hour 'go."

Everyone looked tired and was moving slowly, but I could read the relief on their faces, knowing that the hard work and stress was over for another year. The whole plantation would be quiet for several days while everyone rested, cleaned up their houses, washed their clothes, and regained a semblance of order in their lives.

THE LAST WITNESS FROM A DIRT ROAD

The big barbeque was set for Friday. Mama and Dad, with Shine, Wesley, Rosa and Alex, would do most of the work to make everything ready. Dad would have plenty of wine for everyone who would come to the barbeque at the Big House.

And I was ready, too, for our dirt road to come alive again.

CHAPTER 26

Walking slowly while I passed the toolshed where the tractors were parked, I stopped several times to talk to some of the cutters. They were tired, I could tell, with layers of tattered cloths showing the black soot from the burned cane, and soot marking their faces and the skin on their weathered hands. Still, an air of excitement surrounded us, knowing that another season of hard, dirty work had come to an end.

Alex called and waved for me to come to where he was working under the open shed, changing the oil in a tractor. I thought about Bernice and J.B., and was hoping that he wasn't going to ask me about them. Then I thought about our friend Mag, and Gilbert Frank and Emma. Maybe he would ask about one of them. Gilbert Frank was standing by his tractor at the other end of the shed, talking to some other men, and I figured that Alex hadn't seen hide nor hair of Mag for a long time.

"Hi, Alex, what's up? Y'all are all finished, huh?" He sort of shook his head, but I knew he had to finish whatever he was reaching for at that moment. I waited anxiously for him to speak.

Finally looking at me directly, he smiled and asked, "Ya gonna hep me Friday, Billy?"

"Friday, what about Friday? What's happening?"

"Boy, ya sho forgits easy! Ya know wat's gon be Friday! The barbeque! Evy body talking bout it now."

"Oh yeah, the barbeque. Well, I don't know. I guess I have to go to school." Then I quickly asked, "Alex, why don't you tell Dad that you need me to help you?"

"I'll do dat, I sho will. I sho would 'ppreciate it if ya could. Yo daddy'll let chu do dat!"

I knew Dad was a pushover about staying home from school if the reason was to *work*. He made work when there was none. I figured that he was accustomed to doing that so the field hands would have a payday every two weeks.

Mama would be really mad about my staying home, but I was sure Dad wouldn't say anything to her until Friday morning when it was time for her to take us to school. That way, she wouldn't have time to talk him out of it.

It seemed that the rainy weather had begun as a drizzly little rain kept the students in the lobbies or the basement of the school for three days. Finally, when Thursday came, I was anxious and nervous; waiting for the day to end so we could go home.

The Christmas holidays were only a couple of weeks away, and several of my friends had already started talking about Christmas. Eddie kept saying that his family was going to Canada during the holidays to visit their family. They had come from Canada a few years back, and lived in Eola where his Dad was manager of one of the oil drilling companies. Canada. That was a million miles from Shirley Plantation. I had traveled to Alexandria several times, and a few times to Port Arthur, Texas, a little over a hundred miles from home. That was about as far away as I had ever been, and maybe one day I might go to Canada, but right then, I just wanted Thursday to be over so I could go home. My elbows were sore from rubbing on my desk while my cupped hands held up my chin.

Our old school bus rattled down the gravel road and finally came to a stop at the dirt road about the same time the school bus with the black kids arrived. Bernice and Junior got off the bus with four or five other kids. Several of the little ones walked together with Mickey and Junior, Bernice's little brother. He and Mickey often played together at the Big House or in the Quarters. Bernice was smart and pretty, and seldom missed school to work in the fields, except during cane season.

As we walked side by side, she soon glanced toward me and said, "Billy, don't you believe J.B. He's just a big liar!"

I looked down at the ground while we walked, "Believe what? What are you talking about? I don't believe anything J.B. says, anyway."

"You know what I'm talking about Billy. And I don't like it. If he says anything more, I'm gonna tell my daddy, and he'll beat the devil out of him."

We stopped walking, and I faced her, holding her arm a little above her wrist. She had on a tight pink sweater, completely filled by her bosoms, showing a crease up to where the buttons remained open. Her bronze skin was just a little darker than her dad's; her lips were tinged in a light pink, and her black hair was tied in the back with a green and red ribbon. Staring at her for a second, I thought, "Bernice is really pretty, and except for her skin being a litter darker, she was just like the girls in my class at school, and a lot prettier than most of them."

Looking straight into her dark brown eyes, I spoke softly, "Bernice, I know J.B. He's been picking on me for as long as I can remember, and he'll pick on anybody, but he doesn't mean anything, and besides, nobody pays any attention to him. He just likes to laugh and cut up." She barely smiled, and moved her hand to my chest. The dirt road had taught both of us a lot more about our bodies, our feelings and desires, than kids our age should have known, but I took her hand from my chest and stepped back, while a tear slowly rolled down her cheek. Her chin quivered, and her smile faded away.

We both turned and started walking again, trying to step away from the really muddy spots on the side of the road. She said nothing else as we walked, but

I figured then that J.B. wasn't lying to me when he told me about the noontime meeting with Bernice in the sugarcane. They must have talked again after that meeting, and my guess was that he had bragged to her about telling me about the incident. Over and over in my mind, I could hear him saying it, "Poon-tang, boy, a little poon-tang." After a short time, Bernice turned to walk the narrow path to their porch.

Glancing back toward me, she smiled, speaking softly, "Bye, Billy, I'll see ya later."

I stopped, then called her name, and motioned for her to come back to the road. She was holding her books in the crook of her arm, as I looked again directly into her eyes and spoke softly, "Bernice, don't worry. I'll never tell your daddy anything about it. I promise." She started to cry, while I continued, "You better wipe your eyes, or your mama's gonna ask you what happened. Okay? Don't cry. Everything's gonna be fine!" I wanted to hug her, and to feel her breasts pressed hard against my chest, to feel her warm brown skin touching my cheek, and to know what it was like to wrap my arms completely around her, holding her tight. We had danced with each other, but *this* feeling was different, and my heart began to race. I turned away quickly. If her mother saw us, it would make Veesy angry, and she would surely tell my dad about it, causing all kind of trouble for me and for Bernice, too.

I hurried to the Gaspard house. Wondering what else I was going to find myself involved in that day, I ran my fingers through my hair and spit onto the dirt road. Gritting my teeth, I muttered to myself, "That damn J.B., I hate him, and I hate this damn ole place!"

I went around to the back porch and up the steps. Papa and Cathrine had already started. Cathrine rode the first bus, which would go to Saint Anthony's Catholic School to pick up the kids there, and deliver them to their homes in the country.

Papa was eating his roll, and Cathrine had a tablet and pencil out on the table, commanding, "Hurry, Papa, we don't have all day. Put your roll right here, and let's start writing your numbers," and she pointed to a little plate next to the tablet. He was excited, and he had a jaw full of bread, chomping down on it, and grinning at me.

Quickly backing away from the table, I asked, "Darn, what's that awful smell?"

Papa looked up from his tablet, "Oh, Cathrine don broke wind in huh mama's kitchen."

I laughed out loud. As Cathrine's face turned scarlet, she shouted, "Liar, you did it, not me! You're flat out lying!" And she hit him on the head with her pencil, and shouted again, "You lying stink pot!"

He grabbed the pencil from her, leaned over his tablet, and began writing, starting with one, and chuckling while he concentrated on his numbers. He put the last bite of bread in his mouth. I knew who had "broke wind," and said, "Boy, you'll get your head skinned if Miz Mazie walks in!" Cathrine's face was a bright pink.

Cathrine hit him on the hand and scolded, "You're just being silly, Papa. You can go faster than that! Billy, don't pay any attention to stink pot. He's just showing off for you!"

Papa grinned really big, tilted his head down toward the tablet, and his tongue came out just a little, over to one side of his mouth. I could tell he was trying really hard. By the time he got to twenty, his face was about six inches from the tablet.

Cathrine scolded, "Sit up, Papa, you're gonna go blind that close to the paper. Sit up straight." Cathrine sounded just like a real teacher.

Every day, the three of us met in Mrs. Mazie's kitchen, ate a roll, and worked on numbers, letters and reading. That day, I looked at Papa and thought, "Every day, he gets a little better. Every day, he gets a little more proud of himself, and it seems like his shoulders are broader, and his chin is higher." Just when I was deep into those good thoughts about him, he tilted to one side and farted really loud, leaned over, and fell to the floor, curled up in a ball, and laughed as hard as he could, while both of his hands covered his face. Cathrine looked at me and we started laughing at him. I thought again, "That rascal! He's already got more guts than I have, to fart out loud in front of a girl, and now he'll do that over and over, trying to make us laugh at him." Mrs. Mazie didn't come into the kitchen, thank goodness, but she probably knew, as usual, exactly what was going on.

Cathrine put her hands over her nose and mouth, demanding, "Y'all get outta here. I can't stand it," and she walked to the door and held it open. The lessons were over for that day.

The next morning, before daybreak, I heard Dad call softly to me from the bottom of the stairs, "Billy, get up!"

My feet quickly hit the cold floor. I grabbed by pants, a clean shirt, socks and tennis shoes, and ran down the steps all the way to the kitchen, where Dad and Wesley were drinking their coffee. I stood warming myself in front of the stove, and before I could get my pants on I recognized Alex's voice calling at the kitchen door.

"Come on in, Alex! How bout some coffee?"

"Dat'd be good, Mista Carl."

Alex looked at me and said, "Look at dat, Billy done turned white again. Look at dem legs." My summer tan had faded away, and I was trying very hard to catch a little warmth from the kitchen stove.

Wesley had already gotten up and poured a cup of coffee for me and one for Alex. He had crumbled a biscuit in mine. I knew that coffee and biscuit would be my breakfast, except I would take a can of Donald Duck juice to drink later.

CHAPTER 27

Dad, Alex, and Wesley started planning the day for the big barbeque. Dad asked Alex how much wine he thought we needed, and told Wesley to have all three shoats ready at about ten o'clock. The little pigs were cleaned and dressed on Thursday and seasoned with Shine's special seasoning. Everybody liked it, but word around the plantation was that the seasoning was some kind of *spell maker*, which Aunt Colleen concocted and would sell to anyone who wanted to put a *gree-gree* on someone they might be mad at. J.B. ate her seasoning all the time, and I guessed that was why his brain had shrunk, making him the way he was. J.B. was coming to make the fire in the pit at about eight o'clock, and some others were coming later to help, while Shine and Alex smoked the shoats on the big pit. Rosa and Mama had already boiled a big basket of potatoes, which were kept in the cold on the porch. When Wesley would finish the milking, he and Mama would make the potato salad. Rosa had made three cakes, and Mama was going to donate one of her fruitcakes to the party, also. Aunt Colleen had made about fifty nice teacakes. J.B. had brought them over late the night before, and we both ate one on the porch before he brought them to the dining table.

Dad instructed Alex, "You and Billy take the truck and go down to Harper's Grocery to pick up the rest of what we need," and he handed Alex the list that Mama had made.

It was still dark outside, and Alex asked, "Ya wants us ta go now, Mista Carl?"

"Yeah, Sook will let you in early and help you get all of this together so you can get back here. I already told her you'd be there early." He looked over to me in front of the warm stove and said, "You better get your clothes on if you're going with Alex." I knew he hadn't yet told Mama that I wasn't going to school that day. She would know soon, but I would be gone.

Grinning, I looked at Alex, begging, "You gonna let me drive?"

By the time I backed the truck out of the garage, the sun was showing its light over the trees toward town. This was going to be a nice day for a *cochon-de-lait*. Dad loved to cook *suckling pigs* whole on a closed pit, often inviting church friends and family members from Gold Dust, Eola, and Bunkie.

I felt good when I heard the truck whine each time I shifted gears. I left it in second gear all the way down the dirt road, and every now and then the rear wheels would spin in the mud, making me feel as powerful as the truck itself. It had power, and it gave me power, too, every time I mashed the accelerator. Alex sat silent and watched me.

By about seven thirty we had loaded the groceries and four cases of Nehi pop, and were headed back to Shirley Plantation.

About a mile south of Frithland Plantation, Alex announced, "I needs to take ova from heah. We gon make'a stop in town." I brought the truck to a stop, where the highway crossed the Southern Pacific Railroad, and we switched places.

Alex didn't have to tell me that we were headed to Avoyelles Wholesale Grocery, right off Main Street, on the alley in back of the *The Bunkie Record* newspaper. I had been there many times with my dad. As we pulled up to the loading dock a big door had already begun to rise, making a big black hole that looked like the entrance to a deep, dark, and spooky cave.

Old Mister Ford, as white as a sheet, with his green plastic visor, white shirt and necktie, and baggy gray sweater drooping almost to his knees, covering his wrinkled black pants, walked very slowly, with short jerky steps, from the black hole, calling out, "Y'all here for the wine for Mister Carl?" He sneezed, and rubbed a big handkerchief across his nose, then stuffed it into his rear pocket.

"Yes, sir, dat's us," Alex called to Mister Ford, while he waited on the dock.

I opened the door and stood on the running board, while Alex climbed into the back of the truck. Old Mister Ford finally returned with his dolly loaded with four cases of wine, and came to the edge of the loading dock. Alex took each case and set it neatly near the truck's tailgate. In a few minutes, Mister Ford came out with four more cases, and Alex stacked them carefully on top of the others. There were eight cases, and each case contained four gallons of Port wine.

Old Mister Ford sneezed again, very hard, then asked, "Mister Carl's gonna have his big shin-dig already? It must be something," and he wiped his nose with the same dingy, grey handkerchief.

Alex smiled and said, "Well, sir, Mista Carl always gives us all a big dinna when all da cane's in. We don sent da lass load to da mill Toosdy mornin, and ta days our pawty day!" Alex smiled, looked at me, and said softly, "I betta drive on home."

Old Mister Ford shook his head, smiled, and mumbled, "I shore hope y'all make it. That's a lotta wine!" and he shuffled with his empty cart toward the big black opening. Just when we started pulling away from the dock, the big, squeaking door began moving down slowly, sealing the entrance to the deep, dark, cave, and locking poor old Mister Ford inside.

We were going to make it! I knew we were going to make it, and I smiled to myself, figuring that I was going to "make it," too. J.B. was going to be there. Alex was going to be there. I knew something about J.B. that he didn't want Alex to know. I wanted today to be the day that I would get my first glass of wine, maybe by two o'clock, or maybe even sooner. And I wanted a big one.

It would depend on how I played my hand with J.B.

CHAPTER 28

Alex and I arrived back at the Big House right after Mama had left to take Mickey to school. She usually spent about an hour in town having coffee and visiting almost every day with my grandmother, so I figured that I had a little time before she would be home and would get on to me for staying out of school. I wasn't afraid, even though she would act mad and threaten me with, "I ought to tie you to the mailbox, and sell you." I had heard that threat at least a thousand times, too.

Alex turned in front of the garage and backed the truck in. We both hopped out and I unhooked the tailgate to let it down. We unloaded four cases of wine, putting it in the storage room, and hiding it under a blanket of croker sacks. Alex pulled the truck to the entrance of the barbeque yard, where we started unloading the groceries and the rest of the wine. The two tables were soon pretty well covered with anything we would need for the *cochon-de-lait*.

J.B. came walking toward us down the side of the Big House. He didn't stop, but just raised his hand and walked on toward the back of the yard in the direction of the milkshed, never looking at Alex or me. Wesley was still milking, and I figured that J.B. would probably pester him until it was time to light the fire in the barbeque pit. I figured he probably thought I had already told Alex everything about him and Bernice, and he would wait to see what might happen.

Alex looked my way and said softly, "We gotta watch dat wine in the sto room. J.B.'ll have a jug out fore you know it, hidin in da barn. Shine'll be here dreckly, and he'll keep 'im straight."

Before we finished unloading the groceries, Shine came walking up the driveway and stopped at the truck, and in his thick French accent, asked, "Ya need some hep wit all dat?"

Alex shook his head and said, "Nah, we got it. Man! It sho is a lotta food heah!"

Shine had already turned, and was going toward the screened porch. He hadn't planned to help us anyway. He opened the screen door, crossed the porch and called out, "Rosa, you in dare?" and he opened the kitchen door. I figured he was going to get Rosa to make him a sandwich and give him a cup of coffee.

My dad and Shine had grown up together about ten miles south of town, below Gold Dust and nearer to Whiteville, on Barbaric Plantation. Although Shine was several years older than my dad, they were very much alike in many ways. Shine fussed at all of us kids and threatened to "whip you good," anytime he thought we were doing something that Dad wouldn't like for us to do. He just threatened, but we all knew that he kept Dad informed about whatever we did and whatever went on in the Quarters, the good and the bad. He came to the Big House almost every morning and planned the workday with Dad.

After a few minutes he came out of the kitchen, closed the door behind him, and sat on the top step with his sandwich and coffee, then called to me, "Billy, wur's J.B.?"

I called back to him that he was helping Wesley finish milking. I knew J.B. had to be doing something, or else Shine would get onto him. That was the main way he was like my dad. To both of them, a person had to be *working* all the time; otherwise he would be wasting time.

Still chewing, he yelled to me again, "Go tell'm ta come light da fire. Bring plenty hickry." He never stopped chewing.

Alex smiled and looked at me, "Ya go haad. I'sl git dis unloaded and set up."

I started trotting to the back gate, heading to the milkshed. Wesley, sitting on his milkstool, was finishing his last cow, and J.B. was leaning against the milking stall, jabbering about something. When I told him what Shine had said, he grabbed me and tried to throw me down onto the soft dirt floor, but I struggled with him and broke loose from his grip. He frowned at me, declaring, "Wesley, dis heah boy don got strong. We's gon havta fix 'im up fo he gits too uppity."

I kicked some dirt at him and started running out of the milkshed toward the house. Wiping the dust from his pants legs, he yelled out to me, "Ya betta come back heah an hep me haul dat wood! Yo daddy said yous wuz gon hep me! I's gon sho tell'm wat ya did to me!"

I turned around and started slowly trotting backward and called back to him, "And I'm gonna tell Alex what you did!" and I spit as hard as I could toward him, shook my fist at him, and continued to trot backward. He stopped in his tracks, and his arms and face dropped. He had to think. I knew I had him, at least for the moment, and figured that I had taken my first step toward my glass of wine.

The sun was bright and the day was warm. When I reached the back of the Big House, I sat on the top step, leaning against the screen by the door. Pal came to me, smiling with his ears back and his big tail moving from side to side. I wondered what he was thinking. He knew my every move and most often he could stay a few steps ahead of me. I took my windbreaker off, glancing at the cuffs, and seeing that both were badly frayed at the creases. For at least three years I had worn that jacket every fall, winter, and spring—maybe even longer. Mama always bought shirts and coats way too big so I could grow into them; and when it was new, I wore it with two roll-ups in the cuffs, and it was so long it hung below my butt. Mama was right, though—I had grown into it. I folded the jacket, laid it where I sat on the top step, and looked to where Alex was working; then, I whispered to Pal, "I wish you'd bury my old jacket somewhere, then I would be finished with it." He wagged his tail and barked once, letting me know he understood what I wanted. Poor Rosa had washed and ironed the jacket so many times that I figured she hated it as much as I did and she could be finished with it, too.

The gate rattled open and Wesley brought two buckets of milk from the milkshed. I ran, opened the door to the milkroom, and went inside with him, telling him, "I'll help you strain it and put it away."

"Good, but I gotta skim da cream off dem crocks and wash'um befo I can put up dis."

Mama made me help Hoss every now and then, but he thought I was a lot of trouble and more of a bother than help. Opening the screened cabinet, I took out both the crocks and moved them onto the counter by the sink. The cream on top was thick and yellow, the kind that Mama always wanted to use to make a strong, rich butter.

"Billy, you wanta skim 'um?"

"Sure, I'll do that." Wesley handed a big ladle to me, and a little white bucket with a small wooden grip in the middle of the wire handle, which Hoss and Wesley had used for years to bring the cream from the milkroom to the kitchen. I skimmed the cream from the top of the big bowl of milk like Hoss had taught me. Wesley poured the skimmed milk into two big jugs, which he would take home, giving some of it to his neighbors in the Quarters.

Wesley softly instructed, "Go take dis heres cream to Rosa, fer me." Then he asked, "Billy, would ya go open da gate at the airplane and let da cows in the 'biair' pasture fer me?"

I told him yes, though I really didn't want to go. Still, I brought the cream into the kitchen, and Pal and I headed out to open the gate into the bayou pasture.

Running toward the two big trees, I stopped when I saw the silver plane, and remembered on Thanksgiving eve when I had stood at its cockpit, shivered in the blistering wind and snow, and my stomach had turned upside down. There was something very bad about it that night, and it had made me sick. Today was warm, bright, and sunny. Stopping my run about thirty feet from the plane, I suddenly wanted to climb into its cockpit and play with the instrument panel, which I had done many times before. I wanted to check its clock, making sure again, that time had really stopped forever for Danny McBride, at eighteen seconds past 10:23 on Freedom Day, and I wanted to touch the brownness of what was left of the his blood smeared across the instruments. As I moved closer to the silver ghost, the breeze stopped and I could hear no sounds around me. It looked like the plane had awakened, watching me, and waiting to see what I might do. I knew it would never let go of its dark secrets, and the mystery of why Danny had to die so young and so violently, and if the plane had also killed many others in places far away, flying the skies over the Pacific. My having looked and studied its insides hundreds of times, and knowing every little cranny as I did, I figured it hated me and was afraid that I might tell everything I felt about it. It was guilty—I had long ago believed that—guilty of all kinds of meanness, and it was waiting for me to make a wrong move so it could *get* me, too. Other dark and haunting secrets were hidden in this pile of gray rubble, secrets only I had wondered about and wanted to know every one of them. It was hiding them from me, and it wasn't going to give them up easily. Every time I took in a breath of air, I could hear the silver ghost breathe with me, mocking me, waiting and hoping I would make that wrong move. A demon: it *was* a demon, hurt, wrecked, and ugly, and it had cast a terrible *spell* onto me. I knew it would eat me alive, and Pal, too, if we weren't very careful.

A gust of cold air suddenly blew across me and softly whistled through the branches of the big oaks. I blinked several times, trying to clear my eyes and clear my mind.

Wishing that I had my old windbreaker with me, I felt cold and began to shiver, but I could smell the odor of oil, water, and blood, bright red blood—one of the spells that had rooted itself deep inside my memory. Pal was standing between the plane and me, with his ears standing straight up. He looked at the silver ghost and then at me, plainly warning me, "Stop, don't go there!" Slowly shaking my head *yes*, I knew he could see what I couldn't, and he knew the fear stirring inside me. He whimpered softly, then growled angrily again, raising his black lips above his fangs, daring the demon to make a move toward us. He growled again, barked twice, and continued a long, deep growl while we slowly backed away. Quickly, we began our run to open the gate.

CHAPTER 29

My ole yellow dog and I ran all the way to the barbeque yard, never glancing toward the silver plane when we passed beneath the oaks.

The barbeque yard was a special place, a pretty place protected in the summer from the hot sun by the big pecan trees. Rose of Sharon trees surrounded the barbeque yard, blooming almost all summer and until late fall with purple and white blooms, some a rare bluish color. Uncle Nick kept them trimmed, and the whole yard was always spotless, ready for any gathering of friends or relatives; it was a pretty place for us to sit in the evenings, when a hot summer day was over. That day, the pecan trees were bare and the Rose of Sharon trees were sparsely leafed because of the cold and snow a few weeks before. At the back of the yard was the long hitching rail where we tied our horses. The yard that day was open to the bright winter sun as it gleamed from low in the sky through the leafless trees; it would help warm everyone who came to the barbeque.

Despite meeting the demon under the oaks, and with my heart still racing, I knew the day would be a good one, and I liked it.

J.B. was struggling with the wheelbarrow loaded with wood. He finally reached the brick pit and started setting the wood neatly inside. It took the whole load, and Alex told him to go get some more since it would be needed in an hour or so. The fire had to burn until the hickory turned into hot coals, and there had to be plenty of coals to smoke the three little pigs for about four hours. We wouldn't eat until almost two o'clock. J.B. didn't say anything, but I could see him jerk nervously everytime he heard Alex's voice. He grunted when he leaned to pick up the arms of the wheelbarrow, and slowly moved out of the barbeque yard toward the woodpile near the milkshed. The sun was at its high point for the day when several men started coming into the yard. They stood around the pit to talk. Most had on their work clothes, but everybody was neat and clean. The conversations usually centered on the cane cutting and some of the problems that had come about. Several would laugh loudly and poke fun at someone in the group. It was plain that Alex and Shine were the two leaders, because they talked the least and joked the least. A couple of the younger men, like Leroy and Ebay, both around eighteen years old, were smart and had some schooling behind them. Dad knew who they were and what they could do, perhaps having been there when they were born. He also knew their parents well. He had encouraged their moms and dads to send them to school as much as they could, and Leroy and Ebay had gone to about the fifth or sixth grade. These younger men would become the tractor drivers and the mechanics, quickly learning to use the new farm equipment coming from the factories in the North. Looking at them, I thought about myself going to school every day, and I was expected to do so, but I knew the older kids on the plantation went to school only when there was little or no work they could do. Then, I thought about my good friend, Papa, who had never set foot in a school and probably never would. At about fourteen, he was only three or four years younger than Leroy, but had the stature and nature of a child much younger than me.

Alex walked over to the corner of the yard, where he took his knife from his pocket and cut open a box holding the jugs of wine. Rosa had brought out about fifty pint-sized Mason jars that she and Mama used to put up tomatoes and vegetables. My dad came over, and Alex handed him a jar, already half-filled with the brownish colored wine, signaling to everyone that the party was starting. The other men each picked up a little jar for Alex to pour wine into, and all of a sudden my mouth began to water. I swallowed a couple of times and licked my lips.

J.B. had come back with another load of wood and parked the wheelbarrow near the pit. He got a jar and held it out to Alex, but said nothing, so I picked up a jar and moved directly behind J.B. When he walked off with his little jar half full of wine, I held mine toward Alex. He looked at me, and then he looked toward Dad, who was busy talking to several men. Catching the aroma of the clear brown wine, my mouth began to water more.

"Sorry, Billy, you ain't cut no cane," he said, and he barely smiled.

"Dad's not looking, Alex, and anyway, I've been workin all mornin! Just a little, come on, just *one* swallow, just *one*, that's all." and I shook the little jar toward the jug he was holding away from me.

He looked toward Dad again, shook his head, smiled again, and said to me, "This ain't Mag ya talkin to, Billy. You ain't gittin any uh this wine, and ya holdin up thangs, heah," and he motioned with his thumb for me to move on.

Walking away, and glancing about the yard, I said softly to myself, "Son of a gun, after all I've done this morning, and he won't give me any. I'll move on all right, to my 'J.B.' plan."

I stopped where J.B. was talking with Leroy and whispered to him, "J.B., meet me over behind the bell tower. I have to tell you something," and I took my empty jar with me as I headed in the direction of the tower.

J.B. walked fast with tiny steps, only a few feet behind me, anxious, I guessed, to know if I had told Alex anything, and holding his jar of wine out in front of him, trying not to spill any. I walked quickly to the back of the bell tower where no one could see us; he almost ran into me when I stopped, and asked, "What'cha want, Billy? Wha'cha don said to Alex? I bet ya done got me in a heap of trouble, ain't chu?"

I looked straight at him, firmly. "What I want?" and I took a deep breath, hesitated for a second, and demanded, "I want half of your wine! That's what I want, J.B., or I tell Alex everything you've been doing to Bernice," and I held my jar toward him.

He stepped back, frowned, turned his mouth down, and said in a high-pitched whisper, "Ya mus' be done loss yo mind, boy. Mista Carl'll get me sent to da pen in Angola, me givin' ya some wine. Yous bout crazy, ain't chu."

"Half of your wine, J.B. You're gonna get a lot more today, or I tell Alex everything. I'm warning you, and that's my deal."

He continued to look at me with a frown on his face, weighing my proposition while I moved my jar closer to his, but he quickly covered the top of his jar with his other hand and stammered, "Ya, yous mean, boy, and crazy, too. I wish I would'na told ya bout Bernice, but chu sho ain't gitten no wine from me." He quickly turned, and started walking away. After a few steps, he stopped, turned toward me and said, "I guess ya jis gon havta tell Alex!" and he slowly poured his wine onto the ground, all the while looking straight at me. Gritting my teeth in anger, I watched while he walked toward the barbeque yard, his hand gripping tightly around his empty jar. He never looked back.

Realizing my plan had completely failed, I sat down on the concrete footing holding up one leg of the bell tower. With my elbows on my knees, I dropped my pint jar onto the grass, gritted my teeth again, and spoke softly to myself, "That bastard! I hate his guts! I oughta tell Alex everything and let Alex beat the hell out of him." I kicked the little jar, and it went rolling into a bed of dead calla lilies about twenty feet away.

For the next hour or so, J.B. stayed close to the pit, keeping the fire going until the hickory coals were a hot orange color. He never asked Alex for any more wine, but pouting with a pout fixed on his face and his bottom lip stuck out, he watched me like a tree full of owls.

Shine was getting pretty happy after a couple of glasses of wine, and he asked Alex very loudly, "Ya ready to put on da shoats?" Shine was pretty loud anyway and usually gloated with a lot of confidence and pride. He loved Daddy's sisters and brothers, as well as me and my brother and sisters, but he took a great deal of pride, also, in bossing us kids, just like Dad.

Alex looked at the pit of hot coals, saying, "Yeah, Shine, le's put 'um on," and he pulled his watch out of his pocket, studied it for a second or two, and continued, "We can eat bout two. Evabody'll be good and ready by den."

Alex, Shine, and J.B. went to the screened porch, and each brought back a whole pig on his shoulders. Shine and Alex had cleaned them the day before and hung them at the end of the porch in the cold, with their heads hanging down so all of the blood would drip into a little pan placed beneath each one. Alex and Shine placed theirs on the edge of the hot pit, then Shine placed both of the shoats neatly over the coals on a heavy mesh screen, reached over and took the third one from J.B., and placed it next to the other two. Alex lowered the metal cover over the open pit, closing it to keep the smoke in. Shine smacked his big lips, looked at me and winked. His mouth was already watering, and I smiled. Alex and Shine had done this many times before.

About fifteen or twenty men were standing around talking to each other. None of the women had come yet, and it appeared the little kids would probably stay home. I wondered if Papa and Helen would come. What about Mister Alfonse, Mrs. Mazie and Cathrine? I doubted that any of them would make it. Daddy would make sure that whoever didn't come would get a plate brought to them later in the evening, including some wine. Usually Mister Alfonse had to work late to get the mules and horses in their places in the big barns, and put out hay and feed. He had Papa to help him now. That reminded me about going to help Cathrine with Papa's lesson, but that day I had too much to do. The jugs of wine were being emptied pretty fast, and we still had at least two hours before we ate. Daddy had gone in to take his usual noon nap, and Shine with Alex kept things moving. Someone had set up another table, and Rosa and Mama had brought out the potato salad and a stack of big paper plates. Rosa called to J.B. to come help her. They went into the kitchen, brought Rosa's cakes out on a big tray, and put one cake on each table, while Mama counted the places at the three big tables, commenting that we had enough space for about forty-eight people to sit. I figured we would have close to that many.

But everytime I looked toward the case of wine, Alex was looking at me.

Glancing down the driveway, I recognized Gilbert Frank and Emma coming, and behind them was a fellow who looked a little familiar. He was a little tall with a hat that sat high on his head, and he walked with a gait that said, "Well, here I am everybody. Here's Isaac Vead!" I didn't move for just a minute and waited until Gilbert Frank and Emma came closer to the barbeque yard, then called out to Gilbert Frank, "Who's that you're bringing with you, Gilbert Frank?"

He looked a little bit surprised and said, "Dis heres Emma, Billy."

I said, "Yeah, I know Emma, but I'm talking about that tall fella doing all that struttin behind you."

He and Emma turned and glanced back, then back to me, and he said, "I's don rightly know, but I guess dat use to be Papa, but it sho don' look like'm."

Papa had on his dress pants and a white shirt with the jacket Mama had fixed for him, buttoned up almost to the top, and wearing Hoss's chapeau that Daddy had given to Hoss some time back. It appeared to me that what Cathrine and I had done for the past two weeks was working well for Isaac Vead.

Above the chatter, the loud talking, and laughing, Shine's big voice boomed out, "Let's eat!" Those two words were enough to move everybody toward the three tables. Shine continued, "Evybody sit down and start servin. Me an Alex'll bring da shoats."

Alex swung the heavy lid up from the pit and leaned it against the chimney, and I could see on Shine and Alex's faces that the three little pigs were ready. Mama was standing with Dad near the pit with three red apples. Shine and Alex stopped in front of her, with one of the shoats on a cedar slab, and she pushed an apple into its hot snout. They moved on and set it in the middle of the table where Papa and I were sitting together. They did the same thing with the other two shoats for the other two tables.

Rosa and Jo were the hosts at one table, where Mama was going to sit. Veesy and Alex were the hosts at the second table, where Dad was going to sit, and Gilbert Frank and Emma were the hosts at the third table. Little clouds of steam were rising from each dark brown pig, and all forty-two people there were ready to begin the feast!

Aunt Colleen stood at the end of the middle table and held up her arms toward the bright blue sky with her long fingers pointing upward. Everyone bowed, but eyes were crossing the tables back and forth, with lips being licked and mouths watering almost like open faucets. I hoped she wouldn't pray very long.

Aunt Colleen held her breath for a second while looking across the tables at all the people there. With her strong face of smooth brown skin, and looking high into the clear blue sky, she slowly closed her eyes and softly began, "Dear Heavenly Father," and like everyone else around the three big tables, I closed my eyes, while she continued, "we thank ya for this day of reconciling with this rich and wonderful land, and what it gives to all of us folks. Thank ya for all these strong and honorable people who know the goodness, and also the struggle in this life, but still know the greatness of our rewards when we love you, and when we love one another. We thank ya for the abundance we see heah today, abundance of food and abundance of joy and love. We pray, that because of the power in our hearts for your son Jesus, the lives of all of the peoples of the world will be made betta. Let us show ourselves to each other, open and honest, so we can know who we are. Thank you dear Heavenly Father, in the name of your son Jesus, we pray. Amen." Aunt Colleen could really pray, in fact, as good as anybody in The Eola Baptist Church.

She looked across the crowd again, then slowly sat down, perfectly still with her hands crossed in her big lap, and waited for the hosts to carve the little brown pigs. No one said a word, or moved, until the host sat. That was the signal for the feast to begin.

I could hear Pal whinning while he sat in back of Papa and me, letting me know where he was and he wanted his share, too. I reached back, slipping him a big bite of the *red boudin* that Mama had put on every plate as a treat from her new freezer. Pal liked red boudin, but I didn't. Papa ate his, but Papa ate almost anything, about like Pal.

***

On that beautiful Saturday in December of 1946, J.B. won completely, since I didn't get my glass of wine nor did I tell Alex the secret about his daughter Bernice. But J.B. didn't know that Alex and I had hidden the rest of the wine under the croker sacks, and I knew where it was, and I was going to show Isaac Vead when the time was right.

The cochon-de-lait moved along nicely, and lasted till the sun went down.

CHAPTER 30

My twelfth birthday would be Wednesday. Mama would remember, but it would come and go almost like any other day. School was letting out for the Christmas holidays on my birthday, and I would count that as my best present.

On Wednesday morning, Mama called up to me, "Get up, Billy, we have to hurry!"

It was cold in my room, so I grabbed my pants, shirt, shoes and socks, and ran down the stairs to put them on in front of the fireplace in the family room. I swung open the door, and standing in front of the fireplace trying to get warm were Mickey and my sister Jerry. She had come home the day before, but would be going back to Alexandria on Thursday morning to spend Christmas. I squeezed in between them to catch some warmth from the fire, and Mickey hit me in the stomach. As I shoved him away from the fireplace, he started yelling that he was going to tell Mama, and just then she walked in with four cups of coffee, and, under her arm, a box wrapped in bright colored Christmas paper. She smiled, and all three started singing "Happy Birthday." A little embarrassed, I managed an early morning smile and a whispered *thank you*.

Mama smiled and suggested, "You better put on your clothes before you open it." I slipped into my shirt and pants and put on my socks, then took off for the bathroom. When I got back to the family room, they were already ahead of me drinking their coffee, so I reached for the package and started pulling at the string and paper.

"Well, I hope you like it, Son. It's a different color this time," and Mama raised her cup to sip the final drop of coffee.

I thought to myself, "I sure hope it's not another bathrobe. I never used the one she gave me a couple of years ago." I lifted the box top, and there lay a brand new windbreaker. I could tell it was big, and it was *green* like an army jeep.

"Try it on. You can wear it to school today." I pulled it out of the box, put it on, and stood while Mama rolled a big cuff in each of the sleeves and straightened the bottom, which came a little below my waist. She looked up and down at me, smiled and said, "Very nice, I love the olive green. And you'll grow into it in just a little while," and she patted my arm, still smiling. Jerry didn't say anything, but I could see her snickering at me, making me wonder, "Is this oversized jeep-colored jacket making her snicker, or does she know that her leather gloves are gone, and she's getting ready to let me have it?"

"Mama, this is great. My old brown one is worn completely out! Thanks," and I leaned over and kissed her cheek. She had already put on her Coty powder and red lipstick, and smelled just the way my Mama always smelled. Her blue eyes glistened.

As I turned to go to the kitchen to get a biscuit for my coffee, Mama commanded, "Just a minute, Billy. We're gonna go to Texas tomorrow as soon as Dad can get away, so you need to bring down all of your dirty clothes from upstairs. Rosa can wash and iron them today."

I stopped and turned toward her with my cup of coffee in my hand and whined, "Texas! Mama, I don't want to go to Texas for Christmas. I want to stay home, right here on Shirley!"

She glanced toward Jerry, explaining, "Well, Jerry's going to be in Alexandria with Margie during the holidays, and there's no one to stay here with you."

I hated to go to Texas. There were no kids my age, and everybody kept their houses too hot and all their houses had little rooms and almost no yards to play in. They all lived in town and worked for either chemical companies or oil companies. The few kids who were close to my age already had friends to play with, and besides, I hardly knew my Texas cousins. In fact, I didn't know how they were kin to me, and I didn't care if they were kin or not. To me, the only thing good about going to Texas were the Burma Shave signs along the highway, but I wasn't going to Texas if I could get out of it.

I could tell that Mama was a little bit mad at me. She continued, "Well, Billy, go finish getting ready. Jerry's gonna drive y'all to school today," and she raised her hands as though she was answering her own question: "What am I gonna do with that boy?"

I thought, "Uh oh. Jerry's gonna pen me up in the car, and let me have it about those darn gloves."

Driving slowly down the driveway, and reaching the tool shed, we saw Dad leaning on the front of his truck chewing on the butt of a cigar, talking to Alex.

"Stop here, Jerry. I want to talk to Dad," and I pulled on the car door handle. When the Chevy came to a halt, I jumped out and ran over to where Dad and Alex were talking. "Dad?"

He held up his hand toward me, and continued saying to Alex, "Well, if he can do better out there, I don't blame him for goin," then he turned to me, and asked, "And what's on your mind, young man?" I told him that I didn't want to go to Texas and that I could stay right there on the plantation, then he asked, "So, you think you're old enough to handle it by yourself?"

"Yes, sir! I sure do," and I stood as tall as I could with my chest pumped up.

He motioned toward the car, "You better get going or y'all will be late. Man! I like that new windbreaker, and Happy Birthday!" He would convince Mama to let me stay, since I was being *manly* by wanting to stay all by myself, and he liked that. He thought the new windbreaker was ugly, I was pretty sure, and he wouldn't have been caught dead in it.

I jumped into the Chevy, and Jerry took off down the muddy road and then onto the gravel road going to Bunkie. About the time we reached the Prosser's house, she turned to me, demanding, "Billy, I don't want you fooling around in my room any more, and I'm tired of your doing that. And what happened to my new gloves? They're gone, and I know you did something with them. And don't you deny it!" I had been waiting for this day, but I *still* wasn't ready for her. She was smart and tough.

I held my head up, looked straight ahead over the dashboard clock, and I told her the whole story. The snow. Cold hands. Making snowballs. Gloves that were wet, wet, wet, and finally, my drying them on the fireplace hearth. Then, I added, "You know something, sweet sister? They didn't even help keep my hands warm. They were awful gloves, and like Dad says, it was a waste of money to buy those darn things." I stiffened up in my seat, figuring she was waiting for the right moment to sock me on the head or somewhere, maybe my chest, but through the corners of my eyes I'm sure I saw her smile just a little bit, then she said, "They *were* awful gloves, and I didn't like them, but that's beside the point!" She stopped smiling, "I'm warning you," and she shook her finger at me, "stay out of my room. You don't have any business fooling around in it and taking things that aren't yours. And I mean it!"

Boy, it wasn't so bad after all, and, finally, a load had been lifted. I had carried around the guilt for almost four weeks, and suddenly it was over. I thought that maybe the "sweet sister" words helped calm her down before she got too hot. I thought, "I'll get the gloves out of my room and put them back in her bureau drawer. She'll get a kick out of seeing them all shrunk up. She didn't like them anyway." I decided I'd better leave well enough alone for right now, but maybe I could wrap them in a nice box with a Christmas ribbon and give them to her as a Christmas present. Then, we could all laugh about the way they looked. And she knew that I'd fool around in her room again if I thought I needed something she had. Anyway, the nickels and dimes in her little white box were going away, and I figured she surely knew where they were going, but she kept putting more change in it, and it always disappeared, so she must have known who was taking it. I smiled and thought, "I won, again," and quickly turned toward the rear seat and pinched Mickey on his rosy little cheek. He hit at me and missed, then yelled, "Hit him, Jerry, hit that ole dog! Hurry!" And darn it, she smacked me hard on the side of my head with her knucles. It really hurt, and I yelped like a dog that had just been kicked, but I figured I probably deserved it.

And I felt good.

CHAPTER 31

Our class was a mess. Mrs. Gilroy did her best to keep control, but she lost one time after another. We had a little party at around ten o'clock. The mother of one of the teacher's pets brought some cookies sprinkled with colored sugar just like Aunt Colleen's and Rosa's teacakes, but they called them a fancy name. Another mother brought two jugs of red drink that was pretty good stuff. They called it "Kool Aide." I liked it, but I mostly drank milk or Donald Duck orange juice, so the red stuff was different for a change. After the party, Mrs.Gilroy banged on her desk with her wooden paddle, demanding, "Quiet, everybody, I have an announcement!" We all knew what it was, but even Marilyn stopped talking long enough to listen. Mrs. Gilroy held her paddle up, begging, "Now, I want absolute quiet until the bell rings in about twenty minutes," and she looked at the clock on the wall at the end of the blackboard. The old clock just ticked away, and it never had the right time. She had to wind it every Monday morning and reset it, while the whole class stayed frustrated every day, wondering if the time on the darn thing was right or wrong. Mrs. Gilroy looked at the watch she wore on a chain around her neck, and said, "Oh, I'm sorry, not twenty, just eight more minutes. Get everything together that you're taking home, and after lunch, go straight to your busses. Have a Merry Christmas, and I'll see you next year!" Pandemonium broke out again.

Leaning on my elbows, and in the noise all around me, I thought about going home for two weeks for the holidays. That would be good. And I remembered Sarah Grace's party just when Marilyn tapped me on the back, and asked if I was planning to go. I told her *yes*, that I wanted to go, but I had to get a ride there. Word had gotten around that we would play spin the bottle at the party, and I knew what that was because I had seen my sisters play it at their parties at our house. I was getting hot in my new jacket when the bell rang.

Marilyn and I had been friends since before we started the first grade. Her dad and my dad had been childhood friends, too. Marilyn was about the prettiest girl in the fifth grade.

She looked at me and said, "Where did you ever get a coat that color?" and sort of giggled. I looked up at her from my seat, frowned, and reached to grab one of her long pigtails. She jerked back, and we both laughed; then, smiling, she said, "Merry Christmas, Billy." As she turned and walked toward the door with her books in the crook of her arm, my eyes followed her while I thought, "Maybe one day Marilyn can be my girlfriend. I really like her, but she's sorta like my sister, I guess." I didn't know if I really wanted a girlfriend or not, but maybe later on.

I figured that Mama would have a verdict for me about Texas by the time I got home from school, but she didn't. While drinking coffee early the next morning, she announced that I didn't have to go to Texas, that Dad thought it would be okay for me to stay on Shirley. I had won again.

Right after dinner the next day, we started loading the Chevy. I felt a little sad, knowing I would be alone in the Big House, and Christmas would be over when my family came home from Texas, but I tried real hard to sound and look happy.

Wesley and I helped Dad load the trunk with several suitcases, and then he told Wesley, "You can bring it now!"

Wesley went to the milkroom and after just a few minutes he was headed to the car with a shoat wrapped in a white sheet. Dad placed it in the trunk with the suitcases saying, "That'll keep for the next few hours. I bet everybody's gonna like this for Christmas dinner!"

He slammed the trunk lid and leaned against it with one hand, ordering, "Wesley, keep an eye on this boy for me. If he gives you any trouble, call Shine. He'll straighten 'im out!" I was standing by my Dad and, for the first time, I noticed that I was a little taller than he was. Wesley and I both smiled, then Dad pointed his finger at me and said, "Now, Billy, don't you take my truck off the plantation, and don't even be driving it at all, unless you absolutely have to. Okay?"

I didn't say anything, but I figured that he must have read my mind, because I had already planned that I would take it to Sarah Grace's party Friday night. Her family's house was about two hundred yards from the highway and I could park it there, walk the two hundred yards, and no one would know how I got there but me. Then no one would ask me to go anywhere in it or take them home. I was trying to quickly work out another plan in my mind, when he asked, "Did you hear me, Billy?"

"Yes, sir," and I shook my head. He kept looking at me, squinting his eyes a little, and I figured that he knew that I was trying to think of a way to get to his truck. The warning he gave me was stern, and I understood it well, but I didn't think he had told Alex not to take it off the plantation.

Mama came down the walk to the car. She put her hand on my arm and said, "Bye, Son. Your Christmas presents are on my sewing machine, but you shouldn't open them till Christmas day. Promise?" When she told me that, she hugged and kissed me. I got a lump in my throat, but I knew that if I cried she would make me go to Texas with them.

"Promise, Mama" and I held up my hand like I was taking an oath, and smiled at her. When I stepped back, Mama's sweet aroma was lost in the light breeze, and the lump in my throat got bigger.

As I watched the Chevy turn at the hedgerow for its hundred-mile trip to

Texas, I figured that Alex would be glad to take me to the party Friday night...in Dad's truck.

Wesley went on to the barn. Looking toward the old house, I slowly walked up the brick sidewalk to the wide wooden steps going onto the screened porch. The screened door seemed awfully quiet as I pulled it open, then stepped onto the long and empty porch. There were no sounds from anywhere. With my hand wrapped around the doorknob on the kitchen door, I wondered, "Why am I going in here? There's nobody home," and my stomach suddenly turned over when I pulled hard on the heavy door into the dark kitchen. The kitchen with its big iron stove standing on one side, and its wide window facing to the west, was still warm, even though the fire in the stove had long ago gone out. Glancing all around the big room, which was always the meeting place and center for our family's daily lives, it suddenly became a big square box, hollow with silence and loneliness, making me sad and making me wonder. They were all gone, my family was gone, and I was alone, and there was no chance now to change my mind about going to Texas. Moving slowly to the far end of the dining room, I stood in front of the fireplace, while a dwindling little flame flickered in the ashes. Looking upward into the big mirror in the fireplace mantle, there was the face of a lonely little kid who realized he had willingly jumped into a deep pool where he couldn't touch the bottom, and suddenly he realized he didn't know how to swim as well as he thought he did. I quickly looked back into the little fire, knowing that the fire was going out too, leaving me alone, lonely, and with a broken heart. I thought about the cold outside, and about the silver plane, the haunted ghost, and it being so close to the Big House, close to where I had to sleep all by myself. As my stomach turned over again and again, I looked into the mirror, and hated that dumb kid whose face looked back at me. He had lied to me, making me think I was tough and I was brave, and I wasn't a little kid anymore, but *he* didn't know what *he* wanted either, fooling me badly. And now—now my family was gone. My arms and legs were so heavy I could barely move them, making me feel as though I was going to fall to the cold floor. The tears were coming, and I didn't try to stop them. I let myself drop into one of the big chairs, and watched the last tiny flame disappear into the pile of grey ashes, leaving the fireplace cold, and lonely, too. Wiping away the tears with my hand, I leaned my head against the wing on the chair back, and closed my eyes.

Time would pass faster if I slept.

CHAPTER 32

I heard the kitchen door close. Wesley came into the dining room with an armload of wood, demanding, "Wake up, Billy! Ya gon freeze ta det' in heah! Move da screen fer me!" I got up and moved the fire screen to the side, and he loaded the fireplace with fresh wood. He looked at me, hesitated a moment, then said, "Don'cha worry none. I'sl be heah evy day, and Rosa'll be comin back 'an fore. Is dat a'right?" I was sorry that he recognized that I was lonesome already. I just needed a little time to figure out what I was going to do for the next few days.

Papa and Cathrine, I knew, would give me something to eat, and I thought about maybe getting Alex to take me to Aunt Sook's store, but then I remembered the party on Friday night. I told Wesley, "Aw, everything's okay. Anyway, I can get the wood for the fireplace. Don't worry about me." I figured that I would get a few quilts to make a pallet so I could sleep in front of the fireplace every night, keeping the fire going, and living in the dining room for the entire time my family would be gone. That way Wesley wouldn't have to make a fire in the mornings, and I would stay warmer than in my bedroom. We could make coffee in the fireplace. That would be fun, and he wouldn't even have to stoke the kitchen stove. Knowing that Helen and Papa didn't have much, I figured I could bring plenty of sweet potatoes and Irish potatoes from the root cellar in the calf barn. Papa would like that, too. That could be fun, also. My thoughts rambled.

Wesley was still standing in front of the fireplace, waiting for the fire to start up, when he said, "Yo Mama done said dere's plenty to eat in da ice box. If Rosa don' come, I'sl cook you some'in. Dat ain't no trouble."

"I'm not worried, Wesley, I can find plenty to eat. Cathrine and Miz Mazie will feed me!"

He looked at me sitting in the big chair and explained, "I knows dey will, but ya oughts not ta go ta Helen and Papa's, Billy. Dey don got nothing, and dey's gittin ready to move from heah."

"Move? When are they moving?" I asked. "Dad didn't tell me anything about that, and Papa sure hasn't said anything either! Dammit! Why don't they ever tell me what's going on around here."

He rubbed his head with his hand and said, "I doubts Papa knows jist yet, but Mista Carl toll Alex and me ta take da big truck and hep 'um move da day fo Christmas. Helen sez hers and Papa's gon move ta town wit her sister. And Billy, yous aught not be cussin like dat. Yous ain't old enough to talk dat a way!" I dropped down in the big chair, leaning over with my elbows on my knees and my chin in my hands, watching the fire grow into big, roaring flames, angry that everyone treated me like a little kid and never told me what was happening around me. The kitchen door slammed, and Wesley had left to go home.

"Dammit!" I yelled out, "This old house is awful! I hate this son of a bitch," and I kicked the fireplace screen with my bare foot. It folded and the iron side fell against my shin. I hopped around on my other leg, stopped, pulled up my pant leg and found blood oozing from the skinned spot. Looking away from the red blood, I rubbed it with my hand until it stopped hurting, and until the blood was gone. Quickly, I rubbed my hand on my pant's leg hoping to get the red cleaned from my hand. Maybe the fireplace screen falling on my shin was an omen, or maybe punishment. Maybe I needed to stop cursing. Wesley might have been right.

For a few seconds, I waited for the Big House to make some sort of sound, maybe fussing at me, like everybody else did.But everything was quiet—a lonely, dead silence, and very still. Me and the Big House, just the two of us. That's all.

Everybody had left. They had gone.

My time to teach Papa anything was almost gone, too.

CHAPTER 33

I knocked on the Gaspard front door. No one came, so I went around to the back porch, where I could see through the window, and I saw Cathrine and Papa sitting at the kitchen table. I went up the steps and opened the door. Papa smiled big, and Cathrine looked surprised when she saw me, exclaiming, "I thought y'all went to Texas!"

"No, I didn't wanta go. I'm gonna stay home."

"You gonna stay in the Big House all by yourself? I don't believe that," and she laughed out loud at the thought.

Papa blurted out, "Me neitha, cause he jist a cry baby, anyway." That didn't sound like Papa, but he broke wind in front of Cathrine a few days ago, so who knows what's going through his head right now. He never asserted himself that way. He looked at Cathrine, laughed and started teasing, "Billy, gon be cryin fo moanin, cryin like a big ole baby in da middle of da nite," and he started pointing his finger at me, laughing, causing me to hate him at that moment.

"Ah, shut up, Papa," then I asked Cathrine, "How's 'smarty' doin?" Before she could reply, I said, "Cathrine, I'm sorry I haven't been able to be here for the past couple of days." I knew that I had neglected my part of the bargain to teach Papa. I knew also that Cathrine was in charge anyway. She was doing most of the work, and she could do more with Papa than I could.

She sat up in her chair and said, "Well, Papa, show Billy what you can do," and she handed him a little book.

He opened it to the first page and started reading very, very slowly. Cathrine had to help him with every other word, though both of them were very proud. I asked, "Cathrine, can he write his name, yet?"

Papa looked at me, fussing, "Billy, ma name ain't Nick, lack ya done toll me. Cathrine say ma name is Isaac Vead. I knowed dat all da time. Ya jist don lied to me. Ya jist a big lying crybaby," and he started laughing again.

I whined back to him, "Aw, Papa, I didn't tell you your name was Nick. You just didn't understand what I was saying." I remembered the snow on Thanksgiving Day and how angry he became when I told him "Papa" was his *NICKname*.

Cathrine was laughing out loud by then and said, "Oh, don't get on with that. He knows his real name now and he can spell it."

I said, "He can't either," and I looked at Papa, demanding, "Spell it for me, smart aleck."

He looked out of the window and put on a thinking frown, and slowly spelled,

"I-S-A-A-C V-E-A-D."

I looked at both of them, then said to Cathrine, "I can't believe it! You're the only one who could get him so far along! That rascal's gettin smart!" and I thumped him on his head. He frowned and smiled his good friend smile. He was proud of himself.

Cathrine stood up and said, "Well, we have just a few more days. They're moving next Tuesday."

"Papa, what are you gonna do in town?" I asked.

He looked at Cathrine and then at me and said, "I gotta gits me a job, an hep Mama." I then realized that he did know that they were leaving Shirley in a few days. Everyone knew it except me. Again, I had been left out completely.

"Well, you've got a lot of work to do before we let you go to town! Yeah, a city boy, Papa, that's what you're gonna be, a real city slicker! Nobody'll know you when you come back to visit at Shirley!" Papa grinned from ear to ear, and I figured he liked the idea that going to town would make him different. But it was Cathrine who was making him different!

I told them that I had to go see Alex. Closing the kitchen door behind me, I remembered that Mrs. Mazie wasn't in the kitchen.

I stepped onto the porch at Alexs and Veesy's house and had raised my hand to knock on the door when Alex opened it, asking, "Wat's up, Billy?"

"You know Mama and Dad are gone to Texas?" He was shaking his head *yes*, and I told him, "I need a ride to a party on the other side of town tomorrow night. Can you take me in Dad's truck?"

"Sho, I can do dat. Do I hav'ta pick ya up afta da pawty?"

"Yeah, after about two or three hours."

"Dat ain't no trouble, Billy, I can sho do dat, I sho can. Wat time ya gotta go?"

"Come about six tomorrow evening, and you can pick me up at about nine. I know the way there, and I really appreciate it."

"Okay, see ya bout six, at da Big House," and he opened the door into their house.

That was done. I had a way to the party, and Alex seemed really glad to do it, my big friend.

I walked slowly home and missed Pal beside me, but I guessed that Wesley had him out in the milkshed. After crossing the porch, I put my hand on the doorknob and thought again, "Why am I going in here? There's nobody home!" The kitchen was cold. I got a handful of Saltine crackers out of the big tin can that sat in the corner on the cabinet, poured a glass of milk, and went into the dining room. The fire was still going fairly well, and I thought about hot tea, and the first cup I had ever had, only a week or two ago. I wondered if Margie and Jerry were having a cup of *hot tea* right then. Was my new nephew crying? It didn't matter. In fact, nothing mattered except how quiet everything was, and I had nothing to do. Was I the only person in the world with nothing to do, in a great big, cold, old house, completely alone? Was I the only person who lived so close to a silver ghost of an airplane with all of its mysterious secrets, its demons, a wrecked plane with no wings, lying only a few yards away? And there wasn't a door on this old house that locked. In fact there wasn't even a lock on any door in this old house. Was I the only person who cared if this old house could be locked or not? I figured that I was, at least at that moment. I crumbled my crackers into the glass of milk and went to the kitchen to get a spoon, figuring that crackers and milk would be my supper, since I wasn't going back to the Quarters that evening.

I put a spoonful of crackers and milk in my mouth, and looked into the fire, figuring I needed to haul in a lot of wood and stay up as late as I could. Mama had bought me two new comics before she left, and I could read them a couple of times. Then I would find some quilts and make a pallet, and maybe make Pal come in, though he didn't like to come in the house. Besides, he always smelled bad, and if he warmed up by the fire he would really stink up the place. Mama would be able to smell him when she got back a week later. I went out on the porch and started hauling in the firewood. There was plenty after the fourth load, so I sat back down in the big chair and looked into the fire.

Only a glimmer of daylight was showing through the windows in the dining room when Wesley came into the kitchen with the bucket of cream, placing it in the icebox. He called to me from the kitchen, "I's goin home, Billy. Le'me know if ya needs anythang!"

I said nothing, but thought, "Needs anything...needs anything!" I didn't know if I needed anything or not. I just turned twelve, and my whole family was gone. All I had left was this terrible old cold house, and an ole yellow dog that smelled bad, and wouldn't come inside with me. I heard the kitchen door slam closed. The sound echoed through the dark, empty house and I figured it was trying to say something to me, like, "Yes, we're completely alone now, all by ourselves, just you and me, Billy, and it's gonna be dark in a little while."

With the fresh logs I had placed in the fireplace, the fire started blazing again, but this time the shadows made by the firelight seemed different, odd and crazy, making me feel strange and uncertain. I watched as they crept across the floor, quickly hiding under the big server and beneath the dining table. They seemed unhappy, a little angry and sneaky. Every now and then would dart from their hiding place, then completely vanish, but never dancing across the room as they usually did. The big dining room was changing, becoming so damp and dark, and suddenly it began turning into a dungeon just like the ones I had seen in the picture show. I couldn't move, and my heart started racing as I remembered *Black Beard*, his dugeon, and how evil and mean he was. I imagined that any minute I would see a wooden-legged pirate with an eye patch and a long, bloody sword come charging into the room through the door opening directly onto the porch, swinging his sword and a long piece of heavy chain, all at me. At me—and I couldn't even move my arms and legs. The walls and even the ceiling started moving like they were breathing in and out, gasping for air. I set my glass of milk and crackers on the floor by my chair and put my hands over my face and eyes. My heart pounded harder, and I could barely take air into my nose, my breathing had almost completely stopped, just as I heard a wooden leg clopping on the porch floor, getting closer and closer to the door. With my hands pressing harder over my eyes, I waited, expecting that he would beat me with the chain, and hang me high onto the wall that was gasping for breath, too, mocking me. The air rushing in and out became louder while his steps came closer to the door.

The chains rattled along the floor, and I knew they would break open my skin when he beat me and wrapped them around me. I would bleed bright red blood from everywhere, my wrists, my neck, my ankles, and he would break both my arms, and crush the side of my face…and…my…head, letting my brains fall out. He would laugh out loud each time his sword hit me. Over and over, he would hit me and laugh and laugh. And there would be no one, no one to help me, to pick up my brains in a shovel and bury them. Bury my brains! No one would bother…to bury…my brains.

He would laugh again and again, then unleash his rats and let them eat at my toes, and scratch their way up my legs and body. They would feast on my eyes first, then, they would drink the warm red blood from the flesh of my face. After a little while, he would drag my body to the two big oaks, and cram it into the cockpit of that silver ghost. He would laugh out loud, over and over again, and call out to the demons living inside the plane, giving me to them, and commanding the rain and snow to come, to make the rest of me rot away and disappear. No one would ever find me, and I would be another secret hidden there forever, deep in the cold body of the silver plane…just another terrible secret hidden in the demon under the oaks.

I jumped up from the big chair, ran to the light switch and flicked on the light. I ran to the kitchen and turned on the light there. Then, I ran through the dining room at full speed, to the family room, to the great hall, to Mama and Dad's room, to Jerry's room and to the living room, and turned on all of the lights. Then, I ran onto the back porch and the front porch and turned on all the lights there, too. I felt better and everything around me seemed better. Panting and gasping for air, I went back to the brightness of the dining room, and fell into one of the big chairs in front of the fireplace. My feet were cold, and I could see my big toe sticking through a hole in my sock. My heart was still racing, and after just a second there was a loud knock on the kitchen door. I jumped up from the big chair and faced the door into the kitchen, almost falling into the screen in front of the fire. Black Beard had come, even with all the lights on, and he was going to get to me from the kitchen instead of the dining room door to the porch. My heart was pounding harder; I could hear it in my ears, but I quickly picked up a stick of firewood, knowing that I had to fight him as hard as I could before he would run me through with his sword and bind me in those cutting chains.

"Billy, ya in dare? You, okay?" It was Alex's voice. I ran through the kitchen and opened the kitchen door to the porch. Alex was standing there and asked, "Wat 'cha got all dese lights on fer? We can see da Big House lit up all da way ta da Quarters! Is som'um wrong?"

I shrank into a little, tiny kid and lied, "Nah, I'm just playing around. I wanted to see how everything looked with all the lights on!" I was holding my breath.

He chuckled, smiled, and said, "Yeah, I don blame ya. Da Big House really looks good all lit up like dis. Ya oughts to keep it disaway evy night lack somebody's heah. Dat's good." He looked at me straight in the face and asked, "Ya au right?" I shook my head *yes*, but said nothing.

He turned around, went down the steps, turned the corner at the screened porch, and called back to me, "Let me know if ya needs some'in!" I closed the kitchen door tight and sat at the little table, finally letting my breath explode into the cold kitchen. The night was black through the kitchen windows while I moved slowly into the dining room.

I believed the old house did look good all lit up. It seemed a bit happier, and it wasn't quite as lonely, so I figured I would keep it lit up every night till my folks came home.

I left my comics on the big chair and ran up to my room as fast as I could. Throwing the quilts back, I crawled in bed with my clothes on, and pulled the heavy covers over my head.

Closing my eyes tightly, I shivered.

And I wondered.

CHAPTER 34

I could faintly hear someone calling my name, and then I felt a hand on my shoulder. I opened my eyes in the darkness under the quilts, and the hand shook me, "Billy, wake up!" My heart had almost stopped, and I held my breath until I realized that the voice was Wesley's. He leaned over me; demanding again, "Wake up! I got 'cha some breakfas' cookin." I pushed the quilts back and looked at him. "Come on, I's gotta go get started milkin." I managed to get out an okay, and started to get out of bed. He looked at me and ask, "Wat's all dease lights on fer, and you don slep in yo clothes? Billy, ain't notin' wrong, is it?"

Lying, I mumbled, "No, nothing's wrong. I thought the house looked good, and I decided to leave them on."

He smiled a little, and started toward the stairs, "Com on down fo yo breakfas'gits cold. Evythangs gon be awright." I still had on my socks, and I hurried down to the kitchen, and to the bathroom.

Wesley had made French toast that was still in the skillet on the stove. That reminded me of the bad trick I had played on Mag a while back, and I wondered if she was making French toast in the kitchen at Bubenzer that morning. I poured a cup of coffee, sat at the table, and asked, "Wesley, it's still dark. What time is it?"

He looked over to the icebox at the airplane clock on top, and said, "It's almost five. I needs to git going. Da cows sho don lak to wait none."

I thought to myself, "I can tell the time. I just wanted you to know it was too early to get me up. I don't have school for two weeks," then I told him, "I just want one slice, please." He put a slice of toast on a plate and covered it with cane syrup, then set the plate it in front of me. I leaned with my hand on my cheek and my elbow on the table and looked at my breakfast. I seldom ate this much for breakfast, especially at five o'clock, thinking again, "What in the world am I gonna do all day?" He put the other two slices on another plate, really covered them with syrup and butter, and sat down. We ate our breakfast and drank our coffee. I figured he just wanted somebody to come to the kitchen, and he was lonesome, too. I asked him, "Anybody coming to help you this morning?"

He shook his head *no* and asked, "Ya wan' ta hep me?"

"Yeah, I guess so. I'll take care of the horses and clean the stalls."

We finished the French toast and coffee, picked up our plates and took them to the sink. "Don' worry bouts dis mess. I'sl clean the kitchen later. I don told Rosa not to come till Toosday. Dere's a plenty fer ya in da icebox, and things ain't bad 'round heah, jist yet."

That was okay with me, but I wasn't about to heat up the ole stove and warm up any food from the icebox, figuring that I could get by on crackers and milk and every now and then, I could beg something at Cathrine's house. Aunt Colleen would give me some teacakes, too, if I would go home with J.B.

Wesley went on to the milkshed, and I hung around the warm stove for a few minutes before getting my boots from the porch. I had noticed he had gone throughout the house turning out the lights. It wasn't really very cold, but I put on my heavier jacket and went to the barn. Looking toward Bunkie, I saw that the sun was beginning to peek over the treetops, and the air was cool and brisk. Our four riding horses in the barn were waiting to be let out into the walking pens, but quickly I curried each one and brushed their manes. I removed the droppings left through the night, and put out fresh hay in each manger. They would come back to eat the hay later in the day, and around five o'clock I would give them a few ears of corn before locking them in their stalls for the night.

The party at Sarah Grace's house came to mind. I was anxious to go to the party, maybe seeing some of my school friends, but also, I wanted to get away from the plantation for a little while. Alex would come at six to take me to the party, and Christmas Day would be here on Wednesday. I needed to help Cathrine with Papa every day, and my folks would be home on Thursday. Lining up everything in my mind helped me realize there was a lot for me to think about, and a lot for me to do until my folks came home. And maybe Sarah Grace's party would give me something else to think about beside the silver plane and being alone in the Big House. I went to the milkshed and told Wesley that I had finished the chores at the barn, and I was going to the house. Having decided to go to the bayou pasture to look for a little Christmas tree, I hurried past the silver plane, never looking in its direction. Pal whined, then he barked a couple of times, but I scolded him to shut up and be quiet. Just through the gate, I found a small cedar tree, cut the top out of it with my knife, and took it back to the house.

I felt sure that I could find the old Christmas lights that we had used for as long as I could remember. I wanted a Christmas tree, which didn't have to be big and fancy, but just enough to remind me that Christmas was coming. Cathrine and Papa could come see it tomorrow, and we could have a little party with crackers and maybe some Donald Duck orange juice, just the three of us. I slipped my boots off on the porch, and went through the kitchen into the dining room, deciding that the end of the dining table nearest the fireplace was the best place for the tree. In the big closet in the upstairs hall I found the old lights, and I brought them down along with about a half-dozen colored glass balls, and some tinsel left over from the year before. I put the little tree in the tall vase that always sat in the middle of the dining table. It was perfect. Carefully, I strung the lights on the tree, discovering two of the bulbs were burned out, but the *Santa Claus* bulb was still glowing. It was the prettiest of all the bulbs, and Mama said that it had probably been made in France a long time ago. Every Christmas, I had studied Santa closely, and loved the little bulb since I was a kid. The detail of Santa and the bright, shiny colors were as fascinating and magical as Christmas itself. I hung the glass balls on the tree and carefully laid the tinsel over its branches. Backing away, I looked at all of it very carefully, thinking that it was a fine Christmas tree, and I was proud of it. It wasn't big, and it wasn't like one we usually had, but it was there in front of me, in the dining room where I would stay till Christmas, and I could look at it any time, even during the night if I wanted to. It made the dining room beautiful, alive and filled with color, but it was still cold. Rays of the early morning sun coming through the Eastern window lit up the wall on the far side of the big room. The colors of the bulbs and the smell of fresh-cut cedar all around me seemed suddenly to bring the Big House to life again. It was not so lonely, and not so cold, and I was glad.

Wesley hadn't made a fire in the fireplace, but the little tree stood bright and colorful in the cold room, like the centerpiece in a grand ballroom where a great event was going to happen. Gently touching a deep blue, shiny glass ball with the tip of my finger, I spoke softly, "Y'all are going to be my life, and you'll have to stay with me till my folks come home, so shine bright and make me feel good every day. Now, don't y'all be lonesome, and don't be scared, either. Everything's gonna be okay." Nothing moved, and I heard no sounds, but I waited for a second, smiled to myself, and felt a lot better.

I hurried to Mama's bedroom, and my Christmas presents were there on her sewing machine, where she had told me they would be. I looked at each one. The big one was a shoebox—shoes, I guessed. Another one was a flat box, and the third one was small and also a flat box, probably socks. As I looked at the brightly colored paper, I told myself, "Mama won't know if I open them now or wait till Christmas Day," so I picked up all three and took them to the kitchen, where it was a little warmer. The shoebox looked the most tempting, so I pulled at its strings and tore the paper away. Inside was a pair of brown leather slippers. I had never had any slippers, so I put them on right then, over my socks. They felt pretty good, much better than just the socks that I wore in the house all winter. I picked up the bigger flat box and shook it. There was almost no sound, so I tore the string and paper off, and opened it. It was a pair of wool pants. I hated wool, but they looked nice. Besides, they were in a box from Godchaux's Department Store in Bunkie, so they had to be good. I started opening the last box. Socks, I thought, just aren't very exciting. I could buy those myself at the company store on Main Street in Bunkie. I lifted the top and opened the white tissue paper. Gloves! Leather Gloves! My own leather gloves, and they had a thin layer of brown wool in them. They fit a little bit big, but I figured I would grow into them. Mama really knew how to buy presents for me. But in the bottom of the box, lay a small envelope, and I wondered if I should open it. Mama had told me to wait till Christmas to open my presents, and I gave her an oath that I would, but I picked the envelope up. Recognizing her handwriting, I forced a smile, and read out loud the one little word written on it: *Billy.* I turned it several times trying to decide to open it or not, when I suddenly caught the aroma of Coty powder. Pushing my finger under the flap, I pulled the card out. On the front was a Santa Claus in his sleigh pulled by eight tiny reindeer, flying away from the roof of a house where a chimney was letting out a curling stream of blue smoke. The big moon was glowing brightly, the stars were sparkling in the night sky, and the snow was shiny and fresh. At the bottom of the picture, were the words, "To my son, at Christmas." I sniffed, then said out loud, "I'm sorry, Mama, I'm sorry I didn't wait till Christmas," and I could feel the tears coming. I opened the card and Mama had written: "I know you will open these before Christmas, and that's okay. I wish you were with us. We love you, Dad, Mama, Jerry, and Mickey." Just before I closed the card, a tear spattered onto the pretty little house, and when I raised the card to smell the Coty powder again, the aroma was gone! I didn't want the liar in the mirror in the fireplace mantle to see me crying, so I wiped my eyes with the heels of my palms, wondering out loud, "I wonder what they're doing right now. Maybe I should have gone with them." My stomach turned over.

I took my new slippers off, put everything back into the boxes, and took them to the dining room, where I tried on the trousers. "Yeah, Mama, they're okay! I'll wear them to Sarah Grace's party tonight!" I placed the boxes on the table around the Christmas tree, looked at my Santa bulb, bright and colorful, and spoke out loud, "Thanks, Santa, I like 'um all. You did a good job again this year, buddy. Thank you, too, little Christmas tree!" I left the dining room to find my boots and windbreaker on the porch; then, I headed for the Gaspard house, knowing that it was about the right time for Mrs. Mazie to be taking her freshly baked bread out of the oven. It was getting close to the time, too, for Mister Alfonse to eat his dinner, and I hoped Mrs. Mazie would offer me a plate.

I rounded the corner at the hedgerow, wondering if I should invite Cathrine to my Christmas party. I had made up my mind already that I was going to give Papa my new green windbreaker, and tell Mama that I had lost it, or that Pal had hauled it off somewhere. I could think of something before they returned from Texas. Papa and Helen were moving on Tuesday, which was the day before Christmas, and I figured Mama would never see Papa wearing my new jacket.

When I reached the tool shed, there were several men cleaning, sharpening and oiling the cane knives, getting them ready to store away in the plantation shop until next cutting season. I walked over to the group of men and said *hello.* One after the other, they each said, "Hi," but continued to talk and joke with each other.

Gilbert Frank was standing, telling the group, "Yeah, when I gits out dere and gits me uh job, I's gon send fer Emma," while others in the group just nodded or grunted, some probably doubting Gilbert Frank and even wondering what he was talking about.

"See y'all, later," I said quietly, knowing that I wasn't going to become a part of the conversation. Besides, it looked like to me that they all became a little quiet and the talking slowed, making me think that something in the conversations might have been some sort of secret they didn't want me to hear.

"See ya, Billy," I heard over and over while I walked away, then the sermon from Gilbert Frank picked up again, along with the joking, the grunting, and the laughter.

I wasn't sure about anything right then. My thoughts were rambling about, and I was trying to figure out what Gilbert Frank meant when he said, "When I get out there and get me a job." That was somehow connected to what Dad had told Alex a couple of days ago in front of his truck, when Jerry was taking Mickey and me to school. I would ask Alex about it when he would take me to Sarah Grace's party. It was grown-up talk floating around the plantation, and if I didn't listen carefully or get close to someone like Alex or *bigmouth* J.B., I would be left out completely.

Mrs. Mazie had a good dinner—white beans with rice and a piece of sausage cooked in them. She even put a little butter on my roll. Finally, I thought, it looks like Mrs. Mazie's getting to like me a little, and besides, it seemed like she didn't argue and complain as much as she used to. And when she spoke French, I could catch onto a few more words if she didn't talk too fast.

That day was the last time Cathrine was going to help Papa, and it was Papa's last day to help Mister Alfonse in the barns. Having thought about it for a while, I decided not to invite Cathrine to my little Christmas party at the Big House, figuring that Papa would like that better, and, besides, I wanted to show Papa the wine hidden in the back of the garage storage room. Also, I had a present for Papa, but I didn't have a present for Cathrine, but on second thought, maybe I could find a scarf in my sister's bureau drawer. I needed to give Cathrine a present; she was always so good to me. I should have already thought about that, but I would do it later, and give the present to Cathrine on Tuesday, the day before Christmas. That was a good plan. It was okay.

After we ate our dinner, we talked in the Gaspard kitchen for a little while longer; then, I told Cathrine I needed to go home and see if I could help Wesley. Walking slowly on the dirt road toward the Big House, Pal bit at my hand or tried to lick it, and barked at me, wanting to fight or play. He had been digging again after the armadillo early that morning before I got out of bed, because I could hear him barking at the front steps below my windows. I figured he would catch it one of these days and he would be sorry. My ole yellow dog was tough, really tough, but armadillos were tough, too.

Walking slowly, I rounded the corner at the hedgerow and crossed the yard to the fishponds. Sitting on the grindstone with Pal sitting close beside me, I looked across the big yard to the oaks in front of the house, then down the row of tall pecan trees, and back to the Big House itself. It appeared so old and tired, and all that I could see in every direction was a quiet and cold loneliness. There was no life, no people, no one anywhere in sight, and no sounds could be heard. I hated everything I saw, and I hated the way I felt.

Pulling my jacket tightly around me, I trembled in the cool air, seeing the stillness that lay all around us. No soft breeze, or gently swaying branches, only loneliness, and soft, dim shadows from the big oaks as they reached across the wide yard. I heard myself sigh long and patiently just before a chill shot through me, making me tremble again, knowing that in the Big House the usually warm fireplaces were cold, and the rooms were dark and hollow in their emptiness. Our family, the old Kings, too, was gone. We were alone now, for sure, just the two of us again, the old King and me. And the usual beauty and excitement of our magical kingdom were nowhere to be seen.

I hugged Pal as hard as I could, he grunted, and then he licked my wet cheeks. In a second, we both turned, setting our stares again toward the Big House.

It had fallen into a deep sleep.

CHAPTER 35

Around three o'clock, I lit a fire in the kitchen stove and filled the reservoir at the end of the stove to heat some water. I put two big pots of water on the open burners for it to get really hot, and hoped that it would be plenty to take a good hot bath. I went out to the barn and put a few ears of corn in the mangers for the horses and locked them in their stalls for the night. Then I went to the milkshed to see Wesley, telling him that I had taken care of everything at the horse barn and I was going to a party in town.

With his hand propped on his hip, he looked at me and asked, "Ya ain't gon take da truck, is ya, Billy?"

"No, but I'm gonna leave the kitchen and dining room lights on when I leave about six, so don't turn them off."

Then he asked, "Alex gon drive ya?"

"Yeah, don't worry, Wesley, I'm not gonna take Dad's truck, don't worry," and I thought again, "Everybody thinks I'm a kid, and Dad has everybody watching every move I make."

When I finished bathing, I noticed the pile of dirty clothes getting big in the corner of the bathroom. I thought about putting them in the hamper, but the bathroom was cold, and I was beginning to shiver. Rosa would wash them on Tuesday when she came, and I would make sure to give her the Christmas present from Mama. Naked, I ran all the way up to my room. Shivering in the cold, I managed to dress quickly, putting on my new dark gray wool pants, and a starched and ironed white dress shirt. The pants matched my wool sport coat, as well as if Mama had bought them together. The pants itched some, but I figured I would get used to it in just a little while.

Looking down at my brown shoes, I remembered Jerry said never to wear brown shoes with black or gray pants, so I put on my black shoes. That did look better. I sang under my breath, "Thanks, Jerry. You're right! You're a doll, and 'I loves ya honey,'" and I wished that she would come home for Christmas. I would like that.

It had been dark for almost an hour, and I hadn't heard the Robin Hood clock strike. I figured it probably had run down and I needed to wind it and get it started again, but I could do that little job later. I was standing at the wide kitchen window feeling excited about Sarah Grace's party when Wesley came in to tell me that Alex was waiting out in the truck.

"Thanks, Wesley, I'll see you in the morning. Don't turn off the lights!"

and I hurried to the outside. Alex had already moved to the passenger side so I could drive.

The truck whined when I changed gears and we quickly reached the gravel road going to town. Glancing toward Alex, who was dressed up in a brown suit with a white shirt, I asked him the big question, "Alex, what did my dad mean Wednesday morning when he told you, 'if he can do better out there, then I don't blame him for going?'"

He looked over at me, frowning, "Billy, I don' know wha'chu talkin bout! Why, did ya hear som' in?"

I could tell he was lying, "Well, I didn't hear anything special, but I did hear Gilbert Frank tell some other men that when he gets a good job, he was gonna send for Emma."

Alex looked over at the speedometer and said, "Boy, ya betta slow dis thang down, or ya gon git us bote kilt on dis gravel road."

I looked at the speedometer, which was showing only about twenty-five miles an hour, and I said to him, "You can tell me. I'm not gonna say anything to anyone." I could tell he knew more than he was letting on, and just wanted to divert my attention with that *"going too fast"* crap.

He thought for a few seconds, then said very seriously, "Now Billy, I'sl tel ya, but don'chu tell nobody, specially J.B. or Gilbert Frank, and ya gotta make sho, else I'sll git in a lotta trouble."

"Okay, that's fine. I promise I won't say anything to anyone."

He straightened up in the seat, adjusted his hat firmly on his head, and looked straight to the road in front of us. His lips parted but nothing came out. I waited while he took a deep breath, and he finally began, "Ya know, Billy, dey say our whole contry is'a changin, and dis ole plantation is changin, too. Look at all dem new tractas we's gittin. Yo Daddy's workin wit' dat big tractor comp'ny now, and deys'll be makin a cane cutta purty soon dat'll cut mo cane in one day than fifty of us *hands* can do. Almost evybody on Shirley's been heah fer most of deir lives, or lived round heah close befo dey come to work fo yo daddy. Yo daddy too, say all dat's gon change. Job's are gon be gone and old people like Shine and Uncle Nick and po old Hoss'll be the onliest ones ta do da work dat's lef heah. Won't be much no how. One day, dey won't be no plantations like Shirley, uh Oakland uh Oak Hall. Deys'll jist be land rented out to otha big farmas wit deir big, fancy tractas. Dey ain't gon be no place fer all us folks to find da kinda work we's can do. Evybody's gotta do some'in, dough, to takes care of deys families and try ta make a livin."

"Dad's gonna take care of everybody. He's gonna do that."

He shook his head, looked at me, and said in a high-pitched voice, "Yo daddy can't do it by his- self, boy. He don' even own da land. He's jist a good farma ana kind man, and he'll do all he can, but po fella, he can't do nothin by hisself, specially wis no money and no land. Deys too many folks, a heap of 'um, and we's gotta have work to do, and b'sides, Billy," and his speech hurried, "we ain't want'n no otha folks takin care of us. We's needs jobs, and we's sho ain't no little churin. Nah, we ain't no little churin dat gotta be took care of."

I could see that he was beginning to show some anger about something, bad anger that I had never seen before, like it had been locked away somewhere for a long time, but I continued and asked him, "Well, what is Gilbert Frank talkin' about?"

He looked to the road in front of us, straightened his hat, took a deep breath and continued, "Well, it's gon take awile, but Gilbert Frank wants ta go to California and git some work. Dat's wat he means bout 'sendin fer Emma.'"

CHAPTER 36

Alex was right on that dark December night when he told me the secrets going around on Shirley Plantation. There were many secrets among many who lived there; some secrets developed into reality quickly, while others took years to eventually come about, and for new dreams to be realized.

In the middle of December in 1953, I came home from college for the Christmas holidays, my freshman year. By that time, Gilbert Frank, Emma and their two children had been in California for three or four years. Alex, Veesy, Bernice and Junior had left the plantation; also J.B., Leroy, Ellis and their families were gone. Other field hands from other plantations in the area had cut their roots, too, roots set deep into the history of the plantations around Bunkie, all hoping to find new lives in faraway places, and hoping also to never return to the sugarcane and cotton fields in Louisiana. That day, my dad asked if I wanted to ride to town with him to pick up some cow feed, and I happily said yes. Through the years, I had seen a multitude of changes evolving on the plantation with all of the new equipment that had come into place, and the loss of one family after another to better jobs and better living in California, Arizona, and New Mexico, very far from the plantations. Some years back, the Big House had been renovated with gas heat, a new kitchen, and another bathroom, all with running hot water. The stacks of firewood were gone, only two or three riding horses remained, and the milk cows were down to only two or three. But Rosa and Wesley were still there, still a part of everyday life in the yard and the Big House with Mama, my Dad, and my brother.

As Dad drove slowly through the Quarters on our short trip to town that day, I remembered my high school graduation day in May of 1953. Dad had told me early that morning that he would have to put Pal to sleep, for my old yellow dog could no longer suffer the agony that had taken over his life. Graduation day morning was cool and damp. I walked to my car, opened the door, and laid my suit coat on the seat, waiting for Pal while he limped from his bed in the garage to where I stood. He was thin, and his color had faded into a yellowish gray. Pain had almost completely enveloped him, evidenced by the way he slowly walked with one leg dragging badly. His big tail was no longer his symbol of strength and happiness when he saw me. Sitting on the car's running board, I watched and waited until he sat in front of me. I held his chin in one hand and rubbed his ears with the other, while he whined softly, a sound that I had heard a thousand times. We both knew that his fighting days were gone, and I never knew if he had caught the armadillo under the front steps of the Big House. But I knew for certain that he had been a great fighter, and a great lover, as evidenced through the years by the number of pups all over the plantation, who resembled him in color and stature. As he sat in front of me, I wished that I could have read his mind; I imagined he was telling me that he knew he was old now and he, too, had enjoyed our growing up together—the times when I was a small boy, when he would hold my hand in his mouth while we walked, never letting go until I was ready; how we so often rolled in the grass and wrestled; how he would always stand between me and whatever he construed as an imposing danger. I wished that he could read my mind while I remembered his undying loyalty with never a complaint, and how much I wished that every kid in the whole wide world could grow up with an *ole yellow dog* like him. I leaned forward, and wrapped my arms around his neck. My mind was flooded with a thousand memories, and sadness engulfed me as he kissed the wetness from my cheeks. We said goodbye. I was nineteen years old, and Pal was nearing fourteen.

I had asked my Dad to put him to sleep in his bed in the garage, and to leave him there. Late into the night, I buried my ole yellow friend under a Rose of Sharon tree, deep in a bed of daffodils, on the morning side of the Big House. I cried.

The plantation was vastly changed from the winter of 1946 to my Christmas visit in 1953. The dirt road through the Quarters had been graveled several years before, since the mules and horses had been sold off and the big barns stood empty, while the area around them was growing up in bushes and small trees. Mister Alfonse and Mrs. Mazie had retired and moved into town. Cathrine had married and moved away. Many of the houses on each side of the road were empty, their yards grown up in weeds, and volunteer trees growing against the walls. Some of the houses in the North Quarters had been burned as soon as they were vacated, and where the North Quarters once stood were now fields of sugarcane. What had once been a town, a source of life and livelihood for many, the plantation was like a broken shell, with forbidding jagged edges, laid wide open and completely empty, and abandoned by almost everyone whose life had suffered its rabid purpose. Never again would it vibrate as the focal endeavor of a deranged economic system, which kept a vast segment of humanity captive within its bounds. The silence and solitude along the dirt road now could be broken only by the startled gasp of those who had lived it all and survived.

"Dad, what's going to happen to Shirley and all of the other plantations around here?" I knew he had been a big part in the migration of the plantation field hands because he would allow the men to go find work and become established before they would return to the plantation to take their family to a new home in California.

When I asked him that question, he looked somewhat puzzled, probably believing that, at my age, I wasn't interested or even aware of what was happening in his life at his age. But he replied, "Everybody who ever lived here, black and white, lived an unusual life. We all have." I could tell that the question struck an emotional vein in him, but he continued as though he really wanted someone to listen, someone to hear him. "I doubt that any of us will ever realize what we have been a part of. We were a good part, or maybe a bad part, of the plantations when they were run almost as they were a hundred years ago. We were here when they started dying, and we will probably be here when they are only memories in the minds of a few old people." He sighed heavily, shook his head slightly, and whispered, "That's just the way it is—gone, gone forever." He looked into the distance through the truck window, across the flat, open fields, brown and dreary with wetness and winter. I cried inside for my dad, and for me, and neither of us said anything more.

That day, I believed every word my dad said, but listening to him and feeling his emotions—emotions of sadness so deep in the heart of this strong, aged man, who seldom expressed anything less than a strong and powerful will—made me sad, too. I felt sorry for him, and for me. I remembered how the sudden loss of my older brother in 1944 had changed him so much. It appeared to me that his life, after my brother's death, revolved only around his love for his job and the plantation, and his work in his church and the community. He lost, and never regained, the tender desire to merely hug his children or be a part of their lives while they grew from childhood to their youth, and finally into adulthood. Around the age of twelve or thirteen, I had decided that our ideas and our intentions were far removed from each other, and we had little or nothing in common to bind us to one another. Sadly, neither of us seemed to care, and my mind and heart told me on that winter day in 1953 that the time for building a father-son relationship had long passed and was gone forever.

***

CHAPTER 38

The truck's engine hummed softly as I drove down Main Street in Bunkie, to Sarah Grace's party, as Alex kept looking at the speedometer, waiting to slow me down or correct my driving. We passed the spot where Chief of Police Kojis always parked his shiny black Ford with the big chrome siren on top. I kept waiting for Alex to continue spewing out the secrets that I wanted to hear, but he had stopped. Sighing, I waited a few more seconds, then asked him, "You're gonna do the same thing as Gilbert Frank, aren't you?"

He raised his hand and took his hat off, then shook his head while rubbing the top of it, frowned, and fussed at me, "Boy, ya already knows more'an you aughts to; jist pay 'tention to your drivin! Ya dun pass the poleese and neva even taught 'bout how fass ya was goin. Ya gon get me put in jail, ya drivin dat a way." He looked straight ahead with his chin held high, and I knew that I had asked enough.

We went on to Sarah Grace's party.

I didn't want things to change. I liked them the way they were.

CHAPTER 39

As I turned the truck into the long driveway, I could see the colored lights on the Christmas tree in Sarah Grace's house, where she lived with her parents and several brothers and sisters. I knew most of them. I told Alex to pick me up at about nine o'clock.

Four or five girls came off the porch, and in the dim light I knew they were friends from school. Everyone smiled and said "Hi," over and over, and we walked together toward the porch. The girls were giggling and dancing around. When I asked Elizabeth who was there, she named two or three other friends from our class, plus two or three people from the sixth or seventh grades, my knowing most of them, too. When we reached the top of the steps at the porch, I could hear the music coming from a small radio sitting on a table behind the divan. I stepped inside the big living room, where ten or twelve more kids, mostly girls, were laughing and talking. There were five other boys besides me, and three were from the seventh or eighth grade. I knew them, but mostly by name only. None of them were my close friends like Eddie amd Harold. Everybody was talking and the girls were giggling, with the boys in one spot and the girls in another, each quickly glancing back and forth toward each other. I wondered about *spin the bottle* and when we would play. I licked my lips.

About that time, Elizabeth came over to me and asked if I wanted to dance. Someone had turned the radio to KALB, and a guy with a really loud voice was singing a pretty fast song. I didn't know about dancing with all the lights on, and I surely didn't know this song or the fellow singing so loud and hard. I told her okay, figuring that I needed at least to try, so we moved beyond the divan to the middle of the living room. I could feel all five hundred eyes in the room watching us. We stood there for a second before she pulled me closer to her, and we started moving our feet, short glides across the floor. She knew more about dancing than I did, and it sure was different from the way everybody danced at the Saturday Night Balls on the plantation, but her hand on the back of my neck felt really good, so soft and smooth. When she whispered in my ear, I could feel her warm breath on my neck. That felt good, too.

Smiling and looking into her sparkling blue eyes, I answered, "Yeah, I guess so, if everybody else does." I felt her hand move slowly across the back of my neck again.

She smiled and said, "Well, I'm going to play, and I hope the bottle points to you when I spin it," and her finger lightly touched my lips. I knew my face was turning red, and about then my new wool britches started itching. Time was really moving slowly, and I wished that this fellow would hurry up and finish his song. Besides, I had almost stopped breathing, and I needed to get some air into me. I figured what I really needed was to get my sister, Jerry, to teach me more about that kind of dancing the next time she came home.

A couple of songs later, and with four or five cookies in my tummy, Sarah Grace came in and stopped the music. I hoped she would open a window and let in some cool air, since I had started to sweat; Elizabeth, meanwhile, held the sleeve of my jacket, like I was going to run away or something.

Sarah Grace stood near the Christmas tree, raised a Coke bottle as high as she could, smiled, and slowly called out, "Who wants to play *spin the bottle*?" Every girl in the room squealed out, "I do, I do!" and waved their arms and hands in the air like they were in school and knew the answer to the teacher's question. The boys just looked back and forth at each other, and grinned. I licked my lips again, and smiled when I glanced at Elizabeth. She smiled back at me, making her blue eyes glisten brighter.

Otis elbowed me in the ribs, whispering, "You gonna kiss those girls, Billy?"

"Yeah, sure, if I get a chance."

"Okay. Everybody listen," and Sarah Grace named off several kids to sit on the floor in a circle: one boy, then a girl, another boy, then another girl until there were eight. The other kids just stood around and watched. Sarah Grace seemed to know what she was doing, and by then she was one of the four girls seated on the floor. "I'll spin first," and the Coke bottle turned about ten times and stopped on Elizabeth. I figured that Elizabeth would spin next without having to kiss anyone. Elizabeth spun the bottle around and it stopped on Otis, one of the older boys. I think I saw that Elizabeth was a little disappointed, but I was glad because I didn't want to be the first one to kiss somebody. I had only kissed my mama and my sisters and that was cheek kissing. Lip kissing was different, and I didn't know much about it, but I wondered how tight Elizabeth and Otis would close their lips. If the bottle stopped on me, I had already decided that I was going to close my lips as tight as I could. Otis kissed Elizabeth, holding his lips against hers for a second or two. The other kids clapped and called out, while I watched very closely, but I couldn't tell if they closed their lips really tight or not. Otis held the bottle up as though he had won the *big* prize, laid it back down and gave it a spin. It stopped on Rose Marie and everybody *wowed*. While Otis leaned over, Rose Marie put her arms around his neck and I guess she really gave him a good one, lasting for three or four seconds—in fact, probably longer. Watching closely again, it looked like they didn't close their lips very tight, and everybody wowed again and clapped. Otis clumsily fell back into his place in the circle, and fixed a crooked little smile across his face, all the while staring at Rose

Marie. I could tell he enjoyed kissing her a lot more than kissing Elizabeth. Rose Marie took the bottle and spun it around, and it stopped on me, on the opposite side of the circle from where she sat. I didn't move, so she leaned forward and gently kissed me on the lips. She had some pretty big lips and I did, too. It felt like kissing a half empty balloon. That wasn't bad, but she didn't hug me like she did Otis, making me believe she must have had a big crush on him.

I licked my lips again.

I could still feel my face being red and my darn wool pants itching me all over, even up around my neck, but I took the bottle and gave it a little spin, and was glad when it stopped on Elizabeth. That was the second time the bottle had stopped on her. She was sitting next to me, so I leaned over. She put her arms around my neck, tilted her head and gently put her lips to mine, holding the kiss for at least six or maybe seven seconds, a pretty long time, while I held my breath. My lips were as tight as I could get them, but I could feel something tickling my upper lip. I thought to myself, those damn wool britches were even making my lips tingle, but then I figured that Elizabeth hadn't closed her lips tight enough and maybe her tongue had slipped out a little. That thought didn't do much for me. She had skinny lips and I could feel her teeth on my lips when she pressed harder. Everybody wowed again. I hoped that on my next spin, if I got one, the bottle would stop on Elizabeth again. I could hear my heart beating inside my ears.

Before Elizabeth could spin the bottle again, Sarah Grace spoke real loud, "Billy, you, Elizabeth and Otis have to get out of the circle and let somebody else in. You've been hit twice."

"You've been hit twice." There was a ring to it that said something like "You lucky dog." Elizabeth smiled at me, and we both got up from the floor. I figured Elizabeth must have played spin the bottle a few times before that night.

Spin the bottle continued for about four or five more cookies and a big bottle of Nehi orange pop. The room had gotten warmer, and several people had gone out to the porch where the December air was cool and damp.

Elizabeth came over to me, was fanning her face with one hand, and said, "Let's go on the porch and cool off, Billy." That was a good idea; I thought that maybe the cool air might stop my wool britches from itching so much.

"Okay. Yeah, come on!" and I turned toward the door. Elizabeth took my hand, and I thought, "She's just like Pal, but a lot prettier for sure." Every chance Pal got he would bite at my hand or lick it, and would even lick my lips if I let him. Sometimes I did, but I didn't think I wanted to let Elizabeth lick them, but maybe that's what she was doing when she kissed me down on the floor. Anyway, I let her hold my hand as we left the living room to go to the porch, all the while hoping she wouldn't see my fingernails. They weren't as clean as my sister Jerry would have wanted them to be, but I did brush my teeth before I left home. But the cookies I had eaten? Maybe there wasn't any cookie dough stuck between them. I liked Elizabeth.

One of the older boys was kissing a girl down at the dark end of the porch, away from the light over the front door. I thought to myself, "Uh oh, I bet Elizabeth wants to kiss out here." I stopped and whined to her, "You know something? I bet my ride's waiting for me down at the road. I guess I need to go, Elizabeth."

"Billy, it's only about eight o'clock. The parties gonna last another hour at least. Stay here with me," and she made her eyes glisten again when she smiled.

"Yeah, I know, but I had to bum a ride, and I can't keep 'um waitin," and I turned to go down the steps. Still holding my hand, she pulled on it, and came up close to me. She put her arms around my neck and kissed me. I felt that little tickle on my upper lip again, and I saw that she had even closed her eyes, making me figure, "If I go down to the end of the road, I'll just have to sit on the ditch bank till Alex comes, and that would just get the seat of my new pants wet and dirty, but if I stay here, I'm gonna have to learn how to kiss real quick." I wondered again about my fingernails and my teeth, but figured I could sort of hide them in the dim light so Elizabeth couldn't see them.

Elizabeth and I sat in the swing and talked about school, our friends, and about Christmas. Every now and then, she would touch my cheek or push my hair back off of my forehead. Even in the dim light, I could see her getting prettier and prettier, and I wondered if she would be that pretty when school started again. I had known her for five years at least, and I had never noticed how really pretty she was. She leaned over and kissed me again, and I really felt that same little tickle on my lip. I wondered if she had read some *love* books or something. I needed to think about all of this kissing and holding hands, and I sure needed to figure out if I was doing it right, before we did much more. Maybe I could ask J.B. He could tell me, for sure.

"I just have to go, Elizabeth, or my ride will leave me," and I got up before she could catch my hand. Just when I reached the steps, Sarah Grace came out of the house onto the porch, and I told her what a great time I had. She said that she was glad I came and she would see me after New Years.

"Goodnight! See you later, Elizabeth," and I continued down the steps into the darkness, heading to the paved road. About halfway down the drive, in the black of the night, I felt myself strutting again, but this time to the sounds of some other fellow with a soft, smooth voice. Elizabeth said his name was Perry something or other, and he sang about *temptation*. I felt like I was going on twenty, and I was suddenly ten feet tall, again! Sarah Grace's party wasn't like the Saturday Night Balls, but it was fun and I knew I liked *kissing*. Laughing out loud, I started running toward the highway, all the while knowing that it would be almost thirty minutes before Alex would come to get me, but I could think about Elizabeth, and about kissing, while I waited.

CHAPTER 40

I stood at the end of the gravel driveway, throwing rocks across the highway into the open field, while every now and then a car passed by. After about ten minutes, I heard a horn, looked toward town, and recognized my dad's truck, with its three yellow cab lights on the roof, about a hundred feet away. It was moving very slowly and went off the road into the grass, then back on the road to the other side, then back to the right side again. I knew something was wrong, but after a few seconds it came to a sliding halt in the gravel drive. When I opened the door, I could smell something a lot stronger than the wine we had at the barbeque the week before. I looked at Alex. His eyes sparkled from the dashboard lights, but his eyelids drooped and he suddenly belched, then belched again. He shook his head and squinted his eyes at me, while I opened the door wider to let in some fresh air.

Barely able to talk, he begged, "Ya gon havta drive dis truck fer me, Billy. I's had a little too much ta night, but don chu tell Mista Carl." He smiled a tiny bit, belched again, smiled a little and said, "I's sho glad I found ya, Billy. Where ya been, boy?" and he moved toward my side of the seat.

Quickly, I put my hand over my nose to shut out the odor, telling him, "Move over here, and I'll go around." I got out of the truck and started around the rear. Alex must have left it in gear, and when he took his foot from the clutch, the truck lunged forward, hitting a mailbox a few feet away. Luckily, the engine died quickly, or the truck would have gone over the mailbox into the ditch. I hurried on around and jumped behind the wheel. Alex was already leaning against the passenger door window with his hat crushed around his head. I could hear him mumbling something and groaning. After backing up a little, I turned the switch off, got out again and went to the front to look at the broken post with the mailbox lying in the grass. I figured this probably happened a lot of times on the highway, but I stood it up against another mailbox, and hoped it would stand at least until the mailman came on Saturday. The mailman would probably report it to its owners, and if Sarah Grace said anything about it when school started, then I would tell her. I got back in the truck, started the engine and turned it around to head back to Shirley Plantation. Alex was snoring, and I rolled my window part way down to let out the awful smell.

With a big smile across my face, I thought about Elizabeth, while slowly moving my tongue across my lips, and I wondered if she liked the way I kissed. I felt different. I felt big. I felt good, and I was happy.

As we came to the railroad tracks in Bunkie, I decided I'd go along the North side of the tracks, go past Parrino's Drug Store for a couple of blocks, then cross the tracks toward Bordelon Motors, the Studebaker Dealer, knowing that Main Street would be crowded on a Friday night. Usually, on Friday and Saturdays nights everybody in the area would come to town to shop, and go to one of the picture shows. I thought about The Reo, which had been my favorite, but it had closed right after the war, but we still had the Bailey Theater, and the Joy, right across the street. Maybe that's what I should have done instead of going to a "kissing" party, but Mama was gone and couldn't drop me off to meet my friends at the show. Afterward, we would have gone to Walgreen's and sat around for an hour or so, walked up and down Main Street for a while, and later, our moms or dads would have picked us up. Sarah Grace's party was good, but I liked the Friday night movies and hanging around Main Street, too. Elizabeth was pretty, and she could really kiss, and I liked her. I really liked the way she kissed, and I liked it when she put her hand on my neck when we danced. My thoughts were going in all directions, and I laughed out loud. Alex never moved, and the truck smelled awful.

Leaving the busy Main Street area, I turned onto Shirley Road leading to the plantation, and began to wonder how I would get Alex out of the truck. If he could walk even just a little, I could get him to the steps and lay him on the porch floor. Veesy would be mad at Alex, I felt sure, and at me, too, I figured, and I didn't want to get tangled up with her. I drove very slowly down the dirt road and stopped at the walkway in front of their house. Looking toward the porch through the darkness, I decided I couldn't worry about Veesy and what she might do or say, and besides, I could handle whatever happened, feeling good that I was *big* now, and different, too. And I knew how to kiss a girl, a real kiss and a real girl. I hoped that maybe Elizabeth would like to kiss some more, real soon, if we could get together somehow.

Stopping the truck in the soft dirt, I jumped out and walked around it, up the walk onto the porch and knocked softly on the door.

"Who dat out dare?" came quickly from inside the room.

"It's me, Veesy, it's Billy. I need to talk to you."

The door opened quickly, and in the dim light, I could see Veesy frowning at me, asking, "Wur's Alex?" I pointed to the truck and told her that he had had a little too much. She shook her head and said, "Lawd, I don knows wat I's gon do with dat son of a bitch. Evy chaans he gits, he drink too much, an I gotta takes care of 'im." I hoped she wouldn't get any madder than those "that son of a bitch" words, but she had already started toward the truck, opening the door before I could stop her. Alex almost fell headfirst into the road.

She caught him, demanding, "Billy, ya gon hafta hep me wis dis bastard," and she started shaking him, calling, "Alex, Alex, ya betta wake up, boy. Wake up, Alex!"

He roused a little and dragging out his words, said, "Hey, Veesy, wat chu doin heah, Baby? I sho glad ta see ya," and his eyes slowly closed again.

She just continued to shake her head, turned, spit some tobacco juice on the ground, and said to me, "Ya see, he don loss his mine! Billy, git under his arm dere, ya gon has to hep me. He can walk good some, but he a big man." She grunted a couple of times, sighed and announced, "I oughts to jist leave 'im in da road. He ain't worth a shit!" Then she spoke to him again, "Alex, com on, hep yo sef, come on now. Ya can walk!" After struggling for a couple of minutes, we got him all the way into the house, and let him drop onto the front room bed. Veesy looked at me, frowned, and said, "Well, dis ain't da first time, and I don spec it'll be da lass. I aught ta cut his troat whiles he done passed out. He ain't worth nothin," and she went over and spit out her chew of tobacco into the fireplace, finishing, "Sho ain't...ain't worth a thang," and she wiped her eyes with the sleeve of her big white gown.

I could see why everybody in the quarters left her alone. Having wandered to the door, I was stepping onto the porch when I heard her call to me, "Wait jist a minute, Mista Billy. I wants to tell ya som'in." Veesy seldom had much to say to anyone, and when I heard her call me mister, I knew it was going to be something big, or she might even curse me out right there. I stopped, waiting for her to speak. She came out on the porch, closed the door behind her, then stood right in front of me, glaring into my face, "Mista Billy, I sho needs yo hep!" Her tone was a lot sweeter than what I was waiting for. As I held my breath, she put her hand lightly on my jacket right above my wrist, announcing very distinctly, "Mista Billy, I wan'chu to tell yo daddy dat I buys *rubbas* all da time, an Alex uses 'um on Bernice," and she wiped her eyes again with her sleeve.

"What?" and she started repeating her story. I quickly stopped her, "No, no, no! I understand what you're saying, Veesy! Are you sure, or are you lying to me?"

She squeezed my arm and said, "I knows fer a fack. I ain't lying to ya, Mista Billy. I jist can't stop 'im, an po Bernice, she cries all da time, and he sho gonna ruin her, po thang." Even in the dim light, I could see the tears shinning in her eyes when she added, "it gon kill me if som 'um ain't done real soon," and she started crying.

My knees went weak but I managed to mumble to her, "I'll do what I can, Veesy," and I thought, "She's a lying ole dog! Alex would never do that to his own daughter. She has to be lying." I turned and walked quickly to the truck.

The night was pitch black, but I could plainly see her long white gown, like a ghost with no head or feet, standing all alone, but helpless. The truck whined softly when I slowly pulled away. My hands were sweating and my britches were starting to itch me again.

In a nervous daze, I squinted when I walked into the brightly lit kitchen.

Without thinking, I turned the light off, and went into the dining room. There was my Christmas tree, happy with all of the colored bulbs and beautiful glass balls, waiting for me to come home. Three boxes from my family sat under the tree around the glass vase. I looked at Santa Claus and rubbed the little bulb with the end of my finger, not realizing how hot it was until I felt it burn me. The fireplace in the big room was cold and the familiar smell of cold ashes had spread through the room. I turned one of the chairs around so I could see my Christmas tree, and pulled a straight chair from the table to put my legs and feet on. I thought about Sarah Grace's party. It was great and I figured that someday I was going to other parties that would be even better. And Elizabeth was nice, and was the first girl I had kissed, my first real kiss, but I was a little bit scared, and wondered if I was ready for Elizabeth. But I certainly knew that I wasn't ready to take on the problems that Veesy had just laid on me. And my friend Alex, my *big* friend, had made me feel really bad, being drunk when he came to pick me up in my Dad's truck. I had a lot of things running wildly through my mind when I found myself sucking on the finger Santa had just burned. I told myself again that Veesy was lying to me, that she wanted to get Alex in trouble, and a story like that would do it if my dad ever heard it. I wondered about it all, and I didn't want to even think about all of the things that were handed to me that day—good things and bad things. Gently moving my fingers across my lips several times, and then holding my hand onto my forehead, I thought to myself, "I'm just a kid! Two days ago, I turned twelve, that's all, just twelve years old. I just want to be twelve right now, just twelve." Rubbing my burned finger again, and gritting my dirty teeth, I yelled to the top of my voice, "Even Santa Claus burned me tonight, the little b a s t a r d..." and I dropped into the big chair. Tired and sleepy, I took off my shoes and threw them one at a time through the door, and each tumbled all the way to the far side of the kitchen, slamming against the iron stove. Pulling my jacket collar tightly around my neck, I leaned my head against the wing on the chair back, and scratched my legs.

Sleep was coming fast, and I wished right then that I was four years old again and could cradle on my mama's lap. I wanted to smell the familiar sweetness around her, and feel her arms wrapped tightly around me. She would lean her face to mine while she sang, and I could touch her soft cheeks and black hair with my fingers, while looking into the blueness of her eyes. She would rock me, and as she had done a thousand times, sing softly to me, over and over, "Oh, where have you been, Billy boy, Billy boy? Oh, where have you been charming Billy...

CHAPTER 41

I awakened to the familiar sound of a fire being built in the iron stove in the kitchen. The dining room was in total darkness and I called out, "That you, Wesley?"

"You don got yoself in trouble, dis time, Billy. How much ya had to drink at dat pawdy lass night?" and an iron lid clanged nosily over the stoves firebox.

I was cold and stood up from the big chair, stretched and said, "I didn't have anything except a Nehi pop and a bunch of cookies."

Before I reached the kitchen door, he called back, "Well, I seed ya an' Alex come in. Po ole Veesy had to hep Alex agin, po ole soul. I figured dat ya and Alex musta bote had too much, wit' you done pass out heah in da dinin room."

I smiled, shook my head, and said in a whiney voice, "Wesley, I didn't pass out! I just went to sleep looking at the Christmas tree. That's all!"

"Well, ya know yo daddy'ud git all ova ya fer leavin dose ole Christmas lights on. Ya could burn down da Big House with dose old thangs. Dey needs ta be trowed 'way fore deys sets som'in on fire. Deys shocked me when I took de plug out de wall."

I huddled around the stove to get warm and yawned, "Well, that's all I had, and I wanted a Christmas tree."

He finished stoking the stove and put the last lid over the firebox, looked at me and said, "Don'chu worry none, I ain't gon tell Mista Carl wat 'chu did last night, but ya sho betta hope he don fine out from dem folks down in da Quawtas. Evybody already know it."

I thought to myself, "Just forget it, he's going to think whatever he wants, especially after seeing Veesy having to take care of Alex." I knew he wouldn't say anything to Dad anyway; maybe Veesy would, or even Alex if Dad would ask him, but Wesley wouldn't tattle on me.

He went to the cabinet, reached for the coffee and said, "Ya gon feel a lot betta afta ya gits a couple cups of strong coffee in ya. Is yo haad hurtin any? Maybe ya needs some food in ya."

I rolled my eyes back while shaking my head, "No, my head's not hurting, but I gotta get these pants off, they're itching really bad!"

He looked at them, smiling big, "Uh huh, I knowed ya can't wear 'um, when I sawed you yestiddy. Deys is wool. Ya be jist as well off if ya jist put'um in ole Pal's bed right now."

"Well, I'll have to wear them some. My mama gave them to me for Christmas. I'm gonna go to the bathroom and change my clothes."

179

He was getting the water onto the stove, and fussed again, "Ya oughts not opened yo presents yet, Billy. It ain't Christmas. Miz Florence'll sho be mad at chu. I heard what'cha told huh when dey left. An ya even done raised yo hand to huh like it wuz on da Bible."

I looked at him standing at the sink and whined to him, "Wesley, you're getting just like Hoss, fussing all the time! Just leave me alone, would you? And I'll do the barn again this morning. Will that make you happy?"

He put the kettle of water on the open firebox, answering, "Dat'll be good. I needs to ketch da truck to town t'day and buy me some groceries. It's pay day, an I sho is glad."

As I walked into the bathroom, I called back to him, "Yeah, everybody'll be going to town, I guess, except me," and thinking that there would probably be a party somewhere in the Quarters after "pay day." That would be good, and Papa and I could go, but I wasn't about to ask Wesley anything about it. He was like Mama about the Saturday Night Balls.

I let the horses out, cleaned the stalls, and went back to the house. The air was damp and the sky was cloudy, but it wasn't very cold, making me think that it would probably rain later in the day. Having opened a can of Donald Duck orange juice, I looked for the skillet to fry a couple of eggs and fix some toast, since my supper had been a few cookies and a bottle of pop. The skillet sat on the cooler end of the stovetop, but when I touched it, it was already hot. My burned finger started hurting again, and remembering that Santa had burned it a few hours before, I smiled to myself. My mind started going over all of the events that led up to my touching the hot Santa bulb, but I quickly decided I didn't want to think about any of it. All of it was too much to think about anyway, and my mind needed to rest from thinking about *kissing*, about *Elizabeth* and especially about what ole Veesy had told me. I went to the porch to get my jacket. Next to my heavy coat were hanging my old brown windbreaker and my new one. The old one finally fit me, and I decided that I liked the color better than Army green, so I took the green one to the dining room, folded it neatly, and put it in the box my slippers had come in. Papa's present was ready for when he would come later in the day. He would like the windbreaker, and he would like having a present to open. I found the little box that I had put one of my sister's scarves in, and went to the porch, where I slipped my old windbreaker on, then went down the porch steps. Pal met me at the bottom of the steps, happy to see me and wagging his big yellow tail. He smelled awful, so I kicked at him and scolded him to get away. I didn't want him to rub against me or I would smell like him all day. He dropped his tail and walked a little toward the garage, turned around and looked at me as if to ask, "What's wrong with you?" I picked up a rock and threw it at him. He went on into the garage and lay down in his bed by Dad's truck. I could see him watching me as I rounded the corner of the screened porch. The strong odor of a skunk told me that Pal had had a meeting with one late yesterday or during the night, something he did just about as often as digging for the armadillo. A skunk fight usually made him sick for a couple of days, and it would take about that long for him to clean up and get over it.

I trotted down the driveway and reached the toolshed. Several people, all dressed up, were meandering along the dirt road, waiting for the first truck to take them to the company store in Bunkie. Every other Saturday was payday, and the big truck usually made two or three trips back and forth to town, taxiing the workers. Everybody bought groceries right at the company store on Main Street, where they got paid and where they could buy everything from food to clothing. Most just charged what they bought, and the cost was taken out of their pay on the next payday. During the winter, when only a few workers were used in the fields, and some didn't have much pay coming to them, the company store would allow them to charge whatever they needed knowing that, come springtime, work would be plentiful and their debt to the store could be paid then. Houses in the Quarters and wood for the stoves and fireplaces were furnished by the company, and everyone had enough yard to have a sizable garden every spring and summer. The plantation carpenter did all of the repairs, and most of the houses were in fairly good shape. All had electricity furnished by the company, but no running water, which had to be hauled by bucket from the faucets on the north side of the dirt road through the Quarters. The houses were of different sizes, and my Dad usually tried to give the bigger houses to the workers who had the larger families. All houses had a front porch, which served as living space during most of the year, when the weather was warm. Some front yards were covered in flowers every spring and summer, and others were barren except for a few weeds. Each house had its own outdoor toilet. The entire Quarters were usually neat and clean, and if a worker didn't take care of his yard and house, others might complain and the complaints usually resulted in the yard getting cleaned up. The Big House still had its *fancy* outdoor toilet, now used by the workers around the yard, and had been used by my grandfather, who had refused ever to use the indoor toilet.

I passed the barns and turned to go into the Gaspard's yard, where Cathrine met me at the gate. She was going to town with her cousin and would probably spend the entire Saturday shopping and visiting her relatives in Bunkie. Christmas was only a few days away. I walked to the gate where she stood smiling, greeting her. "Hello, Miss Best Teacher in the whole wide world! Merry Christmas," I said, and I handed the little box to her. The box was unwrapped, but I had tied a red ribbon around it.

She looked at it and replied in her usual sweet way, "Oh, thanks, Billy."

"You have to open it right now," and I smiled, figuring she would like the scarf. I knew my sister thought it was pretty. Cathrine untied the string and opened the box while we stood at the gate, finally draping the scarf around her neck and tying it with a small knot on the side. Cathrine had blue eyes, and the scarf was almost the same color. It looked great, and I told her so. "Cathrine, I want to thank you for helping Papa. I could never have done what you have. Papa wouldn't listen to me long enough to learn anything. All he ever wants me to do is read *Superman* comics to him."

She laughed, adjusted her new scarf a little and continued, "Well, he still likes Superman, that's for certain. I just hope he won't forget everything before he can use it some. He plans to get a job as soon as they move to town, and I hope he can, but it'll take someone with a lot of patience." All the while, she was shaking her head with doubt.

"I'm gonna see if Dad will talk to Mister Juneau about letting Papa wash cars and fill gas tanks. Papa could do that if Mister Juneau would give him a try."

Cathrine smiled again when she spoke, "You know, I think he could probably handle that okay! I hope it works out for him."

"Well, I gotta go see Papa before he leaves for town. See you later." As I turned to walk away, she leaned against the gate to wait for her ride to Bunkie, while the pointed ends of her new blue scarf waved in the light breeze.

I figured that Helen and Papa had little or no money and were getting ready to move. Having saved my nickels and dimes for several months, and figuring that my aunts would give me plenty of money for Christmas, I had counted out four dollars and thirty cents and put the change in a small brown paper bag, which weighed heavy in the pocket of my windbreaker. I waved back to Cathrine and walked quickly along the dirt road, headed to Helen and Papa's house. Holding the bag of change tightly with my hand in my pocket, I quickly reached the steps to the little house, stomping noisily on the old, worn planks of the porch floor. Papa opened the door before I could knock, and the smell of smoke came tumbling toward me along with the aroma of fresh pomade. Papa was shiny clean and dressed in his Sunday clothes, ready to go to town.

"Papa, where's your mama?"

He pointed through the door, answering, "She right dare."

"It's *there*, Papa, not *dare*," and I hit him on the arm.

He grinned at me, "Yeah, I knows Billy," and I shook my head and wondered if all of Cathrine's work was going to be in vain.

"Helen?"

Helen was sitting in her rocker in front of the small fire, and the rocking chair would squeak each time it moved slowly, back and forth. "Com'on in, Billy," and I heard a sigh of tired sadness from my white-haired friend. I took the paper bag out of my pocket, unrolled the top, and took thirty cents out. Papa stood watching, waiting to see my next move.

After rolling the top back around the change, I handed it to her, telling her,

"Helen, I want you to have this when you go to town today," and I handed the thirty cents to Papa. His eyes lit up and he smiled as though I had handed him a ten-dollar bill.

Before I could say anything to Papa, Helen argued, "Oh, Mista Billy, you don gotta do dis. I got a little money I don saved up from when po ole Hoss died."

"Helen, that's my Christmas gift to you. And I wish you and Papa could stay right here on the plantation with all the rest of us," I said, knowing that wasn't possible.

She lowered her head and looked into the flickering little fire, sighing softly, "Me, too, Billy, but I knows we gon be betta off in town, specially if Papa can fine a little work to hep us along."

With as much hope as I could get into my voice, I told her, "Well, I'm gonna get my Dad to talk for him with a couple of people. Maybe someone will give Papa a chance. He'll find something, I bet."

Helen looked up at me with a glimmer of a smile, "Thanks ya so much," and she reached and patted my arm, then announced softly, "I knows you and Papa sho gon miss each otha, but maybe yous can come visit wis us at Mary's house one day."

"Papa, come outside with me! I'll see you later, Helen," and I left to go into the front yard. I felt sadness about what Helen had said, a *strange* sadness, like when you hear a bad thing for the first time and you can't believe it, or something you want, but you know you can never have. There was no way that I could visit at their house in town.

Papa was right behind me, and when I stopped and turned around he ran into me, face to face, and our heads bumped. We both started laughing, but I scolded him, "Now, Papa, don't you waste your money on bubble gum. Just one pack, and the rest of your money, you ought to keep till next week when you move." He just grinned and never committed himself to my suggestion. I waited for him to have some kind of reply, but he just stood there looking at me, so I continued, "Papa, when you get back from town, come to the Big House. I have something for you. Okay?"

He smiled bigger and mumbled, "Yeah, I'll be dare." I sighed and shook my fist at him, knowing that he was testing me and wanted me to start a fight with him.

Instead, I turned and headed toward home.

CHAPTER 42

I walked slowly home from the Quarters. When I reached the hedgerow, Pal came running toward me, with the skunk odor reaching me before he did, but I yelled at him to go away. He dropped his tail, turned around, and started trotting toward the garage as though I had really hurt his feelings. He never turned to look back at me, and I felt sorry for him, while his big tail just hung down.

Stopping in the middle of the gravel drive at the end of the hedgerow, I stared at the Big House.

Glancing around the big yard, it reminded me of the times when Mister Gaspard had talked about when he was a child, the small barges that were loaded with bales of cotton, and docked in the bayou in front of the the Big House. I could see it in my mind, all of it, and I had wished over and over that I would see a barge one day again, right there in the bayou. But I knew those days were gone, along with many other things the Big House and the big oaks had seen, too.

Tall and stately, with wide porches going all around it except on the west side, the Big House, I figured hadn't been painted for probably fifty years or more. Only the sheltered walls under the porches showed several layers of thick, gray paint. From the second floor gables and dormers the paint had long ago been washed away, revealing the bleached-white planks, probably cut from a plentiful supply of cypress trees found in the woods when the land was cleared and gardens were planted, and crops would be grown, and farms and plantations developed. The four big oak trees in the front yard and the long row of pecan trees standing on the east side of the wide yard sourrounding the Big House on Shirley Plantation were planted many years before, and I often wondered who had planted them, all so perfectly spaced and planned, making a well-shaded, great yard for me and my friends to play in for hours. I wondered how many kids had grown up in that house and under those trees, and what was it like on this old plantation when those big oaks were little. If they could talk, would they tell the stories of what they had seen? Fun stories or maybe sad stories? Or maybe they would tell the long-kept secrets about the hardships of so many people who lived around them, those who did the backbreaking work in the fields of cotton and sugarcane. Would they tell about the possible deviousness and meanness of those who lived in the Big House, those whom the big oaks had proteced for so many years? And where were the kids who had grown up there, long before my brothers, sisters and me? I had never heard of any of them, and now, many of my friends who lived on the plantation, were talking about leaving, too, going far away to California or somewhere else far away. Was I going to be the last of the kids to grow up there? Hearing the things my Dad and Alex were saying, everything was changing—the plantation, the people, and the way we lived. My world was small, I knew, but I liked it, and I didn't want it to change. But I knew also that it *would* change, too, and no one could stop it. Yet, I wished many times that my grandfather were still living. He was a young kid about like me during the Civil War, and he knew a lot about changes, friendships and families, about failures, and winning and losing, about wars and bad times and good times. He would have helped me understand what was happening around me, to me, and to my friends on the dirt road.

CHAPTER 43

The kitchen was still warm from the stove, but I decided to light a fire in the dining room fireplace, so I went to the porch and got some kindling. Soon the flames were warming the room. I couldn't remember the last time I had eaten any real food, and I missed sitting around the kitchen table talking with Mama and Dad, my sisters and my little brother. Everyone was gone; even Wesley and Papa had gone to town that day, and I figured I was the only one around.

I went back into the kitchen and put some wood in the stove, and then I went to the cabinets and got out three plates, three forks, three knives, and three glasses. I set the kitchen table, all ready for supper. The only times that I had opened the icebox since my family had left was to get some milk to drink. I pulled the door open and the light came on. Pressing the black button over and over, I watched the light go on and off, remembering that I was at least eight years old before I figured out how the light came on in the icebox, but now knowing that there were a lot of other things I would wonder about.

Mama had left three or four bowls in the icebox with food for me, but I was never hungry enough to heat up the stove to warm the food. Tonight, Wesley could heat up everything when he finished milking, and when Papa came, the three of us would eat supper. I went back into the dining room and plugged in the lights on my Christmas tree, even knowing Dad wouldn't like for me to leave them on, and Wesley wouldn't either, but neither was there. Sitting in the big chair facing the little tree and the big glass-front china cabinet, I remembered Mama's fruitcakes and the Jack Daniel used to soak the cloth that she wrapped around the cakes. I pulled a chair up to the big cabinet and opened the tall glass door. The tin boxes with the fruitcakes were gone, I guessed to Texas, but the bottle of Jack Daniel was there. I worked it to the edge of the shelf and grabbed it with my hand and brought it down. Only a couple of swallows of whiskey were left in the bottle, which was probably just enough for me to learn another adult secret. I unscrewed the cap and smelled the whiskey, its smell reminding me of what Dad's truck was like when I drove it home with Alex passed out on the seat. I thought for a second and decided that Mama would know I had drunk the whisky the minute she looked at the empty bottle. I put it back on the shelf, slid it to the back, and gently closed the glass door. I jumped from the chair, and landed hard on the floor, causing the dishes to rattle in the tall china cabinet, while the Big House seemed to shake, too. Sitting quietly in one of the big chairs, I watched Santa as he glowed brightly on my Christmas tree.

Leaning toward him, I asked very softly, "Santa, what do you think? Should I try that Jack Daniel or not?" I leaned my head against the wing on the back of the big chair and smiled, figuring that even Santa would be mad if I drank that little bit of whiskey left in the Jack Daniel bottle. I waited for an answer, and closed my eyes.

Someone was knocking on the kitchen door. I knew it wasn't Wesley because he was in and out too often to knock, so I jumped up from the big chair, and in a daze, ran to the kitchen. When he knocked again, I quickly recognized Papa's code. I opened the door, and he had his hand up ready to pound it once more. He had on the jacket Mama had given him, and the hat that Daddy had given to Hoss some time back.

"Papa, why are you so dressed up? You goin to church or something?"

He smiled, and in a teasing voice, "Nah, Billy, I's here fer da pawdy! Ya said fer me ta com dis evenin an we's gon hav'a pawdy. Is you gon still have it or not, and is we gon dance any?" I was still a little confused from being awakened so abruptly, and I just stood there looking at him. He leaned his head a little to the side, then asked, "Billy, ya still drunk from when ya com in las night?"

"Drunk, I've never been drunk in my life, Papa! Where'd you hear that?"

"Up and down da Quawtas," he shot back to me. Apparently everyone in the Quarters had heard it, and I figured now that Dad would hear it, too, as soon as he returned from Texas.

I looked at Papa, but knowing what his answer would be, I asked, "Papa, you ever been drunk?"

He grinned and said, "Ya know betta dan dat. My Daddy wooda kilt me for sho, and yo daddy's gon kill ya when he com home, already. Yo mama, too," and he kept shaking his finger at me, laughing.

Pushing him onto the porch, I reached for my windbreaker, commanding, "Come on. I want to show you something." We headed to the far end of the porch, down the steps, and ran into the garage. The garage smelled awful.

Papa grabbed his nose and mumbled, "Billy, uh skunk's hidin' in heah! I can sho smell 'im!" and he grabbed onto the sleeve of my jacket.

"No, that's just Pal. He must have killed one last night, and he's hiding over there in his bed, and Papa, don't be pulling on me," and I jerked my arm from his grasp. Pal was whimpering a little, and I supposed that he was getting sick from the terrible odor. I opened the storeroom door, we stepped inside, and I lifted the burlap sack. There was only one case of wine left. I flipped the cardboard flap and on the inside of the box were only two jugs. Neither one had been opened. I wondered where all of it had gone, and I complained out loud, "I bet J.B. found it after all. That bastard!"

Papa grabbed my arm again, shook it, and said, "Boy, don chu bes cussin like dat. He jist an ole turd. I knows dat fer a fack, cause he smell bad all da time."

"Papa, have you ever had any wine?" His eyes were open wide, and he shook his head.

"Me neither, Papa, but we're both gonna have some tonight!"

He kept shaking his head while his eyes opened wider, saying, "No we ain't. Not me! The preacher says we's gon go to hell if we drink dat wine, for sho. An ya ain't gon make me drink no wine, Billy, ya heah me. Ah jist ain't gon do dat."

"Yes, we are, Papa. I say 'we's gon have some wine tonight,' boy!" and I dragged it out in a long sentence, "We's...gon have...some...wine...to...night!"

I picked up a gallon jug and unscrewed the top. It smelled really good, but not nearly as sweet and powerful as the Jack Daniel bottle. I screwed the top back on, telling Papa to wait right where he was, that I would be right back. Then I added," Papa, if J.B. comes, you'll have to fight him off to save the wine. Don't let him get it."

As I ran to the kitchen to get a pitcher from the cabinet, Papa was calling out, "I ain't fightin nobody, sho not some old turd." Then I heard him yell, "Git outta heah, Pal, git away, dog! Billy, come back heah, hurry! Pal gon rub on me! Hurry!"

We poured some wine into the pitcher and screwed the cap back on the jug. I put it back in the box and covered the box with the croker sack, telling Papa, "Don't you tell anybody about that wine. J.B. will take it if he finds out about it! You hear?" He just nodded, *yes*.

We walked slowly back to the house, with Papa walking a little behind me, and I could smell Pal. When I glanced back, Papa was rubbing Pal's back with his hand, and speaking softly he said, "Dis heah dog sho do stink, Billy. What chu gon do wit him?"

I turned, hit him in the chest with the back of my hand and yelled at him, "Dammit Papa! Don't touch him. The smells gonna get all over you!" It was too late, but I yelled at Pal, "Get outta here, dog!" and he turned and trotted back into the garage.

Papa quickly repeated, "Yeah, git outta heah, dog! Ya stink too bad."

We went into the kitchen, and I fussed at Papa, "Don't you get close to me. You ought to know better than to touch Pal when he's been fightin a skunk. Now you smell just like him! What're you gonna do now?" and I shook my fist toward him. He just looked at me; and I thought for a minute that he was going to cry. Angrily, I scolded again, "Take off your coat and hat and put 'um on the porch, and go wash your hands in the bathroom!" I hid the pitcher of wine in back of the milk in the icebox, hoping that Wesley wouldn't find it. Papa came out of the bathroom and I could still smell him, so I told him to take his pants off and put them out on the porch.

He looked at me with his lips turned down, about to cry, whining, "I ain'ts bout ta git no neked in dis heah kitchen. Rosa'll sho nough kill me. Dat's what ya wants, Billy, fur me to die, don chu?"

"Papa, nobody's here but you and me, and my mama's gonna kill us both if it stinks like this when she gets home. Put your pants on the porch and go stand by the stove where it's warm." He slowly went onto the porch and came back in just his underwear, shirt and socks. I could hear Wesley on the porch coming in with the bucket of cream.

I opened the door for him and the first thing he said was, "Y'all got ole Pal in heah? He been fightin a skunk," and when he saw Papa, "Boy, what chu got yo pants off fer?"

"No, Papa stinks, Wesley. He's been breakin wind here in the kitchen, also, and I'm gonna tell Rosa next time she comes," and I smiled at Wesley.

Papa looked at Wesley and pouted, "I ain't done dat! Billy lying. I ain't broke no wind." With his lips hanging down, he hesitated for a second, then, yelled at me, "Say you's lyin, Billy! Say it, else I's gon go home."

"No, and Rosa's gonna beat the devil out of you, boy. She'll teach you to fart in her kitchen! You aughta be ashamed of yourself, Papa!" All the while, Wesley was putting the cream in the icebox and laughing. Papa looked like he was going to cry again, so I told Wesley, "Naw, I'm just joking. Papa let Pal rub against him. That's why he took his pants off." Papa continued holding his head down with his lips stuck out.

Wesley looked at both of us and said, "Y'all needs ta get calm fo ya breaks something, den ya sho would has some'im to cry bout."

"Ah, don't worry. I'm just pickin at him, the poor little baby. Look at his lips." Then, I suggested, "Wesley, why don't you heat up all that food Mama has in the icebox and you, Papa, and I'll eat supper. I've got the table all ready, and I'm hungry."

He was still standing at the icebox, looking at Papa, and said, "Papa can eat wit'cha. I'sll put everything on da stove, but I's gotta go on home." He started getting the bowls out of the icebox and moving them to the cabinet to put the food in pots that could be heated on the stove.

"While you do that, Papa and I'll go out and finish cleaning the milkroom for you."

He shook his head, agreeing, "Okay, dat'll be good."

I told Papa to come with me, but he wouldn't leave the kitchen. His bottom lip continued to show his pout, and he still looked like he was going to cry. I left him there and went out to the milkroom to wash the milk buckets and crocks. By the time I got back to the kitchen, Wesley was serving three plates, one for each of us.

He chuckled and complimented, "Miz Florence sho left some good stuff, heah. I sho hates to pass it up." I told Papa that was our *party supper*. Smiling at me, I could tell that he had already forgiven me for picking at him. He was hungry, too.

THE LAST WITNESS FROM A DIRT ROAD

The sun had long ago set and the night was pitch black. With the soft sound of raindrops on the tin roof, and in the warmth of the kitchen, we talked and laughed about a thousand things for over an hour.

We all thanked Mama for supper, and I was thankful for my friends.

CHAPTER 44

Wesley had started moving the dirty dishes to the sink when I told him to leave them alone, that I would wash them later. We had been talking about everything Cathrine had taught Papa in the last three or four weeks, so I asked Papa, "Why don't you show us something you can do?" I went to get a pencil and a pad of writing paper from my dad's desk in the corner of the dining room, while Wesley continued to move the dirty dishes to the sink. I sat down at the table next to Papa, commanding, "Papa, show Wesley how you can write your name," and I laid the pad and pencil in front of him.

He slowly picked up the pencil and leaned over the pad, about ten inches from it, and his tongue slowly came out of the corner of his mouth. He held the pencil the way I had been taught in the first grade, and I could tell that he was thinking really hard. He made a capital *I*, then a period. Next, he made a capital *V* and continued with small letters, *ead*. It took him a couple of seconds, but he made it. He looked at Wesley, smiled, and waited, but Wesley said nothing.

Cathrine had done well. Papa could sign his name. I asked him how much was five pennies.

He thought a second and said, "Uh nickel, and two nickels is a dime."

Seeing Wesley's face, I could tell he was surprised, and I could almost see a look that seemed like a look of disgust on his dark brown skin, and a spark of disappointment, maybe mixed with a little anger. Finally he said, "Dat's good, Papa," and he stared at the pad of paper, then at Papa, and finally at me, with the same look I had seen just moments before.

Happily, Papa continued, "It takes fo quawtas to make a dollaw. I gots tree dollaws and ten cents at my house dat I been savin from da money ya done give me, Billy. Ain'ts dat good?" I was surprised, and also glad that I had been wrong in thinking that Helen had been taking his money, or that he would spend it all at the Rolling Store for gum and candy.

Wesley stood up, stretched and said, "I's gotta git on. It's gittin late." I looked at the airplane clock on top of the icebox and it was a bit past six o'clock. Wesley glanced again at the pad of paper where Papa had written his name, said nothing, but then moved quickly toward the sink.

"Go ahead, Papa and I'll clean up," and I motioned toward the door. Wesley went to the porch where the rain was sounding louder on the tin roof. I told him to take Dad's slicker coat, since it was long and had a hood on it. He put it on and left in the dark.

I went into the kitchen and Papa had gone to the dining room looking at the little Christmas tree. I called to him from the kitchen door, "Don't touch those bulbs, they'll burn....," but it was too late. He had already touched Santa Claus and burned his finger. He started whimpering and jigging around, with his finger in his mouth.

"Come on, let's clean up this mess so Wesley won't have to do it in the morning. Then we'll have a little wine," and I stood watching him show off with his jigging about.

He stopped dancing and his smile vanished as he looked at me like I was crazy. He said angrily, "I ain't drinkin no wine, Billy, I don told chu, and ya aughts not be gittin drunk agin tonight eitha." I laughed out loud. By then, he was back in the kitchen, and I figured that if we were going to have some wine, I needed to get it out soon, before he got too upset and left. He started whining again, and then he sang a little while sucking on his finger, and danced.

"I'll be right back, Papa. Wait here!" and I went onto the porch and used the broom handle to take his pants to hide them in the porch closet. I knew he wouldn't leave in just his underwear, especially in the rain.

When I returned to the kitchen, he was sitting at the table, examining me with a big frown creased across his face, and asked, "Wat you don did out dare, Billy?"

I said, "Oh, I was looking for something I lost yesterday."

He continued to frown, "No you ain't. You done didway wis ma cloths, huh? I knows ya, and I ain't drinkin no wine, I done told ya ova and ova. Ya tryin to gits me in trouble, and I knows dat fer fack." His fussing continued. By the time he had finished his little tirade, I had gotten two tall glasses from the cabinet in the dining room, and was getting the pitcher of wine from the icebox.

I poured each glass about three fourths full. "Come on, Papa. Let's go sit by the fire in the dining room. This'll be good for you. Make you feel good, boy." In the the dining room, I set the glasses on the table, knowing that Papa hadn't moved from where he sat in the kitchen. I turned another of the big chairs around to face the Christmas tree so we both could see it while we sipped our wine. Papa finally came to the door and leaned against the doorfacing, crossing his long black legs at his knees. He looked suspiciously at me, but he studied my movements as I took a sip from my glass, smacked my lips, smiled at him, took a long, deep breath and said, "Com 'on Papa, this'll make you a happy boy! You're a big fella now. You can read and write. Come on, let's celebrate."

He slowly licked his lips, lowered his head, and asked, "Billy, yo sho dat wine ain't gon make me go ta Hell when I die? Is ya really sho? I sho don wanna go down dare."

"Yeah, Papa," I said assuredly, "I'm telling you. Don't worry. We're not gonna drink enough to make us go to Hell. Do you think I want to go to Hell?"

He whined back to me and opened his eyes wide, exclaiming, "Mag sayed ya wuz gon go ta Hell. Yous and hers both, cause yous both so mean. Ain't dat right?"

"Naw, she don't know what she's talkin about, Papa! Mag's a crazy woman! Don't you know that?"

He walked slowly into the dining room and sat in the other big chair beside me, still sucking on his burned finger. I leaned over, picked up his glass from the table, smiled, and held it toward him. He slowly reached for it while licking his lips again, and finally, taking the glass of wine, he brought it to his nose and took a deep breath.

"Papa, let's have a little toast," and I held up my glass toward his, smiling at him.

He wouldn't look at me, but stared at the Christmas tree, afraid to look at his wine, then said slowly, "Naw, Billy, I ain't hongry right now. I ain't want'en no toast no ways," and he finally looked down at the glass in his hand. He licked his lips again, swallowed, and said very slowly, "I's guess I's gotta drink dis heahs wine else ya ain't neva gon be happy wis me." Then he smiled big and said happily, "It sho is Christmas, ain't it, Billy. I sho do laks Christmas! Look at dim lights! Dey sho is purty." He continued smiling, looked down at his glass again, then at the Christmas tree, and again at his glass. His tongue came out, slowly crossing his lips, while his smile grew bigger.

"Now, just sip a little at a time. Okay?" I told him while taking a sip from my glass. I recalled that only a week or so before, I had sat right there in that big room, and had my first cup of *hot tea*, and tonight, I was having my first glass of wine. I leaned toward the little tree and whispered, "Thanks Santa. You're a good little fellow," and I held my glass in a toast to Santa and my Christmas tree.

Papa looked at me and announced, "Billy, ya don already got drunk, talkin to dat light like dat," then he quickly raised his glass to his lips and took a big swallow from the tall glass, smacked his lips, smiled and asked, "Ya sho da devil ain't gon get me, Billy?" I smiled back at Papa, assuring him again, that he wasn't going to Hell.

Neither of us said anything for a few minutes, while we looked at the Christmas tree. I knew that we had to take it slowly and figure it out as we went along. Every now and then I would hear Papa smack his lips. After a little while, he tapped me on the arm, complaining, "Boy! Dat old fireplace sho put out a lota heat. I's gittin hot in heah, Billy. Ya needs to do some'um. Whew!" and he wiped his forehead with his hand, and shook his head in a quick motion, then blinked his big round eyes several times.

I, too, could feel the room warming up, so I got up and made a narrow opening in the door going directly onto the porch from the dining room. Sitting in my chair, I reached for my glass on the table, and started counting out loud, the colored bulbs on the tree. I told Papa that there were only six bulbs left, but he said nothing. A few minutes later, I asked him, "Whatcha think of this wine, Papa? It's pretty good, huh?" He grunted something, but had no comment. I looked at him and saw that his eyelids were drooping badly, and it appeared he was dozing off, with his glass tilted in his hand. I reached and took it from him, then realized that Papa had drunk all of his wine in about five or six minutes, and now he was falling asleep with drool seeping from the corner of his mouth. Very loudly, I told him, "You're not worth a penny, Papa! Wake up! The party's not over, boy. Wake up! Papa?" He said nothing, but smiled a little crooked smile for a second while his eyelids looked heavier and heavier. I took his empty glass and set it on the table in front of us, then took another sip from my glass, waiting until I thought I could hear him sleeping soundly. Watching him closely, in just a minute or so he started drooling more, and would snort every now and then, so I figured, "Now's the time." I put my hand about an inch from the top of his head, then very quickly, grabbed and shook his head, and yelled really loud, "Isaac, wake up! Wake up, boy! Rosa's in the kitchen!"

He jumped up, screaming, and fell headfirst onto the dining table. I tried to catch him, and both our glasses hit the table, shattering into a million pieces. As we both fell forward onto the table, the Christmas tree in its big glass vase went flying to the other end, crashing to the floor in front of the tall china cabinet. Sparks from the tree lights flew everywhere, and I thought I could faintly hear the shattering of glass somewhere in the distance, and lasting for a long time. The room was dark except for the light coming through the kitchen door and the dwindling fire in back of us. The wine left in my glass had splashed across the table with the broken glasses, and Papa, who had fallen to the floor, was groaning and mumbling something, just about like Alex was doing the night before in dad's truck. I sat on the floor next to him and tried to figure out what had happened, talking to him, but he wouldn't answer me. Everything around me had come apart, and it was suddenly so quiet, so silent, except for Papa. He was groaning, and I could see him drooling again when he put his hand between his cheek and the floor.

"In my Mama's dining room, half naked on this cold floor? Papa must have lost his mind." "Papa! Papa!" I could hear myself calling, "What's the matter with you, boy? Get up! Get up, Papa!" but he never heard me. I looked around but couldn't find my Christmas tree. Sitting on the floor, I wondered again what had happened, and thought maybe Papa had died right there in the dining room. I sure didn't want Papa to die, but maybe I had killed poor Papa with just one glass of Port wine. Figuring I needed to do something right then, I prayed, "Please dear Jesus, don't let us die tonight. I'm sorry, Jesus, I'm sorry," and I slid over to lie against my friend. I latched my arm through his and closed my teary eyes, figuring that if I died too, and was headed to Hell because of what I had done, I might be able to hold Papa's arm tight enough to take him with me.

THE LAST WITNESS FROM A DIRT ROAD

Shivering, I felt a cold wind blowing over me, so I sat up and looked around the room, trying to figure out where I was. Papa lay curled up in a ball with his long black legs pulled almost up to his chin. I could hear him moan every now and then, and he would shiver from the cold air around us. Smelling smoke, I stood up, held on to the back of one of the big chairs, and looked around. The fire was completely out, and I couldn't see anything burning, but thinking, "Those damned old lights must have set fire to the house. Dad was going to skin me for sure!" In the light coming from the kitchen, I saw the dining room door to the porch had been blown open, and the breeze had spread ashes all around the hearth, the floor, the tabletops, the chairs and the server, and onto the two of us. I walked around the chairs and closed the door, brushing the ashes off of me, and thinking to myself, "What in the devil happened? This is awful," and I started calling Papa, but he never moved. The rascal shouldn't have drunk all of his wine so fast, I figured. Then I started laughing, and not knowing what I was laughing about. We hadn't died, I felt fairly sure, but looking about, I wondered if the devil had come to get us. I could see Hell all around me, it seemed, but we were still in the dining room of the Big House. If Papa would just wake up, maybe together we could figure it out.

CHAPTER 45

The screened door slammed, and someone stepped across the porch. The kitchen door opened and closed, and I recognized Wesley's voice, "Lawd, what don happen heah?" He came to the dining room while I stood at the back of one of the big chairs, and frowned at me, "Billy, wat'in da world ya two been doin? Wat's da matta wit Papa? He ain't daad, is he?"

"Naw, Jesus saved us, Wesley. I guess. I don't feel so good...I guess we had a little *too much*," and I pointed down to where Papa was lying, announcing, "He's sure sleeping really good, that rascal."

"Too much'uh wat?" he asked.

"Well, we thought we'd have a little wine after you left, and that's what we did," and I leaned harder against the chair with my hand holding up my chin, my starting to laugh again, even though things really looked bad. Wesley's frown never changed.

Leaning over, he shook Papa, telling him to get up. Papa had a layer of ashes stuck to his hair and skin. He was shivering from the cold, but he sat up, looked around and then at me, mumbling, "It sho is cold in heah! Wat chu don done, Billy?" Then he glanced up at Wesley ordering him, "Git us some wood fer da fireplace, Wesley, else we gon freeze to det!" He looked back to me and sneezed.

Wesley stood up straight, and angrily snapped at Papa, "Dis ain't yo house, boy! Who you think ya talking like dat to. Ya betta git outta heah and take yo black ass home! Ya don be talking to me like dat!" To me, it sounded like Wesley must have been mad, because I had never heard him talk that way, and he snapped at Papa again, "Ya hear me, boy? Yo mama been waitin fer ya fer over two hour, yous with all dem ABCs and countin dat money like dat. Ya done got to big fer yo britches, boy. Git on outta dis house fo I's gives ya a whippin' myself!"

I went out to the porch closet, found Papa's pants and brought them to the dining room on the end of the broomstick. I could still smell the skunk on them, but he would have to do the best he could. He put his pants on, and I took him to the porch where he put on his boots and coat. He was still shaking from the cold, and had started to cry. I called to Wesley, who had already started picking up the trash in the dining room, to come on, that I would take them home in Dad's truck. He came out to the porch, looked angrily at me, "Billy, I don knows dat ya fittin to drive. Things is bad nough heah at da Big House, and if ya wrecks yo daddy's truck, I don't rightly know what'll happen. We gon all be in trouble, den."

"Ah, come on. I'm okay, and we can clean up that mess tomorrow." I didn't want even to think about it, and he said nothing more. Papa was wiping his eyes, so I told him, "Papa, just stop that crying. Act like man, for a change!" The Robin Hood clock in the dining room finished striking, just as I felt my stomach turn over again.

The three of us piled into the truck, and I slowly backed out of the garage and headed toward the Quarters. The dirt road was muddy after the rain, and the truck slipped and slid from one rut to the other. We came first to Wesley's house; and before he opened the truck door, he leaned forward, announcing, "Ah gotta clean up ole Pal. Ah can smell a skunk in heah! And ya betta git rid of dat wine, Billy. Ya sho don needs to be drinkin any mo of dat stuff."

Papa's eyes got big, and he shouted, "Wat wine? I ain't drank no wine. Billy, ya tells my mama I ain't drank no wine. Uh huh, not me! It all yo's fault, Billy! Yous tryin to gits me kilt," and he started whimpering again.

"Yeah, yeah, just shut up, Papa! All you do is cry like a little ole baby and fuss, just like Uncle Nick, and I'm tired of you crying every time we do something."

He yelled at me, "I sayed I wudden no Nick, so you hush up yoself!" He sniffed really hard.

"Well, stop your cryin, big baby, and try to act like you know something for a change. Go on in the house, and get in bed before your mama even sees you," but I knew that wouldn't happen. Helen probably had her belt out already, just waiting for him to walk in. The truck and Papa both smelled like a skunk, so I figured that Helen might not give him a whipping until the next morning after the sun came up.

Wesley stepped out of the truck onto the dirt road, leaned through the door, and quietly ordered, "Ya boys better stop dat. All dat fussin and dat wine drinkin! Ya don did nough damage fer one night. Mista Carl gon be awful mad bout dis." and he closed the door.

I drove slowly on to Papa's house, telling him before he got out of the truck, "Papa, get up early in the morning and come help me clean up. And by the way, I have a Christmas present for you."

He slowly stepped out of the truck, never saying a word, and slammed the door. As I pulled away, I could see him in the dark, bending over, and throwing up all over the place. I thought, "Boy, how lucky can I get?" If he had vomited in Dad's truck, Dad would have nearly killed me for sure.

Helen might get over his coming in so late if Papa could leave early the next morning before she had time to work up her anger toward him, then I could go later after we cleaned the dining room, to explain to her what happened. I needed a little time to figure it out myself, and I was hoping that Papa had learned a lesson. You just can't drink wine very fast. You have to sip it slowly, like they do in the picture show, especially if you have a big glass full.

THE LAST WITNESS FROM A DIRT ROAD

I pulled the truck into the garage and rolled the windows down hoping it would air out before Dad got back. From the top of the back steps, I ran down the porch all the way to my mama's bedroom, wanting to avoid the kitchen and dining room.

Finding my way through the darkness, I stumbled up the stairs, stripped down to my skivvies and crawled under the cover. Shivering from the cold sheets, I hoped that Wesley wouldn't wake me at five o'clock in the morning. I couldn't move anymore.

But I had to pee really bad. Maybe later...

CHAPTER 46

I raised my head above the quilts to look over the windowsill at a light frost on the grass in the front yard. Hearing the faint sounds coming from the kitchen and dining room, I threw back the covers, and the odor of the ashes in my bed engulfed me. Hurriedly, I put on my clothes and socks, picked up my tennis shoes, and ran down the stairs, hoping that Wesley had not thrown away my Christmas tree. I opened the door between the cold family room and the dining room, recognizing that Rosa was in the kitchen. She wasn't supposed to come till Tuesday, and now she was going to see this mess. I went on into the kitchen, said *hello* to her, and wished her a Merry Christmas, while she worked at the sink washing the dishes left from the night before. She looked over to me and said, "Mista Billy," sounding as though she had caught me in the act of doing something she knew my folks wouldn't like.

I sat at the table, crossed my legs and leaned on my hand and elbow as if nothing was different than any other morning. "Rosa, I didn't think you were coming till Tuesday."

"Wesley sent werd fer me ta come hep him today, that yous had a little accident," and she glanced toward me and smiled a little.

I said, "Yeah, this is quite a mess. I had a little party last night," and I wandered over to the door going into the dining room.

She had already cleaned the big room, and my Christmas tree was gone. The fire in the fireplace was big and the chairs were all in place. "Rosa, where's my Christmas tree?"

Never looking up from her dishwashing, she answered, "Wesley don trowed it 'way. Evything on it was broke, cept a couple lights."

"Where are the lights? What did he do with them?"

She pointed into the dining room and said, "Dey's layin in one of da big chairs. He says deys needs to be trowed 'way, too." I found the lights, and went back to the kitchen door.

"Rosa, would you change my bed today? It smells pretty bad."

She said, "I sho will, soons I finish in heah. I's gon wash yo clothes today, too, fo ya runs out'a some clean underwear."

"Thanks, that would be great, Rosa, I really appreciate it. Thanks!"

Thinking that I would hang them until Christmas, I strung the lights across the windows in my bedroom, and plugged them into the wall socket. All of the bulbs were broken or burned out except Santa Claus. He lit up like a real hero, but I took the lights down and unscrewed Santa from the string, taking him to my closet to hide him in my small trunk where I saved all of my important things, including my nickels and dimes. I lifted the lid on the Tampa Nugget cigar box and laid Santa next to the silver Army Air Force Wings my cousin had given me when he came home from the war. My cigar box was almost full, and it was getting close to the time for me to take everything out; and, in the quietness of my room, lay everything on my bed, study it, wipe it off, and carefully put it back into the cigar box to be hidden away until another time. I closed the closet door, rolled the string of lights around my hand and elbow and took it back to the closet in the hall outside of my room, knowing it would be at least a year before anyone would pull them out and discover that the bulbs were broken, and Santa was gone.

I went back to the kitchen, where Rosa asked me if I wanted some breakfast. "No. I'm going to the barn to let the horses out and clean out the stalls, so Wesley won't have to do it. He was up late last night," and I smiled at her. Wesley had told her what all had happened, I'm sure, and when I glanced toward the table, there sat the pitcher, half full of wine—the only thing on the table. I guessed she didn't want to touch it and, also, wanted to let me know that she knew for sure what had happened last night. I knew she wouldn't tattle to Mama, but if Mama happened to ask her, she would tell her everything she knew. I picked up the pitcher by the handle and went to the sink and poured the wine into the drain. Rosa just stood there, with one hand on her hip, watching me, and I said, "Well, that's over, Rosa. I know what wine is now, and I guess Papa is right."

"Wat's dat, Mista Billy?"

"Well, Papa says that if we drink wine we're gonna go to Hell when we die," and I handed the pitcher to her.

She chuckled a little and said, "Aw, I don't guess dat's true, or Hell'ed be runnin over by now, an enyway, po Papa don knows nuttin," and she chuckled again. Rosa seldom joked around. If that had been Mag, she would have threatened me over and over again, and would have used the little accident in the dining room as a threat against me if I picked on her. I hoped that Rosa was right about Hell and wine, but Mag wouldn't have made fun of Papa.

CHAPTER 47

I let the horses into the pens, cleaned out the stalls, and went back to the house, where Pal met me at the back gate. Smelling as bad as the day before, he turned and walked slowly back into the garage. I guessed he wondered why no one wanted him around, and I think he was beginning to feel ashamed of himself for smelling so bad. While feeling sorry for my poor ole yellow dog, I walked into the kitchen where Rosa was making some teacakes. I opened a can of orange juice and told her I was going to get Papa. She never said anything, but I knew she didn't care to have Papa around. I got my aviator's cap out of my jacket pocket, put it on, and headed out to the Quarters.

When I reached the porch at Papa's house, I called out in a big, deep voice, "Isaac, Isaac Vead. Come outta there, boy, you're under arrest! Put your hands up, boy, and I don't want any trouble out of you!"

The door opened quickly, and Helen stepped onto the porch, "Papa ain't woke up yet, Billy. Wat in da world did yous do las night? He wuz crazy outta his haad and wudden fit to kill. Sides dat, he smell like a polecat and don stunk up da whole house."

Surprised that Helen had come to the door so quickly and had asked me about the night before, I had to think really fast, but I had already decided that if she asked, then I would tell her the whole truth: "Well, first of all, I'm starting to call Papa by his real name, Isaac," and I held up my finger like that was *number one.* Then I continued, "He's not a little kid anymore, and he needs his real name, Helen."

Helen just shook her head in disgust, like she was listening to a silly little kid, but replied "Well, I's gon tell yo daddy bout how much trouble yous causin' me, telling Papa all kinda stuff, and yous an 'im drinkin dat wine. He done told me what ya did lass night, and Mista Carl gon sho find out."

I motioned with my hands, and said, "We found a little wine in a jug, that's right...and I decided that we could drink a glass or two. Now, Helen, Papa, I mean Isaac, didn't want to, but I talked him into doing it, so it's all my fault. I think he must have drunk his a little too fast, and he had a little too much." I liked those words—"a little too much." They made me feel big and grownup.

Helen frowned and put both hands on her hips and said with disgust, "Com on in. I's gittin cold out heah," and we both went into the house. The fireplace was warm, and the light was filtering through the thin white curtains hanging limp over the front window. I sat down on the stool in front of the fire, warming my hands, while Helen tried to wake Isaac in the other room.

"Git up, Papa," she said, "fore I gits my belt ta ya. Ya stinking up da house."

"Dammit, she's gonna give it to him now," I was thinking, so I stood up and turned by backside to the fireplace, ready to try to stop her if she was going to whip Papa. My head was getting hot, so I took my cap off and stuffed it in my pocket. In a couple of seconds, Isaac came through the door yawning, barefooted, and wrapped in a sheet from his head to his feet, dragging part of the sheet behind him. He looked at me and in a soft whisper, asked, "Wat 'chu doin heah so erly? I's was jist gittin to sleep real good. Ma mama sho mad at yous and me bofe."

I whispered back to him, "It's not early, Isaac. It's almost ten o'clock. We have to go back to the Big House." When he got closer to me, I could see the ashes still in his hair, and Helen was right: He did stink like a polecat, and his breath was awful. I put my hand over my nose.

He turned and stood with his back to the fire and spoke softly to me, "I sho ain't drinkin no mo of yo wine. Ya don got us in 'nough trouble."

Covering my nose with my hand again, I explained, "I threw it away, Isaac, so don't worry about the wine. Boy, you stink and your breath's awful. You must have eaten that polecat Pal killed the other night."

He frowned and in a loud voice, said, "Don't be callin me no Isaac, Billy, an don chu be talkin bout no polecat. I be sick all night. I aughta be killin ya right now fo ya gits away." I gave him a little shove, and he landed in Helen's little rocking chair, which was sitting in front of the fireplace.

We both laughed, and I said, loud enough for Helen to hear me, "Your name is Isaac, and that's what I'm gonna call you from now on," and I shook my balled fist in his face.

Helen came into the room, wiping her hands on her apron, and said, "Isaac, yo breakfas bout ready, boy." We glanced back and forth at each other, smiling, and I felt sure that the three of us realized at that moment that Papa had made a couple of steps, crawling out of the shell that had held him captive for all of his life. He was different, and he even looked different. Since Mag's first Saturday Night Ball, Papa had gone from about six to sixteen, and, I think that day, wrapped in a long, white sheet in front of his fireplace, he felt like *somebody*, knowing he had weathered a bad storm with his mother, and neither she, nor anyone else, had given him a beating.

Isaac stood tall, with his back to the fire; he was bigger, and his chin was held high. Helen came over and put her arms around both of us and said, "Thank ya Billy fer evythang yous and Annas don fer Papa, I mean Isaac," and she looked at Isaac and said, "A mama can't be mo proud bout her son, dan I is bout chu, my baby." Big tears quickly came into his eyes, and she hugged him again, reached up and brushed some ashes from his thick hair.

THE LAST WITNESS FROM A DIRT ROAD

I figured that Isaac could not remember ever being hugged by his mother, nor ever hearing those words, that she was proud of him.

With big tears on his cheeks, he smiled at his mother, "Ah loves ya, Mama. Thank ya."

"Papa" had gone away and Issac Vead had become *the man of the house.*

CHAPTER 48

I told Helen that I would see them later, but I had already planned to not return to their house probably ever again since Alex and Wesley would move them on Tuesday. Helen would be busy, and Isaac would have to help her pack their belongings. Knowing their house as I did, I knew there wasn't a great deal to pack, but moving from Shirley Plantation was an awful disruption in the lives of my friends. Every time I thought about it, I had the same fearful, sickening, and empty feeling that I had had when I found Mag packing her things and I told her goodbye. I didn't understand the feeling inside me—this fear as though I were again walking close to a deep, wide chasm with slippery slopes, where strange shadows moved about, continually calling and beckoning to me. Confused, and wondering, I felt like a small child who didn't understand why everytime he looked around everything and everyone was changing, and everything he did refilled his mind with more confusion and more fear. I felt as though I were dangling from the end of a long string, dangling high in the air with nothing to hold on to or reach for to steady me.

I crossed the porch at the Big House, and I could faintly smell the aroma of Rosa's teacakes as I opened the door. She was making them so I would have something to eat for the next few days, and would probably take some of them with her for her children. "Can I have a couple of teacakes with a cup of coffee, Rosa?"

"Yes, suh. Da coffee's from dis mornin, but it's still hot."

"That's fine. I just want to dunk them in the coffee. That'll be my dinner," and I looked at her and smiled. It was Sunday, but the preacher wasn't coming to dinner, that was for sure, so I took my coffee and teacakes to eat them in front of the warm fire in the dining room.

Rosa came to the door and asked if I needed anything else and telling me that she was going home. I asked her, "Rosa, are you sure you're coming on Tuesday?"

"Well, dat's wat I plans to do. Da folks'll be back da day afta Christmas an I's want ta be sho evythangs allright fo dey gits heah."

"Well, I don't know why you need to come. Everything's looking great, and I'm not going to dirty anything before they get home," I said. "Wait here for a minute! I'll be right back." I set my coffee and teacakes on the server and ran to Mama's bedroom, grabbed the Christmas present, and ran back to the kitchen where Rosa was wiping the table for the tenth time. Setting the box on the table, I told her, "Merry Christmas, Rosa. This is from Mama, for you and the girls."

She said "I sho do thank you, Mista Billy. I'sll see Miz Florence in a day or so, and thank her, too." I asked her to get me a paper bag from wherever she and Mama kept them. She bent over the lower cabinets where the box of orange juice was and pulled out one that had printed on the side *Jitney Jungle*. I wondered, Jitney Jungle? Did Aunt Sook know that Mama was sneaking off to Jitney Jungle? I hated ole man Goldman who ran that store, and Aunt Sook was family! I had to talk to Mama about that.

Opening the bag, I went onto the porch to the deep freezer and opened the lid. Not knowing exactly what I was putting into the bag, I filled it about halfway to the top. Rosa was watching me and said, "Mista Billy, Miz Florence gon be mad if ya gives all dat away."

"Rosa, she won't even miss it. This is from me, for the things you do for me all of the time. Come on, let's go. I'll take you home in Dad's truck." She kept glancing at the bag while we walked to the garage.

Rosa looked around and said, "I sho don wan ole Pal to git round me. Wesley need ta rub him down wit som grease and ashes. He betta do dat, fo da folks gits home."

I would tell Mama about giving Rosa the packages from the freezer, and she would be glad. Inviting myself to her house, I said "Rosa, you cook all of this stuff for Christmas, and I'm gonna come get me a big plate on Christmas day. Okay?"

She smiled and said, "Sho do. I'sll have it ready!"

When I got back and parked the truck in the garage, Pal was there lying quietly in his bed, still sick from the skunk odor. It was bad and sickening to me, too. I went to the kitchen, got another Jitney Jungle bag and partly filled it from the deep freezer. That one would be for Wesley, and I set it by the screen door so he could take it home when he finished his chores. Then I thought about how hard Cathrine had worked and how many rolls Mrs. Mazie had given to Papa and me. Maybe I needed to give them a bag, too, so I went back to the cabinet and got another one. I ran to the deep freezer, raised the lid, and partly filled the bag. I looked at what was left and thought that Mama wouldn't miss a little more, so I went back into the kitchen and got another bag. That was going to be for Alex. He was my big buddy, and I wished there was a way that he could keep ole Veesy from having any of it. Wesley could carry his home with him, so I took the other two and put them in Dad's truck. Moving slowly down the dirt road, I stopped first at Cathrine's house. Grabbing one of the bags, I ran around to the back porch and knocked on the door.

Mrs. Mazie was scratching her tummy when she opened the door, and asked, "You want a roll, huh, Billy?"

Quickly, I said, "No Ma'am, I just want to give you this bag of stuff for all those other rolls you've been giving to me and Papa. Thanks, and Merry

Christmas," and I handed the bag to her before she would say anything else. She smiled, and I think for the first time ever I saw her teeth. I pulled the door closed and laughed out loud while I ran back to the truck parked in the middle of the dirt road, thinking, "Wow, Miz Mazie has some teeth! I'm glad." After all these years, I had never seen her smile big enough to see her teeth. I was happy, I felt big again, alive, and ready to go, ready to move on.

I hopped in and drove on down to Alex's house, making the wheels spin in the soft dirt. Leaving the truck parked in the road again, I picked up the paper bag and walked up the little sidewalk and onto the porch. Alex must have seen me coming since the door opened and he came out, quickly closing the door behind him. I could hear ole Veesy yelling, "Who dat, Alex?" And she yelled louder, "Alex, don'chu leave heah, ya heah me!"

I held the bag out to him. He looked in it and asked, "Wat'cha got chere, Billy?"

Giving my big buddy a Christmas present made be feel good, and happy. I replied, "This is a little present from me. Merry Christmas," and I smiled while watching his face.

He looked into the bag, and said, "Boy, I sho do preciate it. Dere's a lot of meat chere!"

"Yeah! And tell Bernice Merry Christmas for me, too."

Before I could turn to go to the truck, he asked, "Wat'cha doin, cleanin out ya mama's new deep freezer?"

"Yeah, I guess you can say that," and I put on a manly strut while I walked back to the truck, still feeling happy, powerful, and grown-up.

Before I reached the road, I heard ole Veesy again yelling something at Alex, but he called to me to wait. He stepped from the porch and followed me to the truck while I thought about what he had said, "There's a lot of meat here." I wondered, was that all meat in the deep freezer, and what was Mama going to say about it? But anyway, she wouldn't be home until Thursday, which was four days away, so I had plenty of time to figure out a plan in case she would ask me.

Standing at the door of the truck while Alex glanced up and down at me, he began, "Ya gitten ta be a mighty big boy, Billy. I bet 'cha kissed dem girls da otha night at dat pawdy when ya danced wit 'um. Ya sho likes to dance, don' chu?" I smiled, and waited for his next comment, but he put his hand on my shoulder, continuing, "Billy, don chu pays no 'tention to wat Veesy told ya da otha night bout me and Bernice. Veesy wuz mad cause I had a lit'le too much. She don lack fer me to drink none, and she sho ought not be talking dat way bout what goes on in my family."

What he said was like his big fist hitting me in the chest and knocking the wind out of me. I could say nothing for a second or two, but I finally got my breath, "Y'all have a good Christmas, Alex. I have to go home. I'll see you," and

I climbed into the truck, pulling away quickly. In the rear view mirror, I could see him standing on the side of the dirt road with a Christmas present from my mama's deep freezer, and watching the truck. I gritted my teeth and cursed out loud while I watched in the rear view mirror. Alex, my friend, my *big buddy*, became smaller and smaller, while I drove farther down the dirt road, away from him. I took a deep breath and held it.

Again, I could feel the jagged edges of the chasm, which kept coming into my mind, and it sickened me again. I was afraid of it and I hated it, and I couldn't figure it out. Tired, I felt so tired and weak. I hated Alex, and when I passed Helen and Papa's house, I wished that I had given Alex's bag to them even knowing that Helen was busy packing to move away. I turned the truck around at the end of the dirt road and drove it home a lot faster than I knew I should, and into the garage. I looked down through the window at my ole yellow dog wagging his tail and looking up at me, waiting for me to open the door and step out. Banging both fists on the steering wheel, I yelled until the tears came, "You fake, you lying son of a bitch, I hate you! I hate you! Why? Why...?"

I sat quietly for a few minutes with my head leaning against the top of the steering wheel, thinking about Alex and what he had said. I knew that Veesy was telling me the truth about him and what he was doing to his own flesh and blood daughter, who was beautiful, so young, and who looked much like him. Alex, my friend, my big buddy, was the bad man. *He* was the bad person, and I didn't want to have to tell my dad. I opened the truck door and kicked at Pal, yelling as loud as I could, "Get away! Get away, you ole...yellow bastard."

Before I opened the door to the kitchen, I walked down the porch and opened the lid to Mama's new deep freezer. She had had it for only a few months, and I had heard her say that it was the best thing we had bought since the war had ended. When I looked in it, I realized that it was about half empty, and I fussed at myself, "What in the devil have I done now? You stupid idiot, what have you done?" and I slammed the lid down. Maybe she wouldn't notice right away. We'd see.

I picked up a few sticks of firewood and put them into the dining room fireplace. The fire was almost out, but I stood there waiting to see if it would catch. The old house was really clean after Rosa had come, but it was cold and I counted four long days till my family would come home. On the server, I found my two teacakes and my cup of cold coffee that I had left there earlier. I dunked them in the coffee, and nibbled on the big cookies until they were gone. Then I ran upstairs to my room, picked up five comics from the stack in my closet, and went back to the big chairs in front of the fire that had begun to blaze. *Superman* looked pretty good, and nervously I opened the cover of the first one where I found four little pieces of paper. All four had scribbled on them, the same little word, P-A-P-A. "Papa" I heard my voice say, and again I looked at each of them, leaned forward in my chair, and laid them neatly on the hearth in front of me. "Papa," I thought, "In just a few short weeks, the little kid with the tall head, whom everybody made fun of, was gone, and I hoped forever. Isaac is his name now, and I hope he grows into a good man." I picked up the four little sheets from the hearth, and threw them over the screen into the fire, watching while each one floated slowly onto the logs. The red flames made them twist, curl and turn black. Very slowly they broke into a million black pieces, fell apart, and disappeared into the hot coals.

I wondered if that was what was going to happen to me when I went to Hell. Would I twist and curl up from the hot flames, turn black and disappear? Thinking about the wine last night and all the trouble I had caused, and I had given away almost half of Mama's meat from her new deep freezer, and I thought about Alex and about Bernice. Papa had disappeared and Isaac Vead was moving away, and I no longer wanted my big buddy, Alex. I leaned my head against the wing of the chair and thought about Sarah Grace's party, about Elizabeth and my first real kiss with a pretty girl, and about my friends at school, wishing that school would be starting the next day. I was tired of the plantation, the Big House, and everything that was happening around me, and I felt good when I thought about leaving the dirt road to be with my friends in town.

The fire and the tangled thoughts running through my mind had put me in a sleepy daze when I heard the phone ring in the front of the house. I jumped up and ran through the family room into the great hall, answering the phone very plainly, "Shirley Plantation."

The voice on the phone sounded loudly, "Bill Beau, this is Aunt Sook. How are you my darling?" Before I could tell her anything, she continued,"Why don't you come help me tomorrow and Tuesday? Could you do that?"

It didn't take me long to answer, "I sure can, but I don't have a ride. Everybody's gone to Texas, except me."

She countered, "I know. Your mama said you'd be by yourself till after Christmas. You can spend Christmas with us. I'll send Uncle Gathard to pick you up in about an hour. Is that okay?"

Happily, I answered, "Yes, Mam. Tell him I'll meet him at the end of the dirt road, so he won't get his car muddy."

As though she couldn't wait for me to get there, she replied, "Oh, that sounds wonderful. I'm just so glad you can come. I'll see you in a little bit, my darling."

"Okay, bye" and I hung up. I had to hurry. It was past four o'clock, Isaac was coming, and I had to get some clothes together to take with me.

I went to the cabinets and got another Jitney Jungle bag to put my clothes in. Then I thought, "No, I better not take that to Aunt Sook's store with me," so I found one with nothing printed on it. I ran upstairs and put some clean skivvies and a couple of shirts in it, then ran back down to the bathroom to get my toothbrush. That was enough. If I needed anything else, Aunt Sook would have it in the store. I grabbed Isaac's present from the dining table and went out to the porch to put on my windbreaker. Wesley was coming up the back steps with the little bucket of cream, and I told him where I was going, and that I had him a little something for Christmas sitting at the screen door.

He walked over to the Jitney Jungle bag, looked down into it and saw the little packages. He looked back at me, asking, "Ya wants me to take yo mama's meat home?"

I was holding my bag of clothes with Isaac's gift, so I just shook my head and said, "Sure! That's my Christmas present for you. Merry Christmas, Wesley!"

He shook his head and opened the kitchen door, walked in, and while he crossed the kitchen to the icebox, I heard him say, "I ain't bouts to take Miz Florence's meat. Dat wine don got 'im fo sho. He don really loss his mind."

I quickly turned, flung open the screen door, and jumped down the steps. Pal was already there, waiting for me, just as I landed on the brick sidewalk. I thought that I rubbed against him a little, but I kicked at him and yelled for him to get away. He turned around and headed toward the garage. I smelled my pants and the arm of my jacket, but I didn't smell anything bad, so I started running down the driveway toward the Quarters. When I turned the corner at the end of the hedgerow, I saw Isaac strutting in my direction. He had on my dad's old hat perched on the side of his head, and his jacket buttoned all the way to the top.

Before I could say anything, he asked with a frown, "Where ya goin, Billy?" I told him. He looked a little disappointed, then asked, "Wat we gon do t'morrow if ya go down dare?"

"Man, you have to help your Mama get ready to move. That's your job, too!"

"Sho, I's gon hep her, but it ain't much ta do. Dat my present, dare?" and he pointed to the box, smiling.

"Merry Christmas, Issac," and I handed the present to him.

He held it for a second, not believing that it was really for him, and asked in a shrill voice, "Billy, ya sho dis fer me?" I shook my head *yes*, and we started walking down the dirt road.

"You gotta open it right now Issac, so get to it!" He broke the string while we walked and pulled open the top of the box, all the time grinning and chuckling under his breath.

He reached into the box, pulled out the green windbreaker, held it up so he could see it well, and asked again, "Dis fer me? Are ya sho, Billy, dis fer me?"

"Yep, it's for you, Isaac, and it's brand new. It's just like mine, except it's green and it's new." Holding it up so we could see it better, the green windbreaker looked great, in fact, a lot better than it had looked before I gave it away.

He again looked at me, sadly mumbling, "Billy, I don got nothin ta give ta ya fer Christmas. I's sho sorry, but I sho don't."

I hit him lightly on the arm, "Aw, don't worry, Isaac, I've got everything I need," and a big tear rolled down his cheek as he took off his old coat, handing it to me to hold with the box and my bag of clothes. A strong whiff of Pal hit me, and at the same time, a whiff of his smoky house. While standing in the middle of the dirt road, he put the windbreaker on and zipped it all the way to the top. Reaching with one hand, I fixed the collar for him, and complimented the way it fit: "That really looks good, Issac. Now we both have a windbreaker, almost exactly alike. Merry Christmas," and I patted him on his back.

He took his coat and the box, ran up the walk to his house calling out, "Mama, Mama, come see my new coat! Me and Billy got one jist-a-lack!" I figured that the new windbreaker was the first time my friend had ever gotten anything new, and maybe it was the first real present anyone had ever given him. Papa quickly crossed the little porch in a new green jacket, and I waited where I stood, motionless, on the dirt road, until the wooden door into their little house closed.

And my friend was gone.

CHAPTER 49

I knew that my life on the dirt road would change…again.

I walked on in the fading light to the end of the dirt road to wait for a ride to take me away. Anxiously, I looked toward town and wondered about some of my friends from school. What would they get for Christmas? Did Eddie really go to Canada? Did Elizabeth think about Sarah Grace's party, or think about me? With the paper bag of clothes under my arm, I slowly turned and looked toward my home, all the way to the other end of the dirt road. I suddenly realized that to go home, every time I must go the entire length of the dirt road through the Quarters. I had no choice, as there was no other way to get there, to home, to my family.

Darkness was coming fast, and the heavy overcast sky seemed to be slowly falling, smothering the rows of little houses and the green oaks, pressing them deep into the dirt road, and leaving me all alone as I stood on the line where the plantation ended. The cold, damp loneliness made me feel sick to my stomach like saying goodbye to my mother, or my best friend, and wondering if I might never see them again. While crossing to the other side of the graveled road, I picked up a handful of rocks, and threw each one as hard as I could, watching as each rippled the water, then sank forever to the deep, sandy bottom of Bayou Boeuf. Turning toward the dark skies in the east, I set my gaze toward town, saying out loud so I could hear my own voice plainly, "In just a few more days, I will be with my friends in town, at school. That will be good, and I am ready. I…am…ready."

In the distance, I saw the headlights coming, and finally the car came to a halt in front of me. I opened the door, "Hi, how you doin, Uncle Gathard?"

He looked over at me and asked in a rumbling voice, "Boy, you know anything good?" I figured he was mad that he had to come get me, but the warm car felt good, the seats were soft, and the dashboard was all lit up, and pretty, too.

"Yes sir, I really like this Plymouth, Uncle Gathard," thinking a compliment might make him at least a little happy. He just looked straight ahead, and then he sniffed a couple of times.

He sniffed again, wrinkled his forehead, and with an ugly frown getting worse, complained, "I bet we hit a skunk back there, I can smell the damn thing."

"Yes sir, I bet we did. I can smell the damn thing, too," and I sort of mocked him with the *damn* word, then, "You sure got it hot in here," and I reached and pulled my aviator's cap off my head.

I smiled, and in the dim light from the dashboard I saw the rascal fix a deep frown on his forehead and rub it under the brim of his hat when he turned his beaded little eyes toward me. With his lips turned down, and by the way he cleared his throat every second or two, I figured he was getting ready to chew me up, and spit me out.

He rolled down his window a little, cleared his throat three more times, coughed, and sniffed at me again.

I figured I needed to watch him pretty close.

CHAPTER 50

The Plymouth hummed along through Bunkie and finally past the Four Way Café at the Eola cross roads, about four miles south of town. Almost everything had been dark along the way, except the soft light coming from the windows of the small, country houses sitting quiet and lonely along the highway. Slowly, the Plymouth came to the little church near the railroad tracks, just before reaching Harper's Grocery. It was Sunday night, and the lights inside the church were bright. Only two or three cars were parked out front, but through the clear glass windows I could see a lot of people standing and singing, my imagining that the sweet sounds of Christmas hymns were exploding in the little church. I wanted to be there...I wanted to hear those sounds, the hymns, and I wanted to *feel* Christmas. Christmas was only three days away.

Harper's Grocery was about two miles from The Eola Baptist Church, where all of my family went—aunts and uncles, cousins and other kin whom I had only heard of as being our relatives. When I asked Uncle Gathard what time church started, he looked at me through the narrow slits of his eyes, and said, "In about an hour or so, but I don't believe we gonna go tonight," and his mouth turned down like an upside-down moon. I figured he didn't want to go because he might have a little bit of fun, or might have to be nice to someone, but I knew Aunt Sook would decide if we went or not.

I said nothing else until he parked the Plymouth near the back door of their house. Still hugging my paper bag of clothes under my arm, I told him, "I appreciate your coming to get me, Uncle Gathard. Thanks!" He said nothing, but he left his car door open.

As I entered the kitchen, Aunt Ida turned toward me and smiled, "Merry Christmas, Billy." I told her Merry Christmas and set my paper sack on the table.

Aunt Sook walked in from the living room and hugged me, "We're so glad you could come. This is gonna be the best Christmas. How are you, sweetheart?" and she held out her arms to hug me, again.

She was tall and beautiful and, as usual, she was dressed in a pair of slacks. I could smell her perfume.

"Aunt Sook, are we gonna go to church tonight?" I asked, hoping she would say *yes.*

"Well, we can if you want to," and she smiled while I nodded yes.

I hadn't been off the plantation for quite a while, except for the party at

219

Sarah Grace's house, and I figured I ought to forget about the party and especially about *kissing*, if we were going to church. Besides, I wanted to see some of my
buddies from school, and I figured some of them would be at church. Aunt Sook
looked over to Aunt Ida and she smiled a *yes*. Uncle Gathard just held up both
hands as if to say, "whatever you women want," and the frown on his forehead
seemed to fall all the way to his turned-down mouth.

I unzipped my windbreaker and took it off, showing my flowered shirt
that Mama had made with the cloth from a sack of feed, my khakis, and tennis
shoes. Uncle Gathard looked closely at me, frowned harder, and fussed, "Fannie,
I thought you bought that boy some decent clothes. He oughta not go to church
looking like that."

Aunt Sook's real name was "Fannie," after the singer Fannie Brice, but
everybody called her "Sook." Mama had told me that Sook was like French for
sugar. I liked that, "Aunt Sugar," and to me, Aunt Sook was pure cane sugar.

Winking at me and smiling, she countered, "Oh, I bet he can go like that if
he wants to. Don't worry about it, Gathard, everything's going to be fine."

"Good," I thought, "she set the old grouch straight," and his mouth turned
down further.

Aunt Sook went into the dark store, turned on the lights, and in a few
minutes came back with a handful of items. Laying them out neatly on the table,
she announced, "Billy, honey, you can take these home with you. Right now, you
can go to my bathroom and clean up to go to church. That would be nice, don't
you think?" She had her own bathroom, and it had plenty of hot water straight
from the faucet.

I looked at all the good stuff laid out on the table. Tooth paste, a comb, a
jar of underarm deodorant, a toothbrush, and a bottle of *Wildroot Cream Oil*. And
even a bottle of after-shave lotion like my dad used. Smiling at her, I said, "Wow,
I've never had any underarm deodorant and what is this...'Wildroot Cream Oil?'
And a bottle of after-shave lotion, like Dad's. I don't shave yet, Aunt Sook." By
then, I had figured she could smell Pal and the skunk, but I couldn't do anything
about it.

She leaned toward me a little. I could tell she was sniffing me, then looking
me straight in the face, "Honey, I'm gonna go draw you some hot water, and you
can take a good hot bath. That'll make you feel great." Uncle Gathard had been
watching and listening to the entire conversation, and with the frown across
his forehead moving up and down, he mumbled, "I think that boy smells like a
polecat. My car stinks godawful! In fact, I had to leave the door open to let the
stink out. He needs more than a bath-a good scrubbin with some lye soap!" Aunt
Ida started laughing really hard with her big bosoms bouncing up and down. I
figured probably everyone could smell Pal and the skunk on me, but until that
time no one had complained about it. Papa sure hadn't said anything, but I knew

he stunk, so I figured he couldn't smell me. But that ole yellow dog was going to get it when I got back to Shirley Plantation.

I put all the items in my paper bag, and Aunt Sook led the way to her bathroom. She turned the faucets on, instructing, "After you wash your hair and finish bathing, call me, and I'll come comb your hair, honey. And too, I've got your Christmas present that you can open right away." She winked at me again, and smiled. I had spent many nights with Aunt Sook and Uncle Gathard when I was a little child. She often claimed that I was her little boy, and I liked that, but Uncle Gathard never claimed anything.

When she said a hot bath, she had really meant it. I usually bathed in barely warm water or we would have had to heat water for two days to get that much in the tub, and especially so hot. I had to turn on the cold water to cool it down. I washed my hair with some real shampoo that she had on the edge of the tub, instead of the bar of soap. Mama and my sisters used shampoo, but Jerry always said that boys didn't use shampoo, except sissy boys, but I figured she just didn't want me to use hers. In a few minutes, I opened the door and called to Aunt Sook that I had finished. She came to her bedroom and told me to come open my Christmas present, explaining, "Now, this is for Christmas, which won't be here till Wednesday, but I think it would be fun to open it now." Smiling, I shook my head and started unwrapping the present. I opened the box and there was another pair of pants with a matching shirt. Brown again, but that was okay, because I liked brown. Besides, I was sure that it was my khakis that smelled like Pal and the skunk, and now I wouldn't have to go to church smelling so bad.

"Aw, thanks Aunt Sook, I can really use these. Thanks, I really appreciate it!"

"Did you put on your deodorant and brush your teeth?"

"Yes Ma'am, and I put some Wildroot Cream Oil in my hair."

She reached up and felt my hair, then asked, "Darling, how much did you use?"

"Oh, I put on plenty!"

She smiled and hugged me, then felt my hair again and said, "Well, I was going to show you how to use it. I think you may have put a little too much, but we can fix that with no problem at all."

After wiping some of the Wildroot out of my hair, and combing it with a part on the side, Aunt Sook sat back a little on the chair, smiled at me, and announced, "Well, you look like a different boy, now." Glancing at myself in her mirror, I wondered what she meant, but I did look a little different, shiny clean and neat, especially with my hair parted and combed down tight on my head.

Uncle Gathard kept his crooked mouth shut all the way to church, but I heard Aunt Ida whisper to Aunt Sook that she had "put them on to soak," figuring she was talking about my khakis and my flowered shirt along with my underwear. That's what Rosa did with Dad's really dirty cloths.

When we arrived at the church, there was no place to park except along the side of the road. Uncle Gathard commented about being late, my figuring that he was blaming me for it, but Aunt Sook just patted him on the shoulder, assuring him, "Oh, Gathard, we're not that late, and besides, we're gonna have a nice time having Billy here with us."

His frown didn't change a bit, but I could almost hear his teeth grind behind his skinny lips.

The church was packed, and the music and singing was starting just when we entered the door. We had to split up, and Aunt Sook and I sat together. The choir was full, except the empty chair where my mama usually sat. They would miss her tonight, like me. Glancing around the crowd, I found all four of my other aunts sitting together. Away to the side, I found my good friend Marilyn, sitting with her mama, which was a surprise for me because they were Methodists and lived farther south in Whiteville. I knew almost everybody there, like a great big family, and all of the hymns were for Christmas. I wondered if Dad, Mama and Mickey were singing Christmas hymns, too, and Margie and Jerry. Were they singing Christmas hymns? They weren't here in our church where my family had gone for so long. What about Isaac and Alex, and my other friends who lived on the plantation? Where were they tonight? Not here, that was for sure, but maybe in a little church of theirs, somewhere. Like the preacher always said, "We all have souls," but why didn't Issac and Alex ever come to our church? It was nice here. They would like it. I went to one of their churches every now and then, especially if they were having a revival meeting at night, and we could walk to it.

The choir suddenly became louder, jarring my brain, and reminding me that the Christmas hymns were better in my church than anywhere in the world, but all of my family was missing out that night. They weren't there.

Looking at my beautiful aunt sitting beside me, I could hear her voice carry far above and beyond the singers around her, all of the sounds of Christmas that I had missed so badly, and she reached over and patted the top of my hand and smiled, knowing, I guess, that I was lonesome.

I slept on the couch in the living room that night. Uncle Gathard was up early to go to work, doing shift work at the gasoline plant in Ville Platte, about twenty-five miles away. When he came through the living room, he glanced at me, commanding, "You better get up, boy. I'm gonna have coffee made in a few minutes."

I didn't want to get up, but he was the last person I wanted to hear complain, so I crawled off the couch and moved over to the big chair, wrapping myself in a blanket. I had on my skivvies and a knit shirt. He walked through the living room toward his bedroom, and came right back with a bathrobe, ordering, "Put this on. You ought to have on pajamas, a big boy like you. You can't go around here naked like that with these women livin here." When he said that, it made me think that maybe that was what made him mad and grouchy all of the time; he had to live with two women, and probably had to do whatever they said or whatever they wanted.

With only my knit shirt and skivvies, I had on more clothes than I wore in the summer, but I wasn't about to contradict him, so I put the robe on, went to the kitchen and sat at the table. After a few minutes, he put a cup of coffee in front of me. That was quick. I had never seen one of those new electric coffee pots, but they had one, as well as a really quick gas stove where you just turn a little knob and the fire comes on. That sure beat the heck out of our ole wood stove, which took forever to make coffee. And the coffee from that shiny coffee pot was really good. I thought about Hoss and about Wesley, figuring that poor old Hoss would never see one, but I bet Wesley would like to have a new coffee pot like Uncle Gathard's; and Rosa, I knew she would like a stove like that.

In just a few minutes, Aunt Sook and Aunt Ida came in, both in bathrobes. Aunt Sook had already put her makeup on, and her black hair was all in place. Uncle Gathard poured them each a cup of coffee, telling all of us, "Well, I'm headin out. See y'all about five." He looked at me while I was yawning and said, "Boy, you betta wake up! You have to sell plenty of groceries today to pay for those new clothes Fannie gave you." I looked at Aunt Sook over the top of my cup, and she winked and smiled at me. Maybe Uncle Gathard wasn't as mean as he wanted people to think he was. Besides, Aunt Sook and Aunt Ida both knew how to handle the rascal.

For two days, I filled the shelves with groceries as fast as I could. Everybody south of town came at least three times to Harper's Grocery on Monday and Tuesday. Aunt Sook had Mister Gauthier running the meat counter, and a black lady named Rebecca helped in the store, gathering items on the list given to her by customers. She went around the store and picked up everything for them and would take the items to the front counter where Aunt Sook would write the items onto a charge pad. Some people did their own shopping and took their items to the counter, like customers did at Jitney Jungle. Aunt Sook had taught me how to work the cash register and write-up groceries some time back. Anytime I wasn't stacking the shelves, I helped her at the front counter, or helped Rebecca take items to the front. If several people were waiting in line, sometimes all three of us wrote up the items and ran the cash register.

Aunt Sook's store was the gathering place for the area. I thought some people came on Saturdays, or days like the Monday and Tuesday before Christmas, just to meet others and talk. Some of the shoppers would go to Aunt Ida's kitchen, sit around the table, and drink a cup of coffee while Rebecca or I filled out their list of groceries, wrote them on the charge pad, and sacked them the up, ready for the customer to take them home.

Whatever gossip was going around could be heard or denied right there in Aunt Ida's kitchen, or up front at the counter. If they wanted to, someone could even start some gossip right there at Harper's Grocery.

And I had made up my mind a long time ago that I wanted a country store like Aunt Sook's.

CHAPTER 51

We ate dinner on Christmas day at another aunt's house in Gold Dust, about ten miles south of Bunkie. All of the aunts had planned it, and each brought something to add to the Christmas table. Bobby Joe and I rode bicycles along the graveled streets, and visited with some of our school friends who lived there. About three o'clock, Aunt Sook said that we needed to go home, and she seemed to be in a hurry. She let me drive the Plymouth, which was six or seven years old, and made before the war. It was getting a little old, and wasn't nearly as nice as our new Chevy. I asked her, "When are y'all gonna get a new car, Aunt Sook?"

"Oh, Gathard's already talking about one, so I guess it won't be long."

"What kind does he want?"

She thought for a few seconds, then, answered, "They're coming out with a new kind of car soon. I think it's going to be called *Frazer*, and I think he wants to try one of them."

I thought to myself, "Boy, my Dad wouldn't try anything but a Ford or Chevy. Uncle Gathard's crazier than I thought," but I said to her, "That sounds good. Aunt Sook, do you think you could take me home after while?"

She forced a little smile and glanced at Aunt Ida, then back to me, "Honey, I'll get Uncle Gathard to take you when he comes in from work. I hope that's okay." That wouldn't be till five o'clock, which meant I wouldn't get home until it was almost dark, and the Big House would be dark and cold.

Uncle Gathard walked in the back door of the kitchen, and before he could set his lunch box on the kitchen table, Aunt Ida quickly ordered, "Gathard, you have to take Billy home so don't take your jacket off."

He looked at me as if he could chew me up again and said, "Well, he ain't worth it! Why didn't Fannie take him home already?"

Aunt Ida was cutting cheese to make a sandwich for me to take home. She put a small piece in her mouth, and started chewing, "Sook's not feeling good. She's lying down with a headache. You'll have to take him, Gathard. It won't take you long, and I'll have supper ready by the time you get back." Smiling when she glanced toward me, she continued, "He's been ready to go for about two hours, just waiting for you to get here. I think he's tired of us women."

He grumbled something under his breath, and then looked at me, commanding, "Come on, boy, let's go!" Aunt Ida wrapped my sandwich in wax paper, smiled and whispered, "Don't pay any attention to that old man," and handed the sandwich to me. Uncle Gathard frowned, coughed and cleared his throat. He didn't have a toothache. He fussed and frowned because he had two women in the house telling him what to do all the time. He and Aunt Sook had separate bedrooms also, so I figured he must have felt about like Pal when Dad locked our girl dogs in the chicken pen every now and then. I knew I was smiling about my thoughts, but he didn't know it.

When we arrived at the dirt road, I told him to let me off there so he wouldn't get his car muddy. The road through the Quarters wasn't really bad, but I knew he wanted to get rid of me as much as I wanted to be rid of him. "Thanks, I appreciate the ride, Uncle Gathard."

Before I closed the door, he said, "Thanks for helping us in the store, Billy. I don't know what Fannie would've done without you." He smiled a crooked little smile and snickered, "Sure hope you don't get scared in that big old house tonight, boy. You better watch out, all by yourself like that. Thanks for coming," and he laughed.

"Yes, sir, I'll help anytime. See ya!" and I gently closed the door. I couldn't believe what he had said. Just when I had worked up a strong reason to dislike *him* and his *sarcasm*, he came out with "I don't know what we would've done without you." I still thought he was always grumpy because he had two women constantly telling him what to do, and he was locked out of Aunt Sook's bedroom. Anyway, I was willing to bet that my dad would agree with me even though the women were two of his sisters.

Crossing the gravel road, I looked to where Mag's house had been, and through the fading light I could barely see the tall chimney. Having walked to the little gate, I found myself opening and closing it, back and forth, and I wondered if anyone picked on her at Bubenzer. There were only small kids in the big house there, so Mag would probably have it a little easier, at least until the kids were older.

"This place is awful," I heard myself saying, and I slammed the gate as hard as I could. The charred post on which it was hinged fell over, the gate with it, and lay flat on the ground in front of me. "Good, now there's nothing left standing but that ugly half-burned tree and that ole chimney, and I'm going to push that damn thing down." I walked to the chimney and pushed as hard as I could, several times, but it wouldn't fall. I left it, and started my walk to the other end of the dirt road, to home.

CHAPTER 52

The sun had set and darkness was coming, while the Quarters lay quiet in the damp, still air. Smoke from the stoves and chimneys looked bluish as it drifted and spread very low along the dirt road, then rose in small, transparent hills, slowly moving in front of me. The long limbs of the oaks reached through the damp air, trying to touch the smoke. When I reached Helen and Isaac's house, I went up the pathway, slowly stepped onto the worn boards of the porch floor, and sat on the swing, placing my bag of clothes and the box with my Christmas present beside me. Carefully, I worked my cheese sandwich out of the pocket of my jacket, and nibbled on it while swinging back and forth, remembering, "If Isaac were here, I would have to give him half of it." That was always understood, and he seemed always to be hungry. I had eaten my half, so I laid the rest at the other end of the swing. With my bag of clothes and my box under my arm, I left the swing moving back and forth, while the shrill squeak of the chain broke the silence around me, and I walked through the yard to the dirt road.

Surprisingly, I felt glad that Isaac and Helen were gone. Isaac would have a chance in town now, a chance that was started right there in the swing, on that porch, about two years earlier with my reading a funny book to him.

Finally reaching the corner at the hedgerow, I could see Pal coming to meet me, barking. I called out to him, and he came up to me wagging his big yellow tail. I figured that he must have cleaned up because he no longer smelled so bad, or maybe Wesley had washed him.

The Big House was completely dark, but Wesley had placed some kindling and wood by the dining room fireplace, so I set it in the firebox and lit the kindling. Finding my money in my pocket, I pulled it out and counted ten dollars. Aunt Sook had given me five for working two days, and one as a Christmas present even after giving me the new clothes. Aunt Ida had given me one, and my other three aunts had each given me one. I turned and headed upstairs to get my little bag of pennies, nickels, and dimes from my trunk. Adding it to my ten dollars, I needed only sixty cents more to make a total of fifteen dollars, figuring there weren't many kids my age with that much money tucked away. Opening my sister's bureau drawer, I discovered the white box was not where she usually kept it, so I went over to her dresser with the big *Hollywood* mirror, pulled out one of the drawers completely, and it fell to the floor. The white box was there, but everything in the drawer had fallen out, scattering about. I opened the box, but it was empty except for a little note: "Billy, I told you to stay out of my room.

Get out!" I thought, "So, that's why she moved the little box, to set a trap for me. That rascal." Getting even with her for that kind of trick would be easy. Getting everything back into the drawer the way she had it was going to be impossible, so I dropped everything back in it and slammed the drawer closed.

Gently, I pulled open the other drawer, and there was her Pat O'Brien hurricane glass from New Orleans, almost filled with nickels, dimes and pennies. Boy! That would be easier than looking for that little white box if I needed a little change from time to time. I believed she wanted to make it easier for me, so I counted out sixty cents, closed the drawer, and ran back to the dining room. Fifteen dollars, and I had earned almost every penny of it. "How many kids had fifteen dollars? Not many," and I laughed out loud.

I had more than I needed to go to the Sweetheart Banquet on Valentine's Day, and I wanted to ask Elizabeth to go with me. For a couple of days, I had been thinking about Elizabeth, the way she kissed me, and I had hoped she would come to Aunt Sook's store while I was there, but she didn't. Maybe in the cloakroom at school we could kiss again, I thought, and I touched my lips with the tips of my fingers.

I put all of my money into the bag and took it back to my trunk upstairs, and carefully put it back where it belonged. Still kneeling on the floor, I raised the lid on the Tampa Nugget box, and my eyes latched onto Santa Claus. I picked up the little bulb and moved it out of the closet, under the light. It was a little bigger than my thumb, and I imagined that a pretty little French girl with long, black pigtails like Marilyn's, and red lips like Elizabeth's, maybe had made it with her hands. And now it was mine. It was so fine and had so many bright colors. Kissing the bulb, like Elizabeth had kissed me, and with my eyes closed, I softly whispered, "You can live in my trunk for a long time, and I'll take care of you." Very gently, I laid the bulb back into its place next to the silver wings, and again I spoke out loud, "I'll keep you forever, Santa, so don't worry. You're my Christmas right now, but tomorrow our family is coming home."

Our family is coming home. That was the best thing I had thought about for several days. Looking at the tall stack of comic books, I took three from the top and ran down the stairs to the dining room.

Standing with my back to the big fire, I watched with excitement while the shadows danced from wall to wall, across the tall ceilings, and the flames glimmered in the glass doors of the china cabinet at the other end of the room. With my arms raised as high as I could reach, and my fingers wrapped tightly around the roll of comics, I leaned my head back and heard my voice echoing through the Big House, "L e t ' s r e a d *Su p e r m a n*, B I L L YYYYYYY...!

And I remembered Papa.

CHAPTER 53

Wesley called to me from the bottom of the stairs. Sleepily, I called back to him, "Okay," and threw the quilts back. The sun was bright, making the dark green leaves of the big oaks glisten, while the long limbs stretched toward the windows in my bedroom. Wesley had not awakened me at his usual time. Finding a pair of clean khakis and a sweater to pull over my knit shirt, I picked up my tennis shoes and slowly went down to the kitchen. There was Rosa, and she asked me if I wanted any breakfast. "No, I'll just have some coffee right now," and I sat at the table while she poured a cup of coffee, setting it in front of me. "Rosa, did you cook all that meat for Christmas dinner yesterday?"

"I sho did, but ya didn't come get yo plate. But I brought chu one fer dinna t'day."

I explained to her that my plans had changed, and I had eaten Christmas dinner with Aunt Sook.

"You know the folks are coming home today," I told her, but figuring that she already knew that.

She looked through the window over the sink and said, "Miz Ethel and Miz Jerry comin too. Deys'll be heah bout noontime. Miz Jerry called fo ya got up."

I smiled to myself, thinking, "Well, today *will* be my Christmas Day, finally."

"Rosa, I'm gonna make a fire in the family room and in Jerry's room to try and get this old house warmed up."

I figured that Mama and Dad would get home around noon, and it was already ten o'clock. That would give me enough time to go to the Quarters for a little while. I told Rosa that I would be back around twelve to eat dinner, and she could heat the plate of food she brought for me.

"Ya reckon I needs to fix some dinna fer evybody?" she asked, making me realize that she was determined to have everything prepared and ready for when my family would arrive.

I told her that it looked as though they would all arrive around dinnertime, so it might be a good idea to have dinner ready. "Why don't you set the dining table, and we'll pretend that it's Christmas all over again." She liked that idea, and I did, too.

I put on my windbreaker and left for the Quarters. Pal met me at the bottom of the steps, and I recalled how much trouble he had caused for me at Aunt

Sook's a few nights before, but he was so happy to see me that I decided not to scold him. I patted him on the head while he tried to lick my hand, and we left together to go visit Cathrine.

Jumping up the steps onto the back porch, I knocked on the kitchen door. Mrs. Mazie called out, "Com on in, Billy." I wondered how she knew who was knocking on her door. Strangeness was a cloud around Mrs. Mazie, and I couldn't see through it. I figured she probably bought her food seasonings from Aunt Colleen, and she, too, could put a "gree-gree" on anyone she didn't like. But I was glad she did have some teeth. I stepped into the kitchen, holding my cap in my hand, and saw that she was getting a roll for me, then handed it to me on a little plate. Before I could thank her, she got onto me, "Why wuzn't 'chu heah when Papa and Helen moved Toosday? Papa and Cathrine waited fer ya ta come, and po lil'ole Papa cried when the truck took off. Cathrine did, too."

"I went down to my aunt's store to work, and for Christmas," my not wanting her to know that I was glad to have been away when Helen and Isaac left the plantation.

She very quickly added, "Po Papa don wanna go, but he knowed he had to. But ya shudda been dere to tell um g'bye all da same," and she looked at me like she was saddened by Helen and Isaac having to move away.

Mrs. Mazie had gotten onto me many times before, but this time was different. She did feel sad for Helen, and especially for Isaac. It was fairly clear to me that she had learned to like him while Cathrine was teaching him in her kitchen. It was easy for me to see, also, because she gave him a roll every day, without his having to ask; when most of the time, I almost had to beg for one. She turned to me, continuing, "Well, dey's gone now. I sho hope dey make it."

I said under my breath, "They'll make it," and I took the last bite of my roll.

Mrs. Mazie was right, and it didn't make me feel good to hear her say it, but I knew I should have been there to say goodbye. But I figured I would cry when the truck drove off, and I didn't want to cry. I was too big, now, and I didn't want to cry, not anymore.

"Where's Cathrine?" I asked, and she pointed toward the front room. I thanked her for the roll and walked in my socks to the front of the house, where Cathrine was reading a book. I told her that I was sorry I wasn't there on Tuesday to say goodbye to Helen and Isaac.

She giggled and said, "Oh, everything went all right. Papa will be okay. I think he was anxious to get to town and become a city slicker. He asked where you were and even cried a little. He'll be okay."

"Yeah, some city slicker he'll be! We probably won't know him when he comes out here to visit," and neither one of us commented further. We knew it was likely that he would never come out to visit Shirley, and like me, I figured that Cathrine, too, was glad that Papa's life on the plantation was over, and that he could start again in town. Cathrine and I talked for a little while, and she told me that Caroline was coming over at about four o'clock to play cards, inviting me to come back. I told her I would, and I left to go home.

CHAPTER 54

Time at the Gaspard's house had passed faster than I thought. When Pal and I reached the corner at the hedgerow, I recognized Margie's Oldsmobile parked at the front steps with our Chevy right behind it. I started running down the driveway to the back of the Big House. Pal was running and jumping, trying to catch my hand, when I tripped over him. Both hands went into the rocks on the drive and both knees, too. The rocks scratched my palms in three or four places, but my knees were okay except that my clean khakis had two big brown spots on them. Pal just stood there and looked at me lying on my tummy, trying his best to act like he had nothing to do with my tripping. I stood up and looked around to see if anybody had seen me fall, then held out both hands while Pal licked a couple of bloody little cuts and a skinned place on the heel of my palm. He was my best doctor. I started to run again, quickly reaching the top step, and swung open the screened door, crossed the porch and went into the kitchen. "Where are they, Rosa? Where's everybody?"

"Dey's in the family room. Spike sho is a cute lit'le baby!" and she was still talking when I reached the other end of the dining room.

Both my sisters and my mama were there, each drinking a cup of coffee. As I leaned through the door into the family room, I said in my deepest voice, "Hello, ladies, y'all need a man around?"

Mama got up and met me with a big hug and a kiss on the forehead, and the aroma of the Coty powder hit my nose. She smiled and hugged me again, "Well, you made it, Son. How did everything go?"

I felt great and excited, but I wasn't about to tell her what all went on, so I lied, "Mama, everything was fantastic," then quickly asked, "Where's Spike?"

Margie smiled and pointed into Jerry's room, "Go look, but don't wake him. I just got him to sleep!" I hugged both my sisters and tiptoed to the bed to look at my nephew.

Mama had followed me, whispering, "Your dad's looking for you. He and Mickey are out at the horse barn."

"Okay, I'll go find 'um," and I quietly left the family room.

When I got back to the kitchen, Rosa pointed to the kitchen table and said, "I fixed yo plate from ma house." I sat and ate a few bites and told her how good it was, but I wasn't really hungry. Mrs. Mazie's rolls were big.

I stepped through the kitchen door onto the porch just as Dad and Mickey were coming up the back steps from the barn. I met them, and while hugging my little brother, I pinched him on his rosy cheek. He hit at my hand with his fist. While shaking hands with Dad, he asked, "Son, did you take my truck off the plantation?" and he had a deep frown across his forehead.

"No sir, but Alex did take me to a party last Friday night. Why?"

Continuing to frown, he shook his head and said, "Well, I noticed the front bumper has a dent in it."

I thought for a second, and told him, "Yes, Sir, I drove, and I bumped a mail box, but I didn't know it made a dent in the bumper. I'm sure sorry."

I couldn't tell him that Alex had had *a little too much*, or he would have gotten pretty upset at Alex, and I sure didn't want to be a tattletale when nothing really bad happened. He continued struggling to get his boots off and said nothing more, but I could wait no longer: "Well, I have fifteen dollars, Dad. Do you think that would be enough to get the bumper fixed?" And I thought to myself, "There goes all my money and the Sweetheart Banquet, too. Poor Elizabeth." I had decided that I really wanted to kiss her again, and now it looked like the school cloakroom might be the only place for sure.

He walked on toward the kitchen door, commenting, "Well, I'll have to look at it again. It's not bad. We'll see." Then he turned to me, asking, "Where in the world did you get all that money, boy? That's pretty good." He smiled at me, but I said nothing.

We went to the family room and talked and laughed for almost two hours. We were all at home. We were all in our places. We were all where I wanted all of us to be, right there in the Big House, warming ourselves by one of its big brick fireplaces. As I looked into the faces around me, and hearing the laughter, I could also see the abundance of caring and love, making me understand, then, that everything I wanted—and all that I was—was all around me. I thought about the great oaks in our front yard, big, strong and always there, nourished by deep and endless roots. My family was like those oaks, with roots spread from Gold Dust, through Eola and Bunkie, and all the way to the dirt road where we lived in the Big House.

Mama hummed softly while looking into Spike's big blue eyes, like hers, while she gently cradled the first-born of the next generation in our family.

I smiled to myself, stood up, and stretched, then left to get more wood for the fireplaces.

CHAPTER 55

Spike was like a little doll, not much bigger, and Mama talked to him with funny little sounds. I heard the Robin Hood clock in the dining room strike thirty minutes past the hour and knew that it was time to go to Cathrine's house to play cards. Jerry, Margie, and Spike were going to stay until Saturday, so I had plenty of time to visit. I quietly left the family room, grabbed my windbreaker off the hook on the porch, and left for the Quarters.

When I reached the tool shed, J.B. was on the wooden bridge crossing the bayou, and I wondered what big thing he was going to drop on me when our paths crossed. We met a little before we reached the gate into the barn lot, and his big, white teeth spread halfway across his face. I asked him where he was going. He answered that he had to help Mister Alfonse with the mules and the barns until groundbreaking started in a few weeks. Then his job on the water cart would start, too. He grabbed my cap from my head, put it on, and demanded, "Jist gives me dis heahs ole aviator cap, den ah could gits me ah airplane and leave dis old place!" J.B. was full of it all the time. I grabbed my cap from him, and put it on. He suddenly became serious, asking, "Ya ain't don told Alex wat we's talked bout, is you Billy?" His big, toothy smile had vanished.

"No, that's none of my business, but you better keep your mouth shut about it. Besides, you ought not be fooling around with Bernice. She's too young for you, J.B.!"

Before I could say more, he smiled again and asked, "Wat'd chu an Papa do wit' dat wine las Saddy night? I don heard all 'bout y'all gittin drunk and messin up Miz Florence's dinin room."

"We didn't get drunk, we just had an accident, and that's none of your damn business."

He laughed out loud and said, "Ya lying lack a snake, Billy! Now I gots som'um on ya," and he thumped me on the upper arm. "Ya gon has to be a good boy from nows on! An quit yo cussin, boy, or I jist might tell yo daddy how ya talks bad all da time." By then, he was laughing out loud while opening the gate to the barn lot. As I hurried along the dirt road toward Cathrine's house, he yelled to me again, "Ya betta listen ta me good, else I's tell 'im evythang. Ya heah me?"

Cathrine and Caroline were waiting in the front room, where we played gin rummy for almost an hour. The entire time, I was nervous and anxious, never being able to concentrate. They were both happy, as I won no games that day.

Mrs. Mazie brought us each a cup of hot chocolate, reminding, "It sho is gittin late out dere. Da sun'll be settin purty soon!" and I knew then it was time to go. Anxiously, I put on my jacket and moved toward the door, again telling them Merry Christmas and I would see them later.

CHAPTER 56

Walking slowly down the narrow brick sidewalk to the road, and glancing about, I wondered why I felt so nervous inside. My mind seemed to wander in all directions; there was disorder inside of me and all around me, and I felt I needed to stop and sort things out, as every thought was cut short with no conclusion. It seemed as though I was looking at everything within sight, but I was seeing only from the corners of my eyes, unclear and unfocused, while dangling again from the end of a long string, and spinning about.

As the gate slammed closed behind me, I pulled my aviator's cap over my head, snapped the leather strap under my chin, and took a deep breath of the cool air. I suddenly realized that I had raised my hands to look at them, with my fingers spread wide apart. Wondering why I had done that, I turned them, and while looking into my palms, I groaned as a hint of Danny McBride's face appeared. I gritted my teeth and clinched both fists, feeling my fingernails, again, bite into the flesh, but quickly telling myself, "No! You're bigger and stronger now. You're bigger and stronger," repeating over again, "bigger and stronger, bigger and stronger."

Glancing down to the soft dirt at my feet, I knew I was "bigger and stronger," and tall, too, as though, suddenly, I had grown within a few hours. And strength and power surged inside me, making me want to go right then to the silver plane and climb into its cockpit. I wanted to fly it at full speed, fast and loud, so everyone for miles around would hear it; then, I would make a big loop high over the fields, just as Danny had done. I wanted to hear its motor roar again and again, while it pulled the plane higher and higher into the open sky, taking me far away, away from the dirt road, to another place. The silver plane would challenge me, and I might struggle, but I was powerful and strong too, and I must take it on and whip it, whip *it*, along with whatever else stood in front of me, stood in my way. I wanted to win, to be a winner, and I believed with all of my might that there was nothing—*nothing*—ever to stop me.

My heart was pounding like the heart of a great fighter, a hero in the midst of a bruising battle. I wanted to be a hero, too, like Danny. I felt a "hero" pounding inside me, eagerly waiting to burst out, to take charge and conquer. But at the same time, I felt other battles inside my mind, difficult and mean battles about change, and about unknowns, things unclear to me, causing fear—fear I couldn't see, touch, or understand, fear for my friends on the plantation. I knew I must figure it out, and fight to win, to move on. I flexed my jaw tightly, hearing my teeth grind against each other, and brought my palms to my lips, letting the warm air burst out, over and over, from deep within me, and my heart pounded harder.

With watery eyes, I looked down the dirt road, where several people were visiting with each other, while the faint sounds of their laughter wandered to where I stood. The figures appeared small, farther away than what I knew they were, and the dirt road seemed much longer. Their laughter slowly died while the small figures spread silently in different directions, from the road into the yards, and finally vanishing into the little houses. I winced quickly when I heard the loud sound of a door slamming closed, and coldness suddenly made my body tremble, while my boots sank deeper into the sandy mud. The dirt road, a place I loved, a place where I had lived for all of my life, was pulling me down, tugging at me, desperately grasping to hold me, to lock me in place, as it had done to my friends. My body stiffened, and I stepped away from where I stood, feeling tall, strong, and powerful. And I began my walk to the Big House, to home.

In my mind, I felt the dark, cold loneliness of Helen and Isaac's house, knowing that the swing on the front porch hung still and silent, but waiting for another family to come and take its place on the dirt road. Was Veesy cursing at Alex about what he was doing to his daughter? I knew I must tell my dad what Veesy had told me about Alex and Bernice. I wondered who had told J.B. about the party and the mess I had made in Mama's dining room a few nights before, but it no longer mattered if my dad was told about it. And if he wanted, I would pay to have his truck bumper repaired, without question, and I wondered what Mama would think when she opened her freezer. Knowing that the courage within me overwhelmed any fear of facing them, these seemed like *nothing* things now; I would handle all of them when the right time came.

The changing world around me, the plantation and my friends who lived there, were changing, too, and weighed heaviest on my heart, and each time I thought about it, sadness seemed to plague me, letting fear creep back into my mind. My good friend Mag, and my friend Papa, both gone, had left a big hole in my life, and now Alex was no longer a big buddy for me to look up to and admire. Worst of all, I knew I must tell my dad what Veesy had told me.

Mag would learn to love the people she would work for at Bubenzer, and they would learn to love her, knowing, too, that she had *power of the heart* and the strength to endure the dirt roads, wherever she lived.

As for Papa, I felt good that he was prepared to do as well as he could to provide for himself and his mother. Getting along would be hard for him all of his life, but he stood a lot taller now and held his chin far above the downward gaze that had been *his* every hour of every day. I knew I was proud for Isaac Vead, but I felt an awkward guilt, realizing that I was glad that Isaac Vead had gone away from my life, probably forever. But I knew, too, that Issac Vead had had no choices when he left, but now he was free from the dirt road and from so much meaness from people who never gave him a chance. He would have a new start, another chance, and I hoped that some day, he would have choices, too.

And Cathrine had done a good thing. She knew it and was proud of herself, as well as for Issac. I knew that Gilbert Frank, Alex, and my other friends along the dirt road were right about the way we lived; it had to change, along with the rest of the world. I knew my dad was right, also, when he told me that our lives as we lived on the dirt road would someday be "only memories in the minds of a few old people."

Confused, angry and sad all at the same time, while walking along the side of the dirt road I realized that my childhood was gone, taken from me, it seemed, without giving me time, and I must give it up forever. Being a child was over, and never would I be able to go back. I was thrust headfirst into my youth that day, headfirst into a tangled world of uncertainties, changes and fears. I had been wounded by so much, so quickly, but I knew also that I must go forward with a daring valor, feeling my way, and looking boldly into a *new era*, into a *new life*. The power within me surged again, and again I quickened my steps toward home.

It came to me clearly that, having lived so long on our dirt road, and at the age of only twelve, I had learned more than most kids might have known at twenty. I had many from whom I had learned as they lived for generations on a dirt road like ours, somewhere, some time. Most of them knew that they would likely die on a dirt road. Every encounter with a dirt road had beaten them down and locked them in place, but with courage and a powerful will, they were slowly finding their way out. Most were black, but some were white. We had lived together on this plantation, our dirt road, but I had believed as a child that our lives were good, and this was just the way life was.

That wide and deep chasm that separated us, cut my heart like a sharp knife as I came to understand that, as a white child, I had choices every time I crossed the line where the plantation ended and I would never be held captive by inequities and limited boundaries because of the color of my skin. I was free, free to go in whatever direction my life and the world presented to me. The chasm that frightened me was wide and deep, and I recognized that it was what separated us, white from black. As I hurriedly walked toward home, I also realized that the separation had been around for a long, long time, for hundreds of years, warping the minds, the hearts and the souls of millions.

Anxious but sad, I knew that my life had reached its time to cross the sharp, dangerous, and decisive edges of that chasm; and I must cross it—cross it entirely—because there was no island, no place where I could be, or for anyone else who had lived as I had, in both a black world and a white world.

Quickly, but sadly, I turned my back to the Quarters, and looked toward home, recognizing that the darkness was coming fast and the damp air was getting colder, feeling its way through my jacket. Over the woods in the west, the big sun was showing only half of itself above the trees in the distance, a bright burning orange casting the glow of a thousand shades of color in every direction. Colorful flashes of a joyous childhood ran quickly through my mind, each a painted canvass of a unique young life, my life, lived on the dirt road. With all of the beauty around me, there was promise, too. While I watched and listened, the sun spoke to me in vivid color, telling me about time...new tomorrows, about change, and about hope.

The whitewashed fences along the road ran all the way past the front of the Big House to the trees hiding the silver plane. Suddenly, they seemed like long white boundaries that had separated the lives of everyone who had ever laid claim to the Big House, from those who lived in the Quarters—a dividing line, long, straight, and white, and now, to me, clear.

Familiar smells of smoke in the damp air greeted me over and over as I moved slowly. I wondered how many times I had walked from one end of the dirt road to the other, and I knew I wouldn't make that walk many more times. But somewhere deep inside me, a feeling that would not lie still kept telling me the dirt road would forever be a part of me, and I would live its length and breadth over and over for all of my life. The memories of my childhood, the games, the laughter, the dances, the faces—strong faces of love, and sometimes anger—and all of the sweet smells that lingered in the pink dusty air of a summer evening would often bring me home to my friends, and to the way we had lived, together, on the dirt road.

With my eyes fixed on the setting sun and mellowing sky, and with every step, I seemed to be moving across the chasm, the separation that I had seen in my mind so many times, while the voices deep inside me murmured over and over, convincingly, that the bigger world, the one in which I must live, wasn't ready to let me cross those lines of separation, the lines between black and white, as I had done as a child.

Having never looked back to the Quarters where my friends lived, I felt the tears, but I took a deep breath, brushed the wetness from my eyes, and exhaled boldly into a cool new air.

My choice was made.

CHAPTER 57

I came to the corner at the hedgerow and Pal was on his way to meet me. The chimneys at the Big House were giving up a light gray smoke, gracefully curling and disappearing quickly into the evening sky. The windows glowed with a beckoning call to come home, while the horizon was quickly turning into shades of lavender and purple.

The great oaks and the old house, I knew, would soon fade away into the blackness of a night with no moon. Walking close beside me, proud and happy, was my ole yellow friend who kissed my hand hello. He barked once, an "I love you" bark, telling me that he was there and waiting at my side. I looked down toward him and smiled. Like the great oaks, the Big House, and my family, he, too, had always been close by.

Through the fading light, the old house seemed different as it hid behind the big oaks. It looked smaller compared to the way it always was, and it tilted a little toward the east, as it sat on its tall pillars of aged brick. With fading grey paint and a rusting tin roof, it was no longer a proud old king, and no longer a part of my being. It was just the house where we lived, the place my family called home.

My slow walk quickened.

At the top of the steps, the familiar sound of the screened door seemed quieter than usual when I pulled it open, stepped onto the porch, then let the door close quietly. The porch seemed smaller, too, narrower, when I crossed it toward the kitchen door. The worn-out knob on the door was lost in the palm of my hand, and the heavy wooden door opened with little effort.

My dad, with his head bowed, was reading, "...these three, but the greatest of these is love." Then, he whispered, "Amen."

My place at the table was waiting.

We were all at home.

And I was different.

✿✿✿

AND,
"MAYBE THEY SHOULD KNOW,
MAYBE I SHOULD TELL THEM.
A LIFE IS A STORY.
I HAD A LIFE WITH FRIENDS. SOME WERE BLACK AND SOME
WERE WHITE,
AND WE LIVED TOGETHER ON A DIRT ROAD A LONG TIME
AGO. I CHANGED, AND I WENT AWAY."
MY NAME IS BILLY."
THE LAST WITNESS
FROM

A DIRT ROAD

THE PEOPLE AND PLACES

The names of the characters have been changed, except for relatives of the author. The information stated herewith about others is taken from hearsay and conversations over many years, with family members and old friends, who still might live in the area.

✿✿

THE PEOPLE

<u>PAPA</u>: Isaac Veed. Isaac pumped gas and washed cars at several service stations in Bunkie for many years. He married, and after his mother's death, he left Bunkie with his family to live somewhere in southwest Louisiana. Though close childhood friends, after Isaac moved from the plantation, Isaac and Billy never renewed their friendship, each living according to the social and economic dictates of the era into which they were born.

<u>MAG</u>: Magdeline Williams. Had Mag been born fifty years later into another time and place, likely she would have been an actress or "show girl." Her vibrant personality, good looks and natural energy kept her from being a victim of the hardships of the time in which she lived. She helped in rearing several children in the Big House on Bubenzer Plantation. Affectionately, they called her "Black Mama." She died around 1983 at the age of 75.

<u>ALEX</u>: Alex Benoit. In 1948, Alex took his family to California and joined others from the plantation. He died around 1965 at the age of 55.

<u>ROSA</u>: Rosa and Jo Voors lived for over forty years in a house granted to them on a farm owned by Carl and Florence Hunt. Their house burned in 1999. In poor health, they entered a nursing home where Jo died in 2001. All of their six children graduated from high school and beyond, and now live from Mississippi to California, and remain very devoted and attentive to their wonderful mother. Today, Rosa, at the age of 84, continues to live in a nursing home, where members of the Hunt family will visit with her when they are in the area.

<u>FRIENDS IN THE FIFTH GRADE CLASS</u>: Marilyn, Eddie, Harold and Janet: These people, along with others, bonded from elementary through high school, into a lifetime of grand friendships. In a group of eight, they frequently communicate with one e-mail address, sharing their lives almost weekly

with each other and meeting annually in their hometown of Bunkie. They rejoice for having spent their childhood, youth and adult lives with no boundaries or limits, in a lifetime of sweet friendship with each other.

AUNT SOOK AND UNCLE GATHARD: Fannie and Gathard Harper. At the age of sixty-five, Fannie suffered from advanced dementia brought on by excessive use through the years of prescribed narcotics to calm her migraine headaches. She was beautiful until her death at the age of eighty-three, in 1993. Gathard lived five years more, and died at the age of 93.

DAD: Carl Monroe Hunt. Carl and Florence retired from the plantation in 1959, joining Rosa, Jo Voors and their children, on the forty-acre farm known to all in the family as "The Little Place" because of its smallness compared to the size of the great plantation. Carl died of a heart attack in 1974 at the age of 72. The country road on which "The Little Place" once was is named "Carl Hunt Road," and "The Little Place" is merely a part of vast acreages owned by big sugarcane farmers.

MAMA: Florence Armand Hunt. Florence left "The Little Place" and moved into Bunkie after Carl's death. She lived there for twelve years, then moved to Lake Charles to live with her widowed daughter, Jerry. Ten years later, and at her choosing and desire to remain independent, she entered a nursing home in Baton Rouge, near her children Margie and Mickey. Having lived a grand life, she maintained her good sense of humor, which continued to be the anchor for her goodness toward others. During her last minutes of life, she complimented the emergency technician for her skill and her beauty, saying she reminded her of her daughter, Jerry. Minutes later, Florence died at the age of 89.

THE SIBLINGS: Margie Hunt Pierce, Jerry Hunt Wright and Marion (Mickey) Hunt.

Margie and Jerry became artist, and now in their mid, and late seventies, they still paint and teach art in Baton Rouge and Lake Charles, each living near their children and grandchildren. Mickey, the youngest, having retired some years ago, travels extensively with other retired friends. The four Hunt siblings remain very close.

BILLY: Bill Ray Hunt. In 1953, Billy left his life and his friends on the plantation forever. After graduation from college, he entered the military and spent two years in the Pacific Northwest and Alaska, eventually returning to Louisiana, where he married in 1959. Six years later, he took his family to a small town in the heart of the Tennessee Valley of North Alabama. Retiring in 1991, he spends much of his time writing the memories of a unique childhood and youth, initially recorded for his four children and their families. Realizing that he was probably one of the last Southerner who grew up as a son of the overseer on a working sugar plantation in Louisiana, with inspiration from his wife of more than four decades he has compiled those memories in "The Last Witness from A DIRT ROAD."

THE PLACES

BUNKIE: A small rural town, Bunkie thrived in the 1930s and 1940s from the oil industry. During World War II, several large nightclubs sprang up, but none were comparable to the great "Blue Moon," where you could hear Harry James and his trumpet, see Cab Calaway dance, or maybe see General Eisenhower when he visited. These nightclubs brought in thousands of soldiers from the training camps that dotted the Central Louisiana area. Being located on Highway 71, which linked North Louisiana to Baton Rouge and New Orleans, imprinted the name Bunkie in the hearts and minds of people all over the country, who remember it from when they were young and were being trained to be soldiers. The town has changed little since 1946, and lies thirty-five miles south of Alexandria, Louisiana.

EOLA: No longer a community as such, and four miles south of Bunkie, Eola, with Bunkie, boasted as the center of the oil industry in Central Louisiana in the late 1930s through the 1950s. At that time, the community of Eola consisted of several hundred people who lived in the Amerada Oil Camp, the Sid Richardson Oil Camp and the Cabot Carbon Plant Camp. In addition, it had several small country stores, several cafes, and two or three nightclubs. Upon depletion of much of the oil, the people left Eola in the 1960s and 70s. Their departure, coupled with the demise of many plantations in the surrounding area, returned Eola, like Bunkie, to its original agrarian and rural economy.

GOLD DUST: Six miles south of Eola was the small community of Gold Dust, consisting in the 1940s of three grocery stores, a railroad depot, a doctor's office, and several hundred people, all within two miles of its Bayou Boeuf setting. Many years before, around Gold Dust lay several large plantations, their "Big Houses" still standing in the 1940s and 1950s, but the land was lost, or bought by other big landowners in the area.

SHIRLEY PLANTATION: Several live oaks remain on the north side of "the dirt road," and with the row of tall pecan trees that made up the hedgerow on the east side of the Big House, they are emotional reminders, to anyone who lived there, of the vibrant plantation it once was. Old stories indicate but with no evidence or documentation to prove it, that its beautiful name came from the original builders, who came to central Louisiana from Virginia before 1850. The 3,500, flat acres of sandy, loamy soil is mostly rented to others now. "Shirley Road," long ago named in honor of the plantation, travels two short miles from Bunkie to where the plantation once lay. Today, Shirley Road is lined on both sides with great homes, built in the past thirty years, and seems, for many, to be a reflection only, of an era long past. Shirley Plantation was only one of the many symbols of the plantation era in the South, an era that molded much of the economic, social and cultural history of Louisiana.

THE SILVER PLANE: The wrecked pieces of the silver plane remained under the two big oak trees until around 1957, when it was taken away. By then, it had become a quiet sanctuary, almost "holy ground," for the author, who wished through the years that it could have remained forever under the trees near to the bank of the slow brown waters of Bayou Boeuf. Being a sad part of many lives, it never gave up the secrets of what happened and why it crashed, violently taking the life of the young pilot and breaking so many hearts in the community. Those secrets will never be known, but the vivid memories of the crash of the silver plane will forever be a defining moment in time for the author, and many others.

✷✷✷

Printed in the United States
67789LVS00003B/238-264